Nottingham Forest FC

Who's Who
1892 to 1939

Garth Dykes

A *SoccerData* Publication

Published in Great Britain by Tony Brown,
4 Adrian Close, Toton, Nottingham NG9 6FL.
Telephone 0115 973 6086. E-mail soccer@innotts.co.uk
www.soccerdata.com

First published 2017

© Garth Dykes 2017

Cover design by Bob Budd

AUTHOR'S DEDICATION

*To Ann,
the lady
on the train*

Printed and bound by 4Edge, Hockley, Essex
www.4edge.co.uk

ISBN: 978-1-911376-07-1

1898 FA Cup winners. Back, left to right; H Hallam (secretary), Frank Forman, A Ritchie, D Allsopp, J McPherson, W Wragg, A Scott, G Bee (trainer). Front; T McInnes, CH Richards, L Benbow, Arthur Capes, A Spouncer.

1919 Football League (war-time) champions. T Holford (reserve), J Mills (reserve), H Bulling, H Lowe, S Hardy, J Jones, H Wightman, P Barratt (reserve), J Armstrong, W Tinsley (reserve). Front; J Rawson (committee), RG Marsters (secretary), J Birch, D Shea, T Gibson, N Burton, H Martin.

FOREWORD BY THE AUTHOR

The Forest club has a very long history. I saw my first match at the City Ground over fifty years ago, in season 1964-65. A familiar figure in the Reds' line up at the time was a former R.A.F. colleague, Jeff Whitefoot, with whom I was stationed at R.A.F. Ringway some ten years earlier. Jeff was an England Schoolboy international and won one cap for England Under-23 against Italy Under-23 at Bologna in January 1954. I recall how anxious we all were to hear how he had got on, but he returned to camp sorely disappointed. Apart from the other Manchester United representatives in the team (Duncan Edwards and goalkeeper Ray Wood) he knew none of the other members of the eleven and admitted that, perhaps unsurprisingly, they had failed to function as a combined unit, and had been, in his own words, "lucky to lose 0-3".

Having left the R.A.F. and moved from Lancashire to the Midlands in the early sixties, I settled into a pattern of watching the home games of Leicester City one week and Forest the next. The Forest of those days, and of the present, can have borne little similarity to the teams who wore the famous Garibaldi jersey from 1892 to 1939, the period covered in this volume. In earliest days, this was the era of our grandfathers and great-grandfathers, when large moustaches and mutton-chop whiskers were the order of the day, and transport was by horse-drawn trams on cobbled streets lit be spluttering gaslight. Typical of the period. a glance at the very first biography in this book reveals that players cooled off, and presumable cleaned up, by jumping into the river Trent at the conclusion of a pre-season practice match in August 1895 at the Town Ground, conveniently situated near to the Trent's Embankment.

Of the 375 players who have qualified for inclusion in this book, neither the author, nor anybody today, will have memories of star internationals such as Grenville Morris and Sam Hardy. However, newspapers of the time have left one with a means to convey an appreciation of a player's abilities (or lack of same) and style of play. On the question of memories however, my late friend Douglas Lamming, who lived to the grand old age of 91, told me that the first football match that he had ever attended, at the age of ten, was a pre-season public trial at the City Ground in 1924, when one of the Forest goalkeepers was the great Sam Hardy. Nottingham Forest Football Club, like all professional sporting organisations, has to look to the future, but it must never forget its past and the traditions built by men like Morris, Hardy *et al.*

Garth Dykes
Leicester
April 2017

NOTES ON THE TEXT

For each player I have attempted to provide the following information: full names, recognised playing position, height and weight, date and place of birth, and date and place of death. It should be mentioned here that the dates of birth and death of some players have been culled from registers that only record such events in three-month periods. Hence the use (for instance) of 'January quarter 1923' denotes a span of January to March of that year. Also included are each player's Bury debut, full career and biographical details, and a breakdown of appearances made and goals scored. Every player who played in a Football League match or an FA Cup-tie has been included.

ABBREVIATIONS
These have been kept to a minimum and are those in general use in works of this type:

App/s	Appearance/s
cs	close season
gl/s	Goal/s
q.v. (quod vide)	denoting a cross reference
FA	Football Association
FL	Football League
WW1	The First World War (1914-18)
KIA	Killed in action

ABBOTT, Herbert 'Bert'
Half-back
Debut v Blackburn Rovers (a) 1.1.1895, drawn 0-0
CAREER: Local junior football. **FOREST 13th September 1894.** Sheppey United 28th August 1897.

One of eight local players engaged for the reserve team, Bert Abbott was first noted for his appearance for the Whites against the Reds in the pre-season practice match at The Town Ground played on Monday 29th June 1895. Played in very hot weather, it was reported that several of the players rushed straight from the match to partake in a cooling swim in the river Trent! Although retained for three seasons, Abbott found few opportunities. Probably the must successful of his first team outings came in the 4-2 defeat of Blackburn Rovers on 28th December 1895. With McCracken and Stewart both unfit, Abbott was drafted in at right-half and Frank Forman on the opposite flank. A match report revealed that Abbott had acquitted himself so well that: "He deserved all of the very general commendations that came his way." An added seasonal bonus was the receipt of 10 shillings, promised to each player of the team "With his usual liberality" by director Mr. H.B. Clayton. Abbott departed to join Sheppey United in August 1897, following Joshua Hollis who had joined the same club some weeks earlier. Their first season in the south brought some success, as Sheppey United finished their first season in Division Two of the Southern League as runners-up to New Brompton.
Appearances: FL: 5 apps 0 gls Total: 5 apps 0 gls

ALLAN, Jack Stanley
Inside-forward   5' 7"   11st 4lbs
Born: Wallsend, 28th December 1886
Died: Wallsend, 4th May 1919
Debut v Leicester Fosse (a) 7.9.1912, lost 1-3
CAREER: Wallsend. Sunderland, amateur, 6th December 1906. Newcastle United 7th June 1908. West Bromwich Albion May 1911, fee £150. **FOREST 28th July 1912.** Worcester City October 1914 to April 1915.

A schoolteacher and son of the Mayor of Wallsend, Jack Allan was described as a "scientific and clever centre-forward" on joining the Reds in July 1912. He had the experience of three seasons with Newcastle United, in the last of which he was twelfth man for their FA Cup final at Crystal Palace. Moving on to West Bromwich Albion he was unfortunate to sustain a training injury after showing admirable form throughout the first half of the season. He played infrequently thereafter but appeared in the FA Cup semi-final against Blackburn Rovers at Sheffield. In a similar season to his last, Allan appeared in most League matches for Forest to the mid point of the season in which the team struggled in the lower reaches of Division Two. At this juncture, a successful experiment

moved full-back Tom Gibson to lead the attack and he responded by netting 18 goals to lead the scoring list for the season. Moving on to Worcester City, Allan played in four matches, scoring two goals, before the outbreak of World War One, in which he served in the R.A.M.C. Sadly, within a fortnight of his safe return to Tyneside he died of pneumonia, he was just 31 years of age.
Appearances: FL: 22 apps 3 gls Total: 22 apps 3 gls

ALLSOP. Dennis Watkin 'Dan'

Goalkeeper
Born: Derby, 13th February 1871
Died: Derby, 6th October 1921
Debut v Wolverhampton Wanderers (h) 14.12.1892, won 3-1
CAREER: Derby Junction F.C. **FOREST 14th November 1892 to April 1900.**

The Derby Junction club challenged Forest's signing of their goalkeeper in November 1892, claiming that he was still on their books, and had not received their authority to transfer. The protests were not upheld and their loss became Forest's gain as the cool and unfailingly safe goalkeeper served Forest with distinction for eight seasons, a highlight being his outstanding performance in Forest's FA Cup win in 1898. Despite his consistently reliable form throughout, Allsop never received international or League honours, a trio of outstanding custodians in Robinson, Hillman and Foulke barring his way. Dennis Allsop took his benefit in December 1900 in the match against Liverpool. Some twelve months later he had assumed a new role, making his bow as a football referee, officiating in his first match in a Derby & District League match. Since leaving Nottingham in the close season he had established himself in a thriving public house in Derby, close to the works where he had been employed for several years.
Appearances: FL: 206 apps 0 gls FAC: 27 apps 0 gls
Total: 233 apps 0 gls
Honours: **(FOREST)** FA Cup winners 1898.

ALSFORD Walter John 'Wally'

Right half-back
5' 11"
11st 11lbs
Born: Edmonton, 6th November 1911
Died: Bedford, 3rd June 1968
Debut v Doncaster Rovers (h) 9.1.1937, won 2-1
CAREER: Lancastrian School. Edmonton Schoolboys. London Schoolboys. Tottenham Hotspur ground staff 1926, amateur May 1929. (Loaned out to Cheshunt and Northfleet.) Tottenham Hotspur, professional, August 1930. **FOREST 6th January 1937 to May 1938**. (Wartime guest player with Aldershot, Arsenal, Doncaster Rovers and **FOREST**). Grantham FC 1946.

After gaining London Schoolboy honours Wally Alsford joined Spurs' at 15 years of age. Following loan spells with nursery sides at Cheshunt and Northfleet he became a professional at White Hart Lane in August 1930. His best season came in 1934-35 when he appeared in 21 First Division matches and five FA Cup-ties, his stylish performances at left-half leading to the award of his England cap against Scotland in April 1935. Introduced into a Forest side in very real danger of relegation from Division Two, he was able to steer the side to safety, four wins in the final seven League matches lifting them to eighteenth in the table. In another relegation-haunted season, Alsford's involvement ended in late October when an injury was found to be osteomyelitis, an inflammation of the marrow of the bone. Although he was advised that his playing career was most likely to be over, he was subsequently able to appear in much wartime football as a guest player for several clubs, Forest included. He was later the licensee of the County Tavern, Nottingham and other hostelries in Brighton and Bedford. In leisure moments he was said to enjoy swimming, a game of tennis and listening to the wireless.

Appearances: FL: 30 apps 0 gls Total: 30 apps 0 gls
Honours: England International, 1 cap v Scotland, April 1935

ANTHONY, Walter

Outside-left
5' 7" 11st 0lbs
Born: Arnold, Nottingham, 21st November 1879
Died: Arnold, Nottingham, 26th January 1950
Debut v Middlesbrough (h) 23.4.04, drawn 1-1
CAREER: Heanor Town 4th August 1898. Osmanton F.C 8th February 1899. Newstead Byron 6th July 1900. **FOREST 18th February 1904, fee £25**. Brighton & Hove Albion May 1905. Blackburn Rovers February 1908. Stalybridge Celtic cs 1914-15.

An early headline in the local press in January 1901 stated that Walter Anthony had fully maintained his reputation as a prolific goal-getter in the Notts. League, after he had scored two of the three goals by which his team, Newstead Byron, had beaten Notts County Reserves. Some three years later he joined the Forest and was given an early run out with the first team in the final fixture of season 1903-04. As understudy to Alf Spouncer for the outside-left berth, Anthony lacked opportunities and, after a stay of fifteen months, he was allowed to join Brighton & Hove Albion where he was immediately impressive. Rarely absent during three seasons at the Goldstone Ground he scored 13 goals in 119 appearances in all competitions. Joining Blackburn Rovers of the First Division in February 1908, he scored his first goal in his third appearance, a 2-0 win against Everton at Ewood Park on March 14th. In season 1911-12 he made 27 League appearances as the Rovers were crowned Football League champions. Additionally, they reached the semi-final of the FA Cup, being beaten after extra time in the replay against West Bromwich Albion at Sheffield. He departed Ewood at the close of season 1913-14 having scored 14 goals in 163 League and Cup matches. During the First World War he served in the Durham Light Infantry

Appearances: FL: 6 apps 0 gls Total: 6 apps 0 gls
Honours: Blackburn Rovers, FL First Division champions 1912

ARMSTRONG, John 'Jack'

Wing half-back
5' 9½" 10st 9lbs
Born: Tollerton, 4th February 1884
Died: Tollerton, 9th November 1963
Debut v Everton (h) 23.12.1905, won 4-3
CAREER: Keyworth United. Keyworth Town. **FOREST, initially as an amateur circa July 1904, professional 1st September 1905.**
Sutton Town player-coach June 1923.

Jack Armstrong was once described as a football 'Admirable Crichton' who could play in any position and play well. Jack by name and a 'Jack-of-all-Trades' as a footballer, he operated mainly at wing-half but also occupied most forward positions and always acquitted himself with credit. Of light build, he relied on speed and skill, was a clever tackler and distributed the ball to advantage. He was one of the finds of season 1905-06 when he sprang out of local football and into the top flight, and fully justified the step. Elected captain of the side after World War One, he surpassed the club's record for League appearances, previously held by Grenville Morris with 423. His lengthy association with the Forest ended in 1923 when he joined Sutton Town as player-coach. Outside of the game, he ran a poultry farm in Keyworth.

Appearances: FL: 432 apps 8 gls FAC: 28 apps 1 gl
Total: 460 apps 9 gls

ARMSTRONG, Richard Johnstone 'Dick'

Half-back 5' 11" 10st 12lbs.
Born: Newburn, 31st August 1909
Died: Nottingham, 10th March 1969
Debut v Stoke City (a) 15.3.30, lost 0-6
CAREER: Easington Colliery School. Stanley United October 1927. Willington September 1929 to January 1930. Huddersfield Town (trial) November 1929. Easington Colliery. **FOREST (trial) December 1929, professional 24th January 1930.** Bristol City May 1935 to 1939. (Wartime guest player with Watford and Queen's Park Rangers in season 1941-42.)

Dick Armstrong's debut in the Football League was memorable for all the wrong reasons. Forest had lost 0-5 at Charlton Athletic on the previous Monday, and the twenty year-old Armstrong was introduced as one of several team changes for the visit to Stoke. Following a very heavy fall of snow, the pitch was in terrible condition despite being cleared, with pools of water standing in the playing area. The Stoke side adapted themselves much better to the conditions and totally dominated throughout, netting six goals without reply. In a stay of five years at The City Ground, Armstrong remained a reserve team player, his best seasonal return being seven Division Two outings, as deputy for Billy McKinlay, in season 1930-31. His fortunes took an upturn following his move to Bristol City in May 1935. In four seasons leading up to the Second World War he netted 18 goals in 112 League appearances. Highlights included a club record away victory by 8-2 at Walsall in February 1938, and 23 League appearances in the campaign that ended with the Robins in the runners-up position in the Third Division South, just one point adrift of the champions, Millwall. An elder brother, James Harris Armstrong was a centre half-back with Clapton Orient, Queen's Park Rangers and Watford in the inter-war period.

Appearances: FL: 17 apps 0 gls Total: 17 apps 0 gls

ASHMORE, Richard A 'Dick'

Half-back/Inside-forward
5' 10" 11st 0lbs
Born: Highgate, Rotherham, 28th November 1892
Debut v Wolverhampton Wanderers (h) 5.2.1921, drawn 1-1 (scored)
CAREER: Swinton Alliance. Bristol Rovers February 1920. Barnsley August 1920. **FOREST 29th January 1921, fee £750.** Doncaster Rovers August 1922. Scunthorpe & Lindsey United (trial) October 1923. Denaby United November 1923, appointed trainer April 1925. Thurnscoe Victoria August 1927. Highgate Halfway House March 1930. Eckington Town January 1930.

It was an impressive performance against the Forest at Oakwell on New Year's Day 1921 that led to Ashmore's transfer to the City Ground later in the same month. A centre-half from Highgate, Rotherham, he began with Bristol Rovers before joining Barnsley at the start of season 1920-21. A regular first team player except when suffering from injuries – which included a broken nose and a damaged wrist – he joined a struggling Forest side whose form evaporated in mid term. Tried in all three half-back positions and at inside-right, he collected just one winning bonus in ten appearances before the end of the season which saw Forest relegated from the top flight. Cast in the role of reserve centre-half in the following season, Ashmore was restricted to a single League outing as Forest bounced back as champions of Division Two. Moving on to Doncaster Rovers he made just four League appearances before moving into non-League football.

Appearances: FL: 11 apps 1 gl FAC: 1 app 0 gls
Total: 12 apps 1 gl

ASHTON, Percy

Goalkeeper
6' 1" 12st 5lbs.
Born: Bolton-on-Dearne, 28th March 1909
Died: Hyson Green, Nottingham, 19th March 1989
Debut v Stoke (h) 15.9.1930, won 3-0
CAREER: Melton Excelsior. **FOREST 8th December 1928.**
(Wartime guest player with Mansfield Town. Grantham F.C. and Notts County.)

Joining Forest at the age of nineteen, Percy Ashton was third choice initially with Langford and Dexter well established, but with youth on his side he was able to bide his time. Big in courage and stature, he was the type of goalkeeper that an opposing forward would hesitate to bump into more than once. A very long period as understudy to Dexter ended when he was finally handed the first team jersey at the mid point of season 1933-34. Forest flirted with relegation in most seasons leading up to the Second World War but managed to hang on to their Division Two status before League Football closed down for the duration. At the end of season 1938-39 the club had promised him a benefit, a match to be played early in the 1939-40 campaign. The outbreak of war prevented the club from keeping its promise, but in July 1943 a payment of £200 on account was despatched to Percy Ashton.

Appearances: FL: 176 apps 0 gls FAC: 9 apps 0 gls
Total: 185 apps 0 gls

ASHWORTH, Joseph Ernest

Outside-left   5' 6"   10st 0lbs
Born: Warrington, 28th January 1902
Died: Peterborough 19th October 1977
Debut v Blackpool (h) 5.9.1925, drawn 1-1
CAREER: Crosfield F.C. Everton (trial) **FOREST 24th August 1925.** Blackpool May 1926. Peterborough & Fletton United August 1927. New Peterborough Sports.

Sixteen goals in reserve team matches was Joe Ashworth's record in his single season at the City Ground. An early run out in the first team came to a virtual full stop when, in September, Forest signed Charlie Jones from Oldham Athletic for the outside-left berth. Ashworth was placed on the transfer list in April 1926, and moved to Blackpool, along with another Forest reserve player, Arthur Tilford.

Appearances: FL: 3 apps 0 gl Total: 3 apps 0 gls

BADGER Herbert Osborne 'Bert'

Half-back
5' 11" 12st 6lbs
Born: Islington, London, 4th October 1882
Died: Clacton, 16th March 1965
Debut v Bury (a) 3.1.1910, lost 1-4
CAREER: Clacton Town. Colchester Town. Ilford F.C. Tottenham Hotspur amateur November 1903. Woolwich Arsenal professional September 1904. Watford July 1906. Brentford July 1908. **FOREST 4th September 1909**. Brentford September 1910 to May 1911.

Bert Badger, who was an Essex Senior Cup winner with Ilford, did not graduate to first team football with either Tottenham Hotspur or the Arsenal, but in two seasons with Watford he made 54 Southern League appearances and scored five goals. A big and sturdy right-half of the bustling type, he joined Forest from Brentford, where he was a team mate of Joe Ryalls (q.v.) Badger in particular had impressed Forest's directors when he gave an outstanding display against the Morris and Spouncer wing in the FA Cup-tie against the Reds in the previous February. Signed as cover for Teddy Hughes, Forest's Welsh international right-half, Badger was restricted to just two first team outings before returning to Brentford after twelve months at the City Ground. An accomplished violinist, he later worked as an assistant hotel manager.

Appearances: FL: 2 apps 0 gls Total: 2 apps 0 gls

BAILEY, Walter George 'Joe' DSC and MC

Inside-forward
5' 7½" 10st 6lbs
Born: Thame, 19th February 1890
Died: Weymouth, 20th July 1974
Debut v Tottenham Hotspur (h) 26.12.1910, won 4-1 (scored one goal)
CAREER: Thame United. Oxford City. **FOREST amateur 24th November 1909.** Oxford City August 1911. Reading amateur September 1911, professional August 1912. Boscombe F.C. August 1921 to 1922. Sittingbourne. Guildford City September 1923 to January 1924.

Despite his scoring debut against the Spurs, England amateur international 'Joe' Bailey made only four appearances in Forest's relegation season, 1910-11. An all round sportsman, he also played cricket for Berkshire, hockey for Oxfordshire, and later became a qualified referee. He served in the Footballers' Battalion in the First World War, rising to the rank of Captain and was awarded the DSC and MC with two bars. He was the scorer of Reading's first goal in the Football League and their first hat trick. His overall record – Football League, Southern League and FA Cup – was 201 matches and 80 goals. He was later cricket coach at Warwick School.

Appearances: FL: 4 apps 1 gl Total: 4 apps 1 gl
Honours: England Amateur international, 2 caps 1913.

BANKS, Frederick William 'Sticker'

Outside-left
5' 8" 10st 10lbs
Born: Aston, Birmingham, 9th December 1888
Died: Nottingham, 16th January 1957
Debut v Chelsea (a) 14.10.1911, lost 0-2
CAREER: Park Road. Myrtle Villa. Birmingham August 1909. Stourbridge 1910. Wellington Town April 1911. **FOREST 29th September 1911.** Stalybridge Celtic July 1914. (Wartime guest with **FOREST**).
FOREST August 1919. Worksop Town September 1920. Ilkeston Town September 1922. Notts County trainer 1929-30.

Rather unhelpfully, the 'Nottingham Evening Post Annual for season 1919-20' announced the signing of Banks as follows: "Forest sign Banks. The ever-popular 'Sticker' is too well known to require further description." Certainly, Banks had enjoyed a lengthy association with the Forest, his appearance figures boosted by 111 matches and 11 goals in wartime football, when Forest were crowned champions of the Midland Section, Principal Competition, in 1915-16 and 1918-19. At the outset of his career, Banks made just one first team appearance for Birmingham, but it was his form in the Birmingham & District League that attracted Forest scouts. Despite a bright start with the Reds, he failed to maintain his form and was replaced by the ex-Crewe Alexandra wingman, Joe Ford. In the seasons leading up to the Great War, Banks enjoyed lengthy spells of first team action, most notably in 1912-13 when he proved an excellent deputy at outside-right during Firth's illness. He appeared in 15 League matches in 1919-20, his final season.

Appearances: FL: 71 apps 5 gls FAC: 2 apps 0 gls
Total: 73 apps 5 gls

BARBOUR, Alexander 'Alec'

Centre-forward
Born: Dumbarton, 7th June 1862
Died: Bonhill, 29th December 1930
Debut v West Bromwich Albion (h) 3.4.1893, drawn 2-2
CAREER: Dalry Primrose. Dalry Albert. Dundee. Renton 1884-88. Bolton Wanderers August 1888 to November 1889. Renton. Accrington 1890-91. Bolton Wanderers September 1891. Glossop North End. **FOREST assistant trainer 31st July 1892.**

Scotland's inside-right in their 8-2 victory against Ireland at 2nd Hampden on 14th March 1885, Alec Barbour scored one of Scotland's goals, but received no further international recognition. A Scottish Cup winner and finalist with the Renton club, he first crossed the border to join Bolton Wanderers, founder members of the Football League. Barbour was at inside-left in the opening fixture of the new competition on 8th September 1888 when visitors Derby County won 6-3 after Bolton had led 3-0 after just five minutes play. Forest registered Barbour for Football League matches but his principal role was as trainer to the reserves. He was called into action quite early when the Forest second team arrived one man short at Matlock on October 1st. Barbour played, and had evidently not lost his touch, the local correspondent noting that the old Scottish international had been "conspicuous with his dribbling."

Appearances: FL: 1 app 0 gls Total: 1 app 0 gls
Honours: Scotland International, 1 cap 1885. (Renton) Scottish Cup winners 1885, finalists 1886.

BARNETT William Thomas

Centre-forward
Born: Sherwood, 29th December 1876
Debut v Stoke (h) 13.10.1900, drawn 1-1
CAREER: Beeston Rovers. **FOREST 26th April 1900.** Newark F.C. 19th September 1902.

Two first team appearances in two seasons was the extent of Barnett's involvement in Division One football. On the occasion of his second outing, a 0-3 defeat at Notts county on 16th November 1901, the 'Nottingham Evening Post' correspondent was scathing in his appraisal of Barnett's performance: "One failed to see wherein the Forest team was improved by the substitution of Barnett for Capes. The old Beeston Rovers player could not possibly have done less on his own account or have hindered Fred Forman more. Barnett is not near 'class' enough for League football, even of the sort shown at Trent Bridge last Saturday."

Appearances: FL: 2 apps 0 gls Total: 2 apps 0 gls

BARNSDALE, John Davison
Centre or Wing half-back   5' 11½"   12st 10lbs
Born: Arnold, Nottingham, 24 May 1878
Died: Farnham, Surrey, 5th August 1960, age 82
Debut v Sunderland (a) 4.4.1904, lost 1-3
CAREER: FOREST amateur 28th March to 1905
A powerfully built and versatile amateur half-back and a serving Army Major, John Barnsdale was one of very few amateurs playing in Division One football. He commenced at centre-half, playing in the final five matches of season 1903-04. In 1904-05 he alternated between right-half and centre-half, playing in all matches until mid term, when he replaced in the side by Bob Innes.
Appearances: FL: 25 apps 0 gls Total: 25 apps 0 gls

BARRATT, Percy Marriott

Full-back   5' 10½"   11st 4lbs
Born: Annesley,
6th October 1898
Died: Ockshaw, Burnley,
6th July 1974
Debut v Stockport County (h)
27.9.1919, drawn 1-1
CAREER: Annesley St. Alban's F.C. **FOREST January 1918**. Grantham F.C. June 1930.
Percy Barratt joined Forest in 1918, securing a position at left-back when the great Bulling and Jones combination was severed. He was a mainstay of the first team until being injured in the match against Grimsby Town on 5th January 1929 and had to undergo a cartilage operation. Subsequently, he was unable to get back into the side due to the brilliance of Jimmy Barrington, the former Wigan Borough left-back. From earliest days it was evident that the Annesley born defender had all the qualities necessary to make a first class full back. Tackling was always his strong suit, but he cleared his lines with strength and precision, and he certainly made the most of his opportunity when he re-established himself into the League side, late in season 1923-24. Thereafter, he was rarely absent, missing only three League matches between 1925-28, in the course of which he netted 17 goals, the majority scored from the penalty spot. In what proved to be his final season of regular first team football, he was suspended for 14 days after being sent off the field in the Bradford match at the City Ground on 8th September. Some four months later his injury and subsequent operation virtually ended his senior career. He was later with Grantham F.C. His brother, Fred Barratt, was a right-arm fast bowler for Nottinghamshire and England. He took 100 wickets in his first season, 1914, and completed the 'double' in 1928. As a lower-order hard-hitting batsman, in 1928 he scored 139 against Warwickshire in 84 minutes.

Appearances: FL: 217 apps 17 gls FAC: 13 apps 0 gls
Total: 230 apps 17 gls

BARRINGTON, James 'Jimmy'

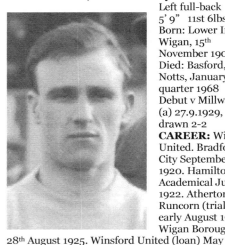

Left full-back
5' 9"   11st 6lbs
Born: Lower Ince,
Wigan, 15th
November 1901
Died: Basford,
Notts, January
quarter 1968
Debut v Millwall
(a) 27.9.1929,
drawn 2-2
CAREER: Wigan
United. Bradford
City September
1920. Hamilton
Academical June
1922. Atherton.
Runcorn (trial)
early August 1925.
Wigan Borough
28th August 1925. Winsford United (loan) May 1927. **FOREST 26th September 1929 (following a month's trial), fee £90. (Released on a free transfer April 1936, but re-signed 31st December 1936, released again on a free transfer April 1937)** Ollerton Colliery October 1937 to August 1938.
Jimmy Barrington began as a youngster in Division One with Bradford City but made only two First Division appearances and was released at the close of the 1921-22 season. A year in Scotland with Hamilton Academical followed, and he next joined Wigan Borough from Atherton of the Lancashire Combination. He was rarely absent in two seasons of Third Division North football at Springfield Park, but was allowed to leave at the close of the 1926-27 campaign, when the Borough finished in 18th place in the table. After a brief loan spell with Winsford United he joined Forest, and costing less than £100 he proved to be an absolute bargain. Despite looking small on the field, Barrington was described as: "Having a kick like a horse, and one who retains his place in the side by sheer ability and hard work." He was eventually crowded out of the first team for most of season 1932-33 by Matt Bell, but despite limited opportunities he showed that the famous left foot had lost nothing of its cunning when he was recalled to regular first team action. He was awarded a well-deserved benefit in 1934-35, and although the club gave him a free transfer in April 1936 they later re-considered their decision and gave him another year. When his playing days ended he settled in Ruddington and worked as a scout for Forest until the late 1950s.
Appearances: FL: 210 apps 1 gl FAC: 18 apps 0 gls
Total: 228 apps 1 gl

BARRY, Leonard James

Outside-left
5' 6½" 9st 12lbs
Born: Sneinton,
Nottingham,
27th October 1901
Died: Mapperley,
17th April 1970
Debut v Brentford (h)
26.8.1933, drawn 1-1
CAREER: Sneinton
Boys' School. Mundella
Grammar School. R.A.F.
Cranwell. Notts County
amateur May 1920,
professional November 1923. Leicester City
September 1927, fee £3,500. **FOREST 5th August
1933, retired April 1934.**

*A major Notts County development, Len Barry
learned the game during the 1914-18 War to such
good effect that the Magpies signed him on
amateur forms and he became an amateur
international. He turned professional on
completion of his RAF service. As one observer
wrote, Len played in the Corinthian style: a tricky
dribbler able to middle the ball at speed and a
scorer of spectacular goals. In addition to his 153
League and Cup appearances and 11 goals for
Notts County, he gave equally excellent service to
Leicester City (214 League and Cup appearances
and 26 goals.) He was almost 32 years of age
when he joined Forest, and lost his first team place
to Billy Simpson in mid term, announcing his
retirement in the close season.*
Appearances: FL: 17 apps 1 gl Total: 17 apps 1 gl
Honours: England International, 5 caps 1928-29.
England Amateur International, 1 cap 1923-24.

BAXTER, William Amelius 'Bill'

Centre half-back
5' 8" 10st 10lbs
Born: Nottingham,
6th September 1917
Died: Nottingham,
21st February 1992
Debut v Burnley (a)
11.9.37, drawn 0-0
CAREER: Berridge
Road School.
Nottingham
Schoolboys. Willson's
F.C. Berridge Road
Institute. Vernon
Athletic. **FOREST
amateur 18th June
1935, professional
8th December 1936**. (Wartime guest player with
Notts County, Derby County, Leicester City and
Mansfield Town). Notts County October 1946.
Grantham May 1954 to March 1955.

*Fair-haired Bill Baxter joined Forest as a
youngster. Strong in the air and with any amount
of stylish touches on the ball, he was nevertheless
unfortunate to sustain cartilage trouble early in
his career, the injury necessitating an operation
and keeping him sidelined for much of season
1937-38. After army service with the RAOC during
the Second World War, he moved across the Trent
to join Notts County for the first post war season.
At either centre half or on the flank berth, he
appeared in 153 League and Cup matches for the
Magpies, assisting them to promotion in 1950, and
later captaining their reserve team.*
Appearances: FL: 15 apps 0 gls Total: 15 apps 0 gls
Honours: Notts County, FL Division 3 South
champions 1950

BEAUMONT, Leonard

Outside-left
5' 10" 11st 6lbs
Born
Huddersfield,
4th January 1915
Died
Nottingham,
23rd July 2002
Debut v
Sheffield United
(h) 27.8.1938,
lost 0-2
CAREER:
Huddersfield
College.
Hopkinson's
Britannia
Works 1929.
Queen Street
Mission 1930.
Golcar Providence 1931. Huddersfield Town
amateur November 1931, professional May 1932.
Portsmouth July 1936. **FOREST 6th July 1938**
(Wartime guest player with Mansfield Town,
Manchester City, Derby County & Lincoln City)
Peterborough United August 1948. Brush Works
(Loughborough) cs 1951, retired cs 1953.
*Len Beaumont underlined his potential when he
made his Football League debut for Huddersfield
Town in a 1-0 victory at Chelsea in January 1933,
just three days after celebrating his 18th Birthday.
It was not until he joined Forest that first team
football became the order of the day, and it was
unfortunate that the outbreak of the Second World
War robbed him of his best years, although he
performed with great credit for Forest during
wartime, scoring 31 goals in 94 matches. He
followed his football career with one in County
Cricket circles, being for many years the official
scorer for the Nottinghamshire club.*
Appearances: FL: 34 apps 3 gls FAC: 1 app 0 gls
Total: 35 apps 3 gls

BEDFORD, Harry

Centre-forward
5' 9" 12st 4lbs
Born: Calow, near Chesterfield,
15th October 1899
Died: Derby,
24th June 1976
Debut v Rotherham County (h) 6.9.1919, won 4-1 (scored two goals)
CAREER: Grassmoor Ivanhoe (Chesterfield League). Rotherham County (trial) August 1919. **FOREST amateur 1919, professional August 1919.** (Wartime guest player with Huddersfield Town 1918-19.) Blackpool March 1921, fee £1,500. Derby County September 1925, fee £3,500. Newcastle United December 1930, fee £4,000. Sunderland January 1932, fee £3,000. Bradford Park Avenue May 1932. Chesterfield June 1933. Heanor Town player-coach August 1934. Newcastle United trainer-coach September 1937. Derby County part-time masseur May 1938. Belper Town manager January 1954. Heanor Town manager March 1955 to May 1956.

A prolifically scoring centre-forward or inside-right, in style dashing and difficult to contain, Harry Bedford netted no fewer that 308 goals in 486 League matches, outstanding figures that included four goals on three occasions and ten hat tricks. He also scored five goals in two Inter-League games, including four against the Irish League at Cliftonville, Belfast, in October 1924. He had commenced in the Chesterfield district with Grassmoor Ivanhoe, with whom he won two cups and four sets of medals. Outside of the game he was employed in Derby as a licensee of the Grapes Inn and, from 1941-64, the Rolls Royce company's fire service. He was also masseur to Derbyshire County Cricket Club for a time, having started his working life as a miner. He served on the committee of the Derby & District (Wednesday) Football League in 1948.

Appearances: FL: 18 apps 8 gls FAC: 2 apps 1 gl Total: 20 apps 9 gls
Honours: England International 2 caps, 1923-25. FL representative, 2 apps 1924-26.

BELL, James

Inside-left 5' 10" 11st 2lbs
Born: *circa* 1900 (Said to be 21 years old when signed)
Debut v Leeds United (h) 30.4.21, won 1-0
CAREER: Army football. **FOREST 27th April 1921.**

Selected for his League debut just three days after signing a professional form, James Bell appeared at inside-left, replacing Sandy Higgins, for the visit of Leeds United to the City Ground. The 21 year-old, who had been demobilised from the Army a month earlier, had played for the Army in all of their representative matches in the 1920-21 season. In what proved to be his only appearance in top-flight football, Bell had the satisfaction of finishing on the winning side, centre-forward Tom Elliott netting the only goal of the game to give Forest the points.

Appearances: FL: 1 app 0 gls Total: 1 app 0 gls

BELL, John Joseph 'Jack'

Inside-forward
5' 10" 12st 0lbs
Born: Basford, Notts,
31st July 1890
Died: Nottingham,
26th December 1943
Debut v Lincoln City (a) 11.10.13, lost 0-1
CAREER: Sycamore Road School. Sherwood Foresters. St. Bartholomew's F.C. Christchurch F.C. **FOREST (trial) August-September 1909.** Sutton Town 1909. Royal Engineers. Reading amateur cs 1911. Plymouth Argyle May 1912. **FOREST 11th October 1913.** (Wartime guest player with Notts County and Birmingham.) South Shields July 1919. Merthyr Town December 1919. Grimsby Town March 1921. Loughborough Corinthians August 1921. Rotherham County February 1922. Weymouth F.C. Hartlepools United March 1924.

A Nottingham man who learned his early football with Sycamore Road School, Jack Bell then played with various local clubs before enlisting with the Royal Engineers, with whose representative team he became a great power. He played for Reading as an amateur, and after leaving the Army joined Plymouth Argyle. He joined Forest and in two seasons, mainly at inside-right, he shone in a poor side that battled to avoid a re-election application. Being on the Army reserve list, he was recalled to the colours during the 1914-15 season, but was able to play in 24 matches during the campaign. In post war years, he was sprightly enough to come second to Pentland in the 1921 Powderhall sprint, and he also won the big sprint open to footballers.

Appearances: FL: 54 apps 6 gls FAC: 3 apps 1 gl Total: 57 apps 7 gls
Honours: Plymouth Argyle, Southern League champions 1913.

BELL, Matthew

Full-back
5' 11" 13st 3lbs
Born: West
Hartlepool,
8th July 1897
Died: Hull,
27th January 1962
Debut v Charlton
Athletic (a) 29.8.31,
lost 1-3
CAREER:
Broughton School.
St. Oswald's Boys.
Army football (East
Yorkshire

Regiment). West Hartlepool. Hull City August 1919.
FOREST 18th August 1931 to May 1934.
Heracles F.C. (Holland) manager-coach to 1939.
*In private life Matt Bell was a confectioner and
tobacconist, but in winter months a full-back of
scrupulous fairness and sound judgment, with a
kick like a mule. A gentleman both on and off the
field and in his way, something of a phenomenon
due to his ability to describe in detail every
movement made in a match, an asset that served
him well in later coaching appointments. A
regular playing member for Hull City in eleven
seasons, and captain for the last four, Bell was
able to take either left or right full-back positions,
and forged successful partnerships with Bill
Thompson and Jimmy Barrington during his three
seasons at the City Ground.*
Appearances: FL: 85 apps 1 gl FAC: 2 apps 0 gls
Total: 87 apps 1 gl

BELTON, Jack

Right half-back
5' 7½" 11st 0lbs
Born:
Loughborough,
1st May 1895
Died: Barrow-
on-Soar, 15th
January 1952
Debut v Bristol
City (h) 19.9.14,
lost 0-1
CAREER:
Loughborough
Holy Trinity.
Quorn
Emmanuel F.C.
Loughborough
Corinthians.
FOREST 12th

**September 1914, released on a free transfer
May 1928.** Loughborough Corinthians September
1928 to May 1930.
*Jack Belton originally played as a forward and
achieved some outstanding scoring feats for both*
*Quorn Emanuel and Loughborough Corinthians,
whom he assisted to the championship of the
Leicester Senior League in 1913 by scoring 34
goals. In his first season with Forest he netted
seven goals in 23 Division Two matches, but
military service with the Leicestershire Regiment
intervened. In post war football, he was tried at
right half-back in an emergency and did so well
that this became his regular position in the side.
His assets were described in the local press as
follows: "Plays a strong, defensive game, and lacks
nothing in determination and courage." Despite
missing four seasons due to the war, Jack Belton
clocked up 348 appearances for the Reds with a
wonderful record of consistency, averaging nearly
35 matches per season.*
Appearances: FL: 322 apps 17 gls FAC: 26 apps 0
gls Total: 348 apps 17 gls
Honours: **(FOREST)** FL Division 2 champions
1922.

BENBOW, John Albert
Inside-right
Born: Newtown, 6th April 1879
Died: Liverpool, July quarter 1926
Debut v Bury (h) 9.4.1898, won 3-1
CAREER: Oswestry United 1895. **FOREST 29th
March 1898 to April 1899.**
*Cousin to centre-forward Leonard Benbow (q.v.)
whom he joined at Forest in March 1898. John
Benbow was built on similar, if slightly more
liberal, lines to his short and stocky relative.
Considered a capable reserve, either forward or at
half-back, John appeared alongside his cousin at
inside-right on his debut, just three days after
Forest's FA Cup Final victory against Derby
County at the Crystal Palace. He was selected at
centre-forward, just two days later, for the away
fixture at Derby County when the Rams took some
revenge for their Cup defeat by winning 5-0.*
Appearances: FL: 2 apps 0 gls Total: 2 apps 0 gls

BENBOW, Leonard

Centre-forward
5' 6" 11st 0lbs
Born: Oswestry, 3rd May 1876
Died: Northampton,
5th May 1946
Debut v Sheffield United (h)
18.9.1897, drawn 1-1
CAREER: Burslem Port
Vale. Oswestry United.
Shrewsbury Town 13th April
1897. **FOREST 1st May
1897.** Stoke 2nd July 1900
Northampton Town 5th

January 1902 to 1906.
*Signed from Shrewsbury Town on a free transfer,
Leonard Benbow was once described as one of the
most dashing centre-forwards in England. His
short and stocky physique seemed to favour his*

sharpness on the ball. Being really quick in his movements, and dangerous in front of goal, his quick perception when faced with difficult positions marked him as a real prospect. He was a regular in two of his three seasons with the Reds, but his two seasons with Stoke were marred by an ankle injury, restricting him to just 20 League appearances and two goals.

Appearances: FL: 54 apps 20 gls FAC: 8 apps 2 gls
Total: 62 apps 22 gls
Honours: (**FOREST**) FA Cup winners, 1898

BENNETT, Alfred

Goalkeeper
6' 1" 12st 8lbs
Born: Clowne, Derbyshire, 13th November 1898
Died: Stoke-on-Trent, March 1967
Debut v Barnsley (h) 18.12.20, drawn 0-0
CAREER: Clowne Rising Star. **FOREST amateur 8th December 1919, professional 20th August 1920**. Port Vale May 1927. Wellington St. George's August 1929.

Once described as: "A lengthy lad whose inches enable him to get to awkward high shots." Alf Bennett commenced as a promising young amateur goalkeeper in the Reds' Reserves. He was afforded an early opportunity to display his abilities in first-class company due to Sam Hardy's injury in 1921-22. In ten League matches he conceded only five goals in Forest's Division Two championship winning side. The tide turned in 1924-25, when he made 31 League appearances in the relegation season. In the following term he lost his place to Len Langford and asked to be placed on the transfer list. He joined Port Vale, initially as understudy to 40 year-old Howard Matthews, the former Oldham Athletic goalkeeper. Ironically, he made his debut in a 2-2 draw against Forest in the opening fixture of season 1927-28, and went on to appear in 36 League and Cup matches in two seasons before moving into non-League football.
Appearances: FL: 83 apps 0 gls FAC: 6 apps 0 gls
Total: 89 apps 0 gls

BETTS, Arthur

Outside-right 5' 9" 10st 5lbs
Born: Huthwaite, 17th May 1916
Died: Sutton-in-Ashfield, 15th June 1978
Debut v Bradford City (a) 28.12.36, lost 1-2
CAREER: Sutton Junction. Huthwaite C.W.S. Birmingham, amateur, September 1934. Huthwaite C.W.S. **FOREST 17th September 1936 to May 1939**. (Wartime guest player with Norwich City.)

Arthur Betts joined Forest from the works team of Huthwaite CWS, and showed such brilliant form in the Midland League that he ended his first season as first choice outside-right. Spoken of as a potential international, several clubs, including Aston Villa and Huddersfield Town pursued him, but Forest refused all offers for his services. Described as: "A born footballer with a natural body swerve", he promised to be one of the finest wingers in the country until he became just another of Forest's unfortunate cartilage injury patients, his final season ending in late January 1939, following an operation on his knee. Ironically, the 'Post Football Guide' for season 1939-40 reported that Betts was fully recovered, but the outbreak of the Second World War effectively terminated his promising career.
Appearances: FL: 65 Apps 10 gls FAC: 2 apps 0 gls
Total: 67 apps 10 gls

BEVERIDGE, Robert 'Rabbie'

Centre-forward 5' 8" 11st 8lbs
Born: Polmadie, Glasgow, 24th June 1877
Died: Glasgow, 11th October 1901
Debut v Preston North End (h) 2nd September 1899, won 3-1 (scored one)
CAREER: Maryhill Harp. Third Lanark 15th October 1895. **FOREST 7th April 1899, fee £130**. Everton September 1900 to his death.

Forest beat Preston North End to the signature of Rabbie Beveridge who in four seasons with Third Lanark had netted 22 goals in 58 Scottish League matches. While finding goals more difficult to come by in Division One, he netted on his League debut, and two goals against Sunderland in the 3-0 victory in FA Cup 2nd round tie helped Forest to ultimately reach the semi-final, in which they lost 2-3 to Bury, after a replay. Early in the following season, Beveridge was transferred to Everton, but by coincidence made his first appearance for his new team at the City Ground, a match won 2-1 by Forest. Tragically, Beveridge was to appear in only a further three matches before his sudden and untimely death at the age of 24.
Appearances: FL: 28 apps 5 gls FAC: 5 apps 2 gls
Total: 33 apps 7 gls

BIRCH, William 'Bill'

Outside-left 5' 8" 10st 10lbs
Born: Rainford, near St. Helens, *circa* 1887
Died: Eccleston, 14th June 1968
Debut v Liverpool (h) 1.10.08, won 5-1
CAREER: Atherton F.C. 25th May 1907. Blackpool 14th February 1908. **FOREST 24th September 1908**. Reading

August 1909. Eccles Borough August 1910. Grimsby Town July 1912. Gainsborough Trinity May 1914. (Wartime guest player with Rotherham County.)
Bill Birch spent less than a season with Atherton of the Lancashire Combination, and was immediately impressive on moving to Blackpool. In the late stages of their Division Two campaign he netted the only goal of the game on his second appearance against Stoke, and further goals against Bradford City and Grimsby Town helped lift his team from the lower reaches of Division Two. Moving up a Division on joining Forest, he started brightly, scoring against Chelsea in a 2-1 win in his second appearance. A ten-match winless run quickly followed, and Alf Spouncer reclaimed his first team spot on the left wing. A move to Reading proved unrewarding, as they were relegated from Division One of the Southern League in 1909-10, winning only seven of 42 League matches. He next featured in the Second Division of the Lancashire Combination with Eccles Borough, but was then given another opportunity at League level by Grimsby Town, and appeared in 34 matches and scored one goal before leaving to join Gainsborough Trinity on the eve of World War One.
Appearances: FL: 14 apps 2 gls Total: 14 apps 2 gls

BLYTHE, Sidney R
Centre-forward
Debut v Chelsea (a) 14.10.11, lost 0-2
CAREER: FOREST 3rd November 1910.
*Blythe's debut was made in place of the injured Grenville Morris at Stamford Bridge, and a match report in the 'London Daily News' considered that the absence of Welsh international Morris accounted for a good deal of the team's ineffectiveness in front of goal. Blythe was said to be largely held in check by Ormiston, Chelsea's centre-half, and with the line well out of gear, Chelsea were comfortable winners. In this match, incidentally, George Dodd the former Notts County forward, made his debut for Chelsea and scored one of his teams' goals. Blythe's name cropped up later in the season, when he was praised for his display in the semi-final of the Notts Senior Cup against Sutton Junction, played at Meadow Lane. He did not get another first team call, however, and was placed on the open-to-transfer list in the close season. **Note:** Details of this player have proved elusive. He was listed in most records as James R Blythe, but he appears in Football League registration documents as Sidney R Blythe. Unfortunately, no trace of one of this name has been found in birth or death records.*
Appearances: FL: 1 app 0 gls Total: 1 app 0 gls

BOOT, Leonard George William 'Lennie'
Goalkeeper 5' 11" 11st 4lbs
Born: West Bromwich, 4th November 1899
Died: West Bromwich, 23rd November 1937
Debut v Preston North End (a) 5.3.28, lost 0-5
CAREER: Army football (Durham Light Infantry). York City August 1923. Huddersfield Town October 1923, fee £300. Fulham August 1925. Bradford City November 1926. **FOREST 24th November 1927.** Caernarvon Town (trial) August 1928. Worcester City September 1928, retired May 1931.
Lennie Boot featured very briefly with York City before joining Huddersfield Town as cover for Ted Taylor and Billy Mercer as successive League championship were won, Boot making five League appearances in both campaigns. Moving on to Fulham, in a similar scenario he made just nine League appearances, and it was a case of diminishing returns with Bradford City (seven appearances) and finally two with the Forest. Moving into non-League football he finally found some success, winning consecutive Birmingham League championships with Worcester City. At the early age of 38, Lennie Boot lost his life in a motorcycle accident at West Bromwich. He had been travelling as the pillion passenger.
Appearances: FL: 2 apps 0 gls Total: 2 apps 0 gls

BOWDEN, Oswald 'Ossie'

Inside-forward
5' 10" 11st 0lbs
Born: Byker, Newcastle-on-Tyne, 7th September 1912
Died: Newcastle-on-Tyne, 20th May 1977
Debut v Fulham (a) 2.9.35, lost 0-6
CAREER: Meldon Villa. Newcastle United Swifts. Newcastle United, amateur, October 1929. Derby County May 1930. **FOREST 8th June 1935.** Brighton & Hove Albion June 1937, fee £400. Southampton June 1938. Cowes (I.O.W.) August 1939.
The third new player signed by Forest within the space of two days in June 1935, Ossie Bowden had spent five seasons with Derby County, but played in only ten League matches. Although tried in all three inside forward positions during his two seasons at the City Ground, his only real first team involvement came in the final month of his first season, when he appeared in six matches within the space of three weeks in April 1936. Called upon only four times in the following campaign, he nevertheless commanded a fee of £400 when he moved south to join Brighton & Hove Albion. He played in just one League match for the Seagulls before joining Southampton on a free transfer. Two appearances for the Saints rounded off his very modest senior career.
Appearances: FL: 14 apps 3 gls Total: 14 apps 3 gls

BOYMAN, William Richard
Centre-forward 5' 8" 11st 7lbs
Born: Richmond-on-Thames, 10th August 1891
Died: Colindale, 3rd March 1966
Debut v West Ham United (h) 29.10.21, won 2-0
CAREER: Gillingham, amateur. Cradley Heath St.
Luke's June 1914. (Served in Royal Navy during
WW1 and made guest appearances for Sheffield
United.) Aston Villa August 1919. **FOREST 29th
October 1921.** Stourbridge January 1923.
Kidderminster Harriers June 1923. Worcester City
June 1925. Kidderminster Harriers committee
member August 1926.
*Six goals in his first five matches – including a hat
trick at Middlesbrough – was a blistering start to
Boyman's Aston Villa career and early indications
suggested that he would make a fine replacement
for England international and Villa legend Harry
Hampton, the scorer of in excess of 200 League
goals for the club. Sadly, he failed to maintain his
flying start, but in 22 League matches scored 11
goals, prompting Forest to obtain his services. He
was showing excellent form for the Reds when he
had the misfortune to break a bone in his shin in
the match against Bury at Gigg Lane on 31st
December. He was out for the remainder of the
season as Forest went on to lift the Second Division
championship trophy. He failed to dislodge Pat
Nelis as attack leader in the following season,
when Forest narrowly avoided a quick return to
Division Two, finishing in 20th place in the table.*
Appearances: FL: 12 apps 3 gls FAC: 1 app 0 gls
Total: 13 apps 3 gls

BRADSHAW, Thomas Dickinson

Inside/Outside-right
5' 8" 11st 12lbs
Born: Stalmine, Lancs.
15th March 1876
Died: Fleetwood,
4th October 1953
Debut v Stoke (h) 19th
February 1898, won 3-1
CAREER: Lostock
Hall. Preston North End
14th August 1896.
Blackpool 27th
November 1896.
Sunderland May 1897.
**FOREST 24th
January 1898, fee £120.** Leicester Fosse March
1899. New Brighton Tower May 1900. Accrington
Stanley March 1901. Swindon Town August 1901.
Reading November 1901. Preston North End
September 1902. Wellingborough May 1903.
Southport Central June 1904. Earlestown
December 1904. Lytham Institute January 1905.
Workington February 1905. Leicester Fosse
October 1905. Rossendale United March 1906.
Lancaster Town September 1906. Glossop May
1907. Penrith November 1907. Peterborough City

December 1907. Darlington August 1908. Darwen
November 1908.
*A glance at the career details above confirm that,
for whatever reason, he was a player who liked to
keep on the move. In terms of Football League
appearances Tom Bradshaw totalled 104 matches
in the services of seven different clubs, and scored
19 goals. He cost Forest a not inconsiderable sum
in January 1898, but failed to reproduce his best
form, being a reserve in the Reds' Cup Final team
of 1898. His time with the club ended in
suspension, the details of which were not made
public, but throughout his career he had serious
lapses. These included failure to train properly,
and a conviction for wife beating in 1908. In 1920s
he posed as a beggar. Between times he played
cricket professionally for Preston CC and was
cricket coach at Harrow for a short time.*
Appearances: FL: 18 apps 0 gls FAC: 3 apps 0 gls
Total: 21 apps 0 gls

BRENTALL, Arthur Allen
Right full-back
Born: Basford, Nottingham, April quarter 1877
Died: Ilkeston, April quarter 1948, age 71
Debut v Manchester City (a) 9.4.1900, lost 0-2
CAREER: Heanor Town. **FOREST 29th January
1900.** Alfreton Town 6th September 1900. Ripley
Athletic 19th December 1900. Pye Bridge United 6th
November 1902.
*As deputy to Ted Peers, the former West Bromwich
Albion and Walsall full-back, Arthur Brentall was
restricted to just two First Division outings during
his short stay at the City Ground. These came
towards the end of the season when the team won
only one of their final seven matches. In addition
to his debut at Manchester City, his second and
final appearance came in the 1-3 home defeat by
Sunderland on 17th April 1900.*
Appearances: FL: 2 apps 0 gls Total: 2 apps 0 gls

BRODIE, John Charles
Inside-right
Born: Crosshouse, near Kilmarnock, *circa* 1868
Died: Dalmellington, 9th July 1901
Debut v Darwen (a) 23.12.93, won 4-0 (scored one
goal)
CAREER: Hurlford. Kilmarnock. Burnley
November 1890. Kilmarnock May 1891. Third
Lanark May 1892. Kilmarnock. **FOREST 14th
December 1893.** Kilmarnock September 1894.
Kilmarnock Athletic August 1895 to 1899.
*Between four separate spells with Kilmarnock,
John Brodie played in two matches for Burnley,
and in 1892-93 scored 14 Scottish League goals for
Third Lanark, his tally including hat tricks against
St. Mirren and Abercorn. He impressed during a
relatively brief stay with Forest, scoring on his
debut and continuing to find the net in League, FA
Cup and United Counties League engagements.
His overall contribution being 10 goals in 16*

matches. He was later noted as an Ayrshire Cup winner with Kilmarnock Athletic in 1897. He tragically lost his life, in his early 30s, in an explosion at Dalmellington Ironworks.
Appearances: FL: 9 apps 5 gls FAC: 3 apps 2 gls
Total: 12 apps 7 gls

BROMAGE, Enos

Outside-left
5' 7" 10st 8lbs
Born: Mickleover, Derbyshire, 22nd October 1898
Died: Derby, 20th April 1978
Debut v West Bromwich Albion (a) 12.10.29, lost 0-2
CAREER: Mickleover School. Firs Estate School. London Road Congs. Burton All Saints. Stapleton Town. Sheffield United 1922. Derby County August 1923. Gillingham May 1927. West Bromwich Albion March 1928. **FOREST 10th October to 29th November 1929.** Chester January 1930. Wellington Town July 1930, retired cs 1936.
In a stay of less than two months, Enos Bromage made his Forest debut at his previous club, West Bromwich Albion, and it proved to be his final appearance in senior football. He had played in only four League matches in as many seasons with Derby County, but followed with 21 appearances and six goals for Gillingham. His West Bromwich Albion figures were 10 appearances and two goals. Enos was a member of a big footballing family, the first of which was Enos Bromage (senior), a goalkeeper with Derby County between 1888-89. Enos junior's brother Bill played for Gainsborough Trinity and Sheffield United and was assistant trainer to Derby County.
Appearances: FL: 1 app 0 gls Total: 1 app 0 gls

BROUGHTON, Matthew
Outside-right
Born: Grantham, 8th October 1880
Died: Grantham, 23rd January 1957
Debut v Wolverhampton Wanderers (h) 7.12.01, won 2-0
CAREER: King's School (Grantham). Grantham Avenue F.C. **FOREST 15th November 1901.** Grantham F.C. May 1903. Notts County amateur October 1904. Watford amateur November 1904. Grantham F.C. 1907.
In season 1901-02 Matt Broughton played in a little under half of Forest's First Division matches, after taking over on the right wing from Fred Forman in mid term. A well-known Grantham sportsman – he represented the town in both football and cricket – he additionally worked as a clerk in an iron foundry, and played most of his football as an amateur. In addition to representing, and scoring for, both Nottingham clubs in First Division football, he had a two-and-a-half year association with Watford, but made only occasional appearances in Southern League matches.
Appearances: FL: 27 apps 5 gls FAC: 1 app 0 gls
Total: 28 apps 5 gls

BROWN, Albert **Richard 'Dick'**

Winger 5' 9" 11st 0lbs
Born: Pegswood, 14th February 1911
Died: Pegswood, March 1985
Debut v Burnley (a) 29.8.36, lost 0-3
CAREER: Northumberland Schoolboys. Alnwick United. Rochdale (trial January, professional July 1929. Sheffield Wednesday June 1930, fee £1,050. Alnwick United September 1931. Blyth Spartans January 1932. Queen's Park Rangers May 1932, fee £150. Blyth Spartans July 1934. Northampton Town August 1934. **FOREST 23rd May 1936 to April 1937.**
One of the first signings made by Forest's new manager, Mr Harold Wightman. Speedy wingman Dick Brown arrived in May 1936 from Northampton Town, to whom he graduated via Rochdale and Sheffield Wednesday. Originally signing as a professional with Rochdale, he scored 10 League goals in 40 matches, his form attracting Sheffield Wednesday and a four-figure fee changing hands. After a year of reserve team football he joined Queen's Park Rangers, for whom he scored 20 goals in 60 League matches. He was similarly successful with Northampton Town, netting 23 goals in 79 matches. After a bright start with Forest – he scored on his home debut in a 1-1 draw against Aston Villa – he played in little first team football in the second half of the season, losing out to the emerging talents of Arthur Betts for the right wing spot. Dick Brown was a miner and track sprinter, and his hobby was pigeon racing.
Appearances: FL: 19 apps 2 gls FAC: 1 app 0 gls
Total: 20 apps 2 gls

BROWN, Albert **Roy**

Outside-left
5' 6½" 10st 7lbs
Born: Sneinton, Nottingham,
14th August 1917
Died: Mansfield, 10th
February 2005
Debut v Norwich City (a)
13.4.36, lost 0-4
CAREER: Nottingham
Schoolboys. Sneinton F.C.
**FOREST amateur 20th
September 1935, professional 8th February
1936**. Wrexham June 1939. Mansfield Town July
1947. Stafford Rangers 1948. Goole Town 1948-49.
*Following an early first team debut in the final
weeks of the 1935-36 campaign, Roy Brown had a
lengthy wait for a second appearance. Drafted in
an the expense of Billy Simpson on the left wing,
his introduction lifted the side and a 6-1 win
against Swansea Town – in which he scored one of
the goals – marked an upturn in results that took
Forest to safety in Division Two. Although lacking
any physical advantage, the Sneinton product
never stopped trying and was capable of dazzling
footwork. Regular first team football aided his
development, but when he moved on it was to
Wrexham of the Third Division North, who
snapped him up after he had declined Forest's
terms and was placed on the transfer list. He had
played in just three matches for his new team
when the outbreak of World War Two suspended
League football. Six and a half years of army
service followed, and he rejoined Wrexham for the
1946-47 season, during the course of which he
scored three goals in 24 matches. He remained for
just one season, joining Mansfield Town for a final
season in senior football in which he scored two
goals in 17 League matches. Roy Brown was a
better than average cricketer if his display in a
charity cricket match, played in August 1937, in
aid of Nottinghamshire's Arthur Staples, was any
indication. Forest opposed Notts County who won
by 51 runs. Star of the match was Reg Halton,
Notts County's cricketer/footballer who scored 105
in his team's total of 176 all out. Roy Brown took
four wickets and held one catch, and followed with
a knock of 37 in Forest's total of 125 all out.*
Appearances: FL: 52 apps 7 gls FAC: 3 apps 0 gls
Total: 55 apps 7 gls

BROWN, Oliver Maurice 'Buster'

Centre-forward
5' 10½" 12st 2lbs
Born: Burton-on-Trent,
10th October 1908
Died: St. Pancras, 17th
January 1953
Debut v Burnley (a)
8.9.30, lost 2-5
CAREER: Broadway
Central School. Trent
Villa. Robirch Athletic.
Burton Town July
1929. **FOREST
February 1930.**
Norwich City December
1931. West Ham United June 1933. Brighton &
Hove Albion March 1934 to April 1937. (Wartime
guest player with West Ham United.)
*As a boy 'Buster' Brown captained Broadway
School Rugby XV at Burton-on-Trent. Leaving the
handling code, he played for Trent Villa and
Robirch Athletic before joining Burton Town, for
whom he scored 30 goals in season 1929-30. A
centre-forward with all the necessary physical
attributes, he lacked opportunities with Forest, but
scored freely elsewhere – 33 goals in 51 League
matches for Norwich City, and 38 in 58 League
matches for Brighton & Hove Albion. A former
miner, he later worked in the London prison
service. His younger brother, Ambrose, was an
inside-forward who played for Chesterfield,
Portsmouth and Wrexham in the 1930s.*
Appearances: FL: 9 apps 6 gls Total: 9 apps 6 gls

BROWN, William

Goalkeeper
Born: Nottingham
Debut v Everton (a)
3.8.92, drawn 2-2
CAREER: Notts. Rangers.
**FOREST August 1890,
registered for FL
matches 18th July 1892**.
Notts County (loan)
November 1894.
*Forest's first goalkeeper in
the Football League,
Brown had missed only
one match in the previous
season when the
championship of the
Football Alliance was
secured. A leg injury
proved troublesome in
1892-93, when he was
praised for some splendid displays, considering
the fact that he was carrying the injury that gave
him pain and greatly restricted his movements.
His habit of falling on the ball during goalmouth
scrambles rendered him liable to serious injury, as*

was noted in the match against Sheffield United in November 1893 when he was once or twice quite roughly used when on the ground. Eventually losing out to Dennis Allsop for the first team jersey, he had a brief involvement with neighbours Notts County, for whom he played in one match, on loan, in a 5-1 win against Crewe Alexandra in November 1894. Several years later, in November 1921, the 'Nottingham Football Post' reported the sad news that the old goalkeeper was lying dangerously ill, suffering from neuritis and heart trouble. However, the lack of further bulletins in subsequent issues of the newspaper hopefully indicated that he had made a recovery.
Appearances: FL: 22 apps 0 gls FAC: 10 apps 0 gls
Total: 32 apps 0 gls
Honours: **(FOREST)**, Football Alliance champions 1892.

BROWN, William

Right half-back
5' 7½" 12st 0lbs
Born: Cambuslang,
10th May 1897
Debut v Stoke City
(h) 25.8.28, lost 1-5
CAREER:
Flemington Hearts.
Cambuslang
Rangers. Partick
Thistle. Everton
amateur August
1913, professional
July 1914. **FOREST
26th May 1928, fee
£200.** Prescot
Cables player-coach
August 1930

William Brown made his first and last appearance for Forest against Stoke City and both ended in heavy defeats. In what proved to be his final Forest appearance, at Stoke on 15th March 1930, the Reds were beaten 6-0 and, in the following month, Brown was one of six players placed on the open to transfer list. In earlier days, the engineer's fitter made his Everton debut as a 17 year-old. A cultured wing half, he totalled 170 League and nine FA Cup matches for Everton, but had played only twice in his final season, 1927-28, when Everton became Football League champions, greatly assisted by a record 60 League goals scored by centre-forward 'Dixie' Dean.
Appearances: FL: 4 apps 0 gls Total: 4 apps 0 gls

BULLING, Harold Montague M.M.

Full-back 5' 11" 12st 0lbs
Born: Martin, Lincolnshire,
29th September 1890
Died: West Bridgford,
9th November 1933
Debut v Rotherham County
(a) 30.8.19, lost 0-2
CAREER: West Bridgford
Boys. Heanor Town 1910.
Watford April 1911.
(Wartime guest player with
FOREST September 1915.)
FOREST August 1919.
Shirebrook F.C. cs 1926.

Harold Bulling joined Watford, along with his elder brother, Chris, in May 1911. Harold made 99 Southern League appearances for the Hornets, a total that included regular appearances in the 1914-15 Southern League championship side. He then assisted Forest as a wartime guest player before leaving to join the army in the autumn of 1916. During active service he was awarded the Military Medal and was demobilised in February 1919. Watford offered him maximum terms to re-sign, but with business interests in the Nottingham neighbourhood he declined. Forest were said to have paid a 'good sum' for his transfer, and he proved to be one of the finest full-backs that Nottingham had produced, being a great defender with a strong kick, who met vigorous attacks with coolness and precision. Despite being kept out of the side by injury for several months in his debut season, he was fully recovered to make maximum appearances in Forest's Second Division championship side. He was awarded a benefit match in November 1924, against Burnley at the City Ground. He was released in April 1926, but in 1927-28 a familiar name appeared in the ranks of Forest Reserves – J. Bulling, a local inside-forward, aged 18 and a nephew of Harold.
Appearances: FL: 186 apps 2 gls FAC: 13 apps 0 gls
Total: 199 apps 2 gls
Honours: (Watford) Southern League champions 1915. (Forest) FL Division 2 champions 1921.

BULLOCK, John Henry

Right half-back
Born: circa 1870
Debut v Bolton Wanderers (a) 31.3.93, lost 1-3
CAREER: FOREST debut April 1892, registered for FL matches 29th July 1892.
After making his first Forest appearance in the final Football Alliance fixture of season 1891-92 – a 1-1 draw at Grimsby Town, it was almost a year later when Bullock made his Football League debut at Bolton Wanderers. This being his final appearance in a Forest shirt.
Appearances: FL: 1 app 0 gls Total: 1 app 0 gls

BURDITT, George Leslie

Centre-forward
5' 10½" 11st 12lbs
Born: Ibstock,
Leicestershire,
27th February 1910
Died: Nottingham,
5th December 1981
Debut v Newcastle United
(h) 25.8.34, won 5-1
(scored two goals)
CAREER: Ibstock
Penistone Rovers.
Norwich City April 1931. Leicester City (trial.)
Ibstock Rovers. **FOREST 16th April 1934.**
Millwall May 1936. Wrexham November 1937.
Doncaster Rovers April 1939. (Wartime guest
player with Leeds United March 1941.)
*A tall, well built, fair-haired centre-forward who
played a brilliant game on his Forest debut, when
the more enthusiastic considered him an
international in the making. He had scored 70
goals for Ibstock Rovers in 1933-34, and when first
playing for Forest Reserves versus a Hucknall &
District X1 in a charity match in April 1934 (under
the name of Fraser) he scored three goals. Aside
from his debut and the Christmas Day match
against his former club, Norwich City, when he
scored a hat trick in a 5-2 win, he never quite
touched the same form again. It was felt that with
more experience he was likely to make a name for
himself, for as a marksman there was little that he
had to learn. A move to Millwall did not enhance
his reputation, but he later scored 35 goals for
Wrexham in 67 League matches. George's elder
brother, Ken, won two Third Division South
championships with Norwich City in 1934, and
with Millwall in 1938.*
Appearances: FL: 18 apps 10 gls FAC: 2 apps 0 gls
Total: 20 apps 10 gls

BURGIN, Meynell

Inside-forward
5' 11" 12st 0lbs
Born: Sheffield,
29th November 1911
Died: Sheffield, July 1994
Debut v West Ham United
(h) 3.10.36, won 1-0
CAREER: Rossington
Main Colliery May 1919.
Sheffield Wednesday
(trial). Huddersfield Town
(trial). Bradford City
(trial). Hathersage F.C.
Wolverhampton Wanderers May 1933. Tranmere
Rovers (loan) October 1934. Bournemouth &
Boscombe Athletic May 1935. **FOREST 2nd July
1936.** West Bromwich Albion 28th May 1938, fee
£1,065. (Wartime guest player with Chesterfield

and Sheffield Wednesday). Retired due to injury
May 1943.
*Described as: "A robust player, hard to knock off
the ball," Meynell Burgin began as a professional
with Wolverhampton Wanderers, but did not
make his Football League debut until joining
Tranmere Rovers on loan in October 1934. He
scored twice on his home debut, and his 21 goals in
31 Third Division North matches assisted the
Rovers to sixth place in the table. He also collected
a Welsh Cup medal following the Rovers' 1-0
victory against Chester in the final. He next scored
just one goal in five matches for Bournemouth. His
two seasons with the Forest were spent in the
lower reaches of Division Two, but his form in late
season 1937-38 led to his four-figure transfer to
West Bromwich Albion, for whom he scored nine
League goals in 14 League matches.*
Appearances: FL: 22 apps 11 gls Total: 22 apps 11
gls
Honours: Tranmere Rovers, Welsh Cup winners
1935

BURTON, John William 'Billy'

Full-back
5' 10½" 12st 0lbs
Born: Ashbourne,
Derbyshire,
1st April 1908
Died: Mansfield,
17th August 1975
Debut v Bury (h)
19.12.31, lost 0-2
CAREER: Mansfield
Woodhouse Albion.
Woodhouse Comrades.
Sutton Junction.
**FOREST 22nd
November 1929.**
Brighton & Hove Albion July 1936. Bilsthorpe
Colliery 1937. (Wartime guest player with Lincoln
City November 1943.)
*As the 'Post Football Guide' put it "This well-built
right-back has not been given many opportunities
of showing his paces in the first team, but his
Midland League record speaks for itself." Billy
Burton's lengthy association with the Reds ended
when he was transferred to Brighton & Hove
Albion in July 1936. He was again cast in a reserve
role at the Goldstone Ground, as understudy to
regular right-back Ernie King he was restricted to
just six Football League appearances. After a
season he returned homewards to join Bilsthorpe
Colliery, where he was employed.*
Appearances: FL: 36 apps 0 gls FAC: 4 apps 0 gls
Total: 40 apps 0 gls

BURTON, Noah

Inside-forward
5' 9" 11st 4lbs
Born: Old Basford, Notts.
18th December 1896
Died: Bobbers Mill, Nottingham, 16th July 1956
Debut v Crystal Palace (a) 27.8.21, lost 1-4
CAREER: Bulwell St. Alban's. Ilkeston United. Derby County amateur December 1915 (**Wartime guest with FOREST September 1916**). Derby County professional August 1919. **FOREST 23rd June 1921; retired May 1932,** but noted with Nottingham East End F.C. October 1934.

During earlier days with Derby County, Noah Burton distinguished himself as a sprinter and a rare opportunist. He first assisted Forest as a guest player during World War One, scoring the goal that sealed the Victory Cup in 1919. He also scored hat tricks in two consecutive matches against Notts County at Easter. He was offered maximum terms to remain with Forest, but he opted to sign a professional form with Derby County, and he was the Rams' leading scorer in the first season after World War One. Before the war he played for Bulwell St. Alban's and Ilkeston United, scoring 96 goals in the season and a half prior to receiving a trial with Derby County. He returned to Forest in June 1921, and commencing at outside-left, missed only one match in his first season when the Reds won the championship of Division Two. Able to fit in any forward position and equally at home at wing half-back he was a mainstay of the Forest side for ten seasons. He was unlucky to be injured early in the 1923-24 season and his enforced absence certainly attributed to the anxieties that were caused as the Reds failed to win any of their final eight League matches, narrowly avoiding relegation from the First Division. Certainly one of Forest's most popular players of the 1920s, he retired from the senior game at the age of 36 and was later a tobacconist in Nottingham. A brother, T.H. Burton, was on Derby County's books in 1919-20 but did not reach first team level.

Appearances: FL: 296 apps 57 gls FAC: 24 apps 5 gls Total: 320 apps 62 gls
Honours: **(FOREST)** FL Division Two champions 1922.

BUTLER, Richard 'Dick'

Wing half-back
5' 7" 10st 6lbs
Born: Shepshed, Leics. 7th December 1884
Died: Leicester, 3rd October 1956, age 71
Debut v Burnley (h) 19.1.07, won 2-0
CAREER: Shepshed Albion. **FOREST 27th November 1906**. Leicester Fosse December 1910 to May 1912. Loughborough Corinthians.

Dick Butler's form in Forest's Reserves won him recognition when he represented the Midland League in his first season at the City Ground. He was, however, unable to break into Forest's first team, his sole appearance being made on the right wing in the 1906-07 season, when promotion from Division Two was secured. Moving on to Leicester Fosse, initially on trial, he found more opportunities, appearing in 28 League and Cup matches. He subsequently captained Loughborough Corinthians.

Appearances: FL: 1 app 0 gls FAC: 1 app 0 gls Total: 2 apps 0 gls

CALVEY, John

Inside or Centre-forward
Born: South Bank, Middlesbrough, 23rd June 1876
Died: Poplar, London, 14th January 1937
Debut v Preston North End (h) 2.9.99, won 3-1 (scored one)
CAREER: South Bank juniors. South Bank F.C. Millwall Athletic May 1895. **FOREST 3rd May 1899**. Millwall Athletic September 1904 to May 1905. Chelsea January 1906.

John Calvey was born at South Bank, a few miles from Middlesbrough. Between the ages of 15 and 18 he twice assisted South Bank Juniors to win two important local competitions. Playing with him was Priest, the Sheffield United winger. Later on with South Bank Seniors, he played in many amateur Cup-ties including a semi-final against the Cup holders, Old Carthusians, in which he scored in the replay, but South Bank lost 2-3 after extra time. He was transferred to Millwall in the latter part of the 1895-96 season and while there was chosen to represent the South versus the North at Crystal Palace in February 1899. Three months later he became a Forest player. Clever on the ball, good in combination, and with an eye for goal, he was leading goal scorer in his first three seasons with the club, form that earned him his England cap against Ireland at Belfast in March 1902. Two other Forest players, Jimmy Iremonger and Frank Forman, were in the England X1 that won 1-0, Settle of Everton scoring the only goal of the match. Calvey returned to Millwall after playing in just 11 League matches in 1903-04, and a final season with the Southern League side took his overall record with the club to 98 goals in 152 matches, covering all competitions. He was a dock worker after his playing career ended.

Appearances: FL: 131 apps 48 gls FAC: 19 apps 9 gls Total: 150 apps 57 gls

Honours: England International, 1 cap v Ireland, March 1902. Southern League representative. International trial, South v North at Crystal Palace in February 1899.

CAMERON, David F

Centre half-back
5' 9½" 12st 10lbs
Born: Middleton, Borthwick, 12th September 1902
Debut v Stoke City (h) 25.8.28, lost 1-5
CAREER: Heart of Midlothian cs 1925. Portsmouth (loan) November 1926. Heart of Midlothian August 1927. Dunfermline Athletic October 1927. **FOREST 1st June 1928.** Colwyn Bay United July 1931.

"A grafter, not afraid to use his weight" was the 'Post Football Guide's' opinion of David Cameron, whose physical proportions were thrown usefully into the fray. Despite his experience in Scottish football, and a loan spell with Portsmouth, the burly Scot did not hold down a place in the League side in his first season with the Reds. He also failed to seize his opportunity following the sale of centre-half Albert Harrison to First Division Leicester City in December 1929, when Tommy Graham, previously at left full-back, was switched to the role of centre-half with great success.

Appearances: FL: 21 apps 1 gl Total: 21 apps 1 gl

CAPES, Adrian

Inside-forward
Born: Burton-on-Trent, 18th April 1873
Died: Smallthorne, 29th September 1955
Debut v Derby County (a) 5.9.96, drawn 1-1
CAREER: Burton St. John's. Burton Wanderers September 1892. **FOREST May 1896.** Burton Swifts September 1897. Burton Wanderers January 1899. Burslem Port Vale November 1900. Stoke November 1905. Burslem Port Vale December 1908 to April 1911, then appointed to coaching staff, later to backroom staff, retiring in May 1934.

Adrian Capes' form in the ranks of Burton Wanderers attracted unusual attention, and a number of top-flight clubs were anxious to obtain his services. Intending buyers, however, discovered that they had either to take Adrian's brother as well or get neither. Arthur, at this point, was considered of little account, and West Bromwich Albion, amongst others, refused to take both. When Forest entered the bidding, they decided that rather than miss Adrian, they would take Arthur as well. Strange to say, Adrian through health issues did little in the Red jersey, while Arthur was quickly established in the team, forming a splendid left-wing partnership with McInnes. Returning to Burton, Adrian made 13 League appearances and scored seven goals for the Swifts. His best spell came with Burslem Port Vale for whom he was leading scorer from 1901 to 1904. He left to join Stoke in November 1905 but after just 17 League appearances and two goals he returned to Port Vale. An injured knee enforced his retirement at the close of the 1910-11 season, when he was appointed to the club's training staff.

Appearances: FL: 30 apps 7 gls FAC: 3 apps 0 gls Total: 33 apps 7 gls

CAPES, Arthur John 'Sailor'

Inside-forward
5' 8" 11st 4lbs
Born: Burton-on-Trent, 23rd February 1875
Died: Burton-on-Trent, 26th February 1945
Debut v Derby County (a) 5.9.96, drawn 1-1
CAREER: Burton St. John's. Burton Crusaders. Burton Wanderers September 1892. **FOREST May 1896.** Stoke April 1902. Bristol City May 1904. Longton Hall September 1905. Swindon Town November 1905 to May 1906. Oldfields November 1910.

Considering that in earliest days Arthur was the man that no one wanted, he turned out to be a big success. It took some time, however, for his qualities to be recognised by the City Ground crowd, who refused for some time to warm to his strenuous efforts. An outstanding utility player, initially a left wing partner for McInnes and Spouncer, when Grenville Morris arrived, Capes filled a temporary gap on the left wing, and then crossed to the inside berth. He really had no stated position, having played anywhere and everywhere, according to emergencies, and with invariable success. The undoubted highlight of his career was his scoring of Forest's first two goals in the 1898 FA Cup Final win against Midland rivals Derby County. On leaving Forest, the club were granted permission by the FA to present Arthur with the amount received for his transfer to Stoke. He was installed as captain of the Potteries club, and was awarded his England cap, after representing the Football League one month earlier in March 1903. A season with Bristol Rovers was followed by a season in the North Staffordshire Combination with Longton Hall, but he spent a final season in senior football with Swindon Town, scoring on his debut. In terms of Football League matches, his career figures were 316 appearances and 81 goals.

Appearances: FL: 169 apps 33 gls FAC: 23 apps 9 gls Total: 192 apps 42 gls

Honours: England International, 1 cap v Scotland April 1903. FL Representative, 1 app. March 1903. **FOREST**, FA Cup winners 1898.

CARGILL, James 'Jimmy'

Outside-right
5' 7" 10st 7lbs
Born: Arbroath, 13th January 1914
Died: Arbroath, 28th October 1979
Debut v Notts County (a) 29.9.34, won 5-3
CAREER: Arbroath High School. Arbroath Roselea. Arbroath Woodside. Arbroath F.C. (trial.) **FOREST 16th August 1934**. Brighton & Hove Albion July 1936. Barrow June 1939. Newton F.C. committee member July 1954.

Following a memorable Forest debut – an eight-goal thriller at Meadow Lane – 20 year-old Scottish winger Jimmy Cargill held his place for a further three matches before Arthur Masters was re-introduced on the right wing. Recalled in the late stages of the season Cargill scored in a 4-1 home win against Barnsley, ending his first season with seven League appearances and one goal. Failing to win a place as the side struggled in his second season, he departed to join Brighton & Hove Albion and gave them excellent service for three seasons, scoring 19 goals in 66 League matches. A move to Barrow saw him play regularly for one season, although he had played only once before the outbreak of war, but continued in regional football throughout the 1939-40 campaign. Jimmy's brother Tom also played for Arbroath.

Appearances: FL: 10 apps 1 gl Total: 10 apps 1 gl

CARNELLY, Albert

Inside-forward
Born: Nottingham, 29th December 1870
Died: Nottingham, 1st August 1920
Debut v Burnley (h) 1.9.94, won 2-1
CAREER: Beeston St. John's. Westminster Amateurs (Nottingham). Mapperley F.C. 1889. Notts County May 1890. Loughborough December 1890. **FOREST 30th April 1894**. Leicester Fosse May 1896, fee £50. Bristol City July 1897. Ilkeston Town 29th August 1898. Bristol City 6th December 1898. Thames Ironworks 4th May 1899. Millwall Athletic 3rd May 1900. Ilkeston Town 29th August 1901. Nottingham Corporation Tramways October 1902.

A designer in the local lace industry, Albert Carnelly was a registered player with Notts County in May 1890 but they had failed to include him on their retain and transfer list in 1893. A meeting of the Football League management committee in July 1894 discussed his position and it was decided that his transfer to the Forest would be allowed to stand. His form with Loughborough in the Midland League, 44 goals plus 10 in FA Cup-ties, had earned him his upward move and he was leading Forest scorer in his first season with 16 goals in 29 matches. A season with Leicester Fosse brought 10 League goals in 28 matches, before he embarked on a wandering path covering Southern League and non-League football. He was later a motorman with Nottingham Corporation Tramways.

Appearances: FL: 52 apps 24 gls FAC: 4 apps 1 gl Total: 56 apps 25 gls

CHAMBERS, Robert James 'Jimmy'

Winger
5' 7" 10st 7lbs
Born: Bessbrook,
5th January 1897
Died: Bessbrook,
13th April 1977
Debut v Charlton
Athletic (a) 29.8.31,
lost 1-3
CAREER:
Bessbrook Athletic
1919. Belfast Celtic
1920. Broadway
United. Distillery
1920. Queen's Island
1921. Willowfield
June 1923. Newry Town 1924. Bury amateur April
1921, professional October 1925, fee £625.
FOREST 13th June 1931. Grantham August 1932.
Portadown November 1933. Newry Town
November 1933 to May 1934.
*Despite playing in little first team football with the
Forest, Jimmy Chambers won the final three of his
12 Irish caps while at the City Ground. A former
soldier with the 1st Irish Rifles, he was awarded the
DCM for his service during the First World War.
He was first capped when on Distillery's books,
and won a further eight during a lengthy
association with Bury for whom his appearances
were strictly limited, as Wally Amos dominated
the left wing spot throughout a 13-year association
with the club.*
Appearances: FL: 9 apps 1 gl Total: 9 apps 1 gl
Honours: Northern Ireland International, 12 caps,
1921 to 1932; also Ireland Amateur International.

CHAPMAN, Frederick William
Defender
Born: Nottingham, 10th May 1883
Died: Newstead Abbey, 7th September 1951
Debut v Small Heath (h) 12.11.04, lost 0-2
**CAREER: FOREST amateur 8th September
1904 to 1907.** Oxford City.
*An amateur reserve defender and local
manufacturer of ladies' gowns who was called
upon very infrequently for first team duties during
a three-year association with the Forest club.*
Appearances: FL: 3 apps 0 gls Total: 3 apps 0 gls

CHARLTON, Arthur Herbert
Inside-right
Born: Paisley, 29th December 1876
Died: Ealing, 24th October 1956
Debut v Stoke (h) 15.10.1898, won 2-1
CAREER: Ashtead juniors (Middlesex). Brentford
amateur 1896. **FOREST 19th January 1898 to
May 1899.**
*Arthur Charlton joined Brentford, one of the best
amateur teams in London, in 1896 when they were
still three years away from gaining admission to*

*the Southern League, Second Division. He joined
Forest in the season that they lifted the FA Cup, but
he had to wait until the following term before he
was tried in the first team. Despite a winning
debut, he made only a further two first team
appearances and was not retained at the end of
the season.*
Appearances: FL: 3 apps 0 gls Total: 3 apps 0 gls

CLARK, John Robert 'Bob'

Inside-right 5' 10½" 13st 0lbs
Born: Newburn, Newcastle-on-
Tyne, 6th February 1903
Died: Newburn, Newcastle-on-
Tyne, April quarter 1970
Debut v Charlton Athletic (a)
29.8.31, lost 1-3
CAREER: Spencer's Welfare.
Hawthorn Leslie. Newburn Grange. Newburn F.C.
Prudhoe Castle. Newcastle United February 1923,
fee £130. Liverpool January 1928, fee £3,000.
FOREST 4th July 1931. North Shields August
1932. Newburn August 1934.
*With a weight variously reported to be between 13
and 14 stones, Bob Clark was not the most mobile
performer, but he was said to be skilful on the ball
and the possessor of a powerful shot. He scored 16
goals in 77 League appearances for Newcastle
United, and was part of their Football League
championship team in 1927. He cost Liverpool a
hefty fee in 1928, and appeared in all three inside-
forward positions and on the left wing in the
course of 40 League appearances and 11 goals. His
signing by Forest was intended to form an entirely
new right wing for the 1931-32 season, alongside
Chambers, the Irish international wingman,
signed from Bury. Unfortunately, the pairing was
not a success and was scrapped after just three
matches, Cyril Stocks resuming at inside-right
following his recovery from injury.*
Appearances: FL: 5 apps 2 gls Total: 5 apps 2 gls
Honours: (Newcastle United) FL champions 1927

CLARK, Thomas George
Left half-back 5' 10" 11st 0lbs
Born: Trehafod, Glamorgan, 31st October 1913
Died: Southampton, 13th August 1994
Debut v Manchester City (h) 26.11.38, lost 3-4
CAREER: Trehafod Welfare. Abereynon. Bolton
Wanderers, amateur June, professional August
1933. **FOREST 26th November 1938.** (Wartime
guest with Cardiff City 1939-40.)
*Forest were reported to have spent a large fee
when they recruited George Clark, Bolton
Wanderers' clever and constructive right half-
back, whose best season at Burnden Park was
1936-37 when he appeared in 18 Division One
matches. His introduction into the Forest middle
line did much to stiffen a defence that had been
decimated by early season injuries to key
personnel. Retained at the close of the season,*

Clark appeared in the first three League matches of the 1939-40 season, and remained until mid term, adding a further five outings in regionalised football. He then returned to Wales and assisted Cardiff City as a guest player.
Appearances: FL: 27 apps 0 gls FAC: 2 apps 0gls
Total: 29 apps 0 gls

COLEMAN, John George 'Tim'

Inside-forward
5' 6" 11st 4lbs
Born: Kettering, 26th October 1881
Died: Kensington, London, 20th November 1940
Debut v Birmingham (a) 2.9.14, drawn 1-1 (scored)
CAREER: Kettering St. Mary's. Kettering Town 3rd May 1900. Northampton Town 21st May 1901. Woolwich Arsenal 16th May 1902. Everton 28th February 1908, fee £700. Sunderland May 1910. Fulham July 1911. **FOREST 23rd July 1914 to May 1915.** Tunbridge Wells Rangers September 1919-20. Maidstone United manager May 1921-22. Coaching in Enscheda, Holland, in 1925.

A short thought sturdily built inside-forward, Tim Coleman was a consistent goal scorer throughout a somewhat nomadic career. For his five different League clubs he scored 189 goals in 405 matches, a total that included 79 in 172 matches for Arsenal, where he won his England cap against Ireland in 1907. He assisted Everton to the runners-up position in the First Division in 1908-09, scoring 30 goals in 69 League matches. He subsequently assisted Sunderland (21 goals in 31 matches) and Fulham (45 goals in 94 matches.) Said to possess brains and skill in plenty, and with a thrilling first-time shot, he had an excellent season at the City Ground before enlisting in the Footballers' Battalion. He retired from playing during the World War One period, but resumed at the age of 38 with Tunbridge Wells Rangers. He lost his life early in the Second World War through an industrial accident.
Appearances: FL: 38 apps 14 gls FAC: 2 apps 2 gls
Total: 40 apps 16 gls
Honours: England International, 1 cap v Ireland, February 1907. FL representative, 3 apps. 1907-11.

COLES, Frederick **Gordon**

Left half-back
Born: Sherwood, Nottingham, 17th November 1875
Died: City Hospital, Nottingham, 22nd April 1947
Debut v Bury, FAC semi-final (at Stoke) 24.3.00 (drawn 1-1)
CAREER: Nottingham Post Office F.C. Notts County 3rd May 1895 to May 1896. **FOREST amateur 8th April 1899.** Woolwich Arsenal 17th August 1900. Grimsby Town 24th June 1904 to 1907. FC Gothenburg (Sweden) coach. FC Haessche Veotbal Vereeniging trainer-coach 1909-11.

Gordon Coles had to leave his native city in order to make his mark in the football world. Never more than a reserve with both Nottingham clubs, he quickly established himself as a first team regular with Woolwich Arsenal, appearing in 86 League and Cup matches before losing his place in 1903-04. Some consolation was gained during his spell in the reserve team, who lifted both the South-Eastern League championship and the London League Reserve championship. Moving on the Grimsby Town, he added a further 44 League outings to his record before becoming one of the pioneer British coaches in Europe. Appointments in Holland and Denmark ended when he enlisted into the Army and was drafted to Egypt with the Royal Army Medical Corps.
Appearances: FL: 1 app 0 gls FAC: 2 apps 0 gls
Total: 3 apps 0 gls

COLLINS, James 'Jimmy'

Inside-left
5' 9" 11st 2lbs
Born: Scotland, 1872
Died: Rochester, Kent, 2nd January 1900
Debut v Wolverhampton Wanderers (h) 2.9.93, won 7-1 (scored three goals)
CAREER: Shawfields Athletic. Newcastle East End 1888. Newcastle West End January 1891. Newcastle United May 1892. **FOREST July 1893.** Newcastle United 14th June 1895, fee £20. Sheppey United 15th October 1897. Chatham 20th May 1899 to his death.

Jimmy Collins made his Newcastle United debut in a Northern League fixture at Sheffield United in September 1892. In two spells at St. James' Park he appeared in 34 Football League matches and eight FA Cup-ties, scoring 11 goals. On joining Forest, he missed only one match in his first season, in which he introduced himself with a hat trick against the Wolves in a 7-1 opening-day victory. He returned to Newcastle after two seasons and was operating in the Southern League when he died in tragic circumstances of tetanus after being injured whilst playing for Chatham against New Brompton on Boxing Day 1899. He had fallen on the field and gashed his knee on a sharp flint stone. He was taken to hospital where his wound was attended to but he was not detained. He returned to his lodgings and appeared to be progressing satisfactorily during the week, but alarming symptoms developed on the Sunday, and he died at the St. Bartholomew's Hospital on Monday night,

Appearances: FL: 40 apps 15 gls FAC: 4 apps 0 gls Total: 44 apps 15 gls

COMERY, Harry
Outside-left
Born: Nottingham, 29th June 1885
Died: Toronto, Canada, 4th October 1979
Debut v Notts County (h) 25.12.03, lost 0-1
CAREER: FOREST 20th March 1903, re-signed 30th January 1904. Arnold F.C. 6th May 1904 to 1905.
In two separate spells on Forest's books, Harry Comery was restricted to just one first team appearance. With regular outside-left Alf Spouncer still recovering from a knock sustained in the 3-7 defeat at Aston Villa six days earlier, Comery was pitched in for the Christmas day 'Derby' against neighbours Notts County at the City Ground.

Appearances: FL: 1 app 0 gls Total: 1 app 0 gls

CONDREY, James **Frederick**
Centre-forward
Born: Wrexham, *circa* 1888
Died: Crewe, October quarter 1952
Debut v Birmingham (h) 4.11.11, lost 0-1
CAREER: Nantwich Town. Wellington Town. **FOREST 31st October 1911 to April 1913.**
Fred Condrey was given an early opportunity, leading the line in place of Frank Saunders within a week of arriving at the City Ground from Wellington Town. Despite a quiet debut, he held his place for a run of six matches, and scored both of Forest's goals in the 2-1 win against Blackpool on his third appearance. There then followed two goalless draws and a 0-1 defeat, and Frank Saunders was reintroduced. Fred Condrey made his final appearance in the season's last match, a 1-1 home draw against Fulham.

Appearances: FL: 7 apps 2 gls Total: 7 apps 2 gls

CONNOR, James
Right half-back
Born: Birmingham, 1st April 1867
Died: Birmingham, 1929
Debut v Burnley (a) 4.11.93, lost 1-3
CAREER: Warwickshire County. Aston Villa August 1889. Burslem Port Vale (trial) August 1891. King's Heath F.C. September 1891. **FOREST 13th October 1893.** Heanor Town October 1894.
A reserve wing half-back with Aston Villa, James Connor made his first senior appearance in a 1-2 home defeat by Bolton Wanderers on 25th January 1890. In the following season he played in three first team matches, departing Villa Park for a trial with Burslem Port Vale and, one month later, a contract with King's Heath. On joining Forest, although finishing on the losing side on his debut at Burnley, the 'Nottingham Evening Post' reported that he had: "Fully justified his selection in the half-back division, and will doubtless figure again in the first team. He gave nothing away, and tackled splendidly," In the event, Connor made infrequent League appearances thereafter, failing to win a regular place in the middle line that featured McPherson, Stewart and McCracken as the favoured trio. Almost a year to the day of his arrival, Connor was transferred to Heanor Town and made his Midland League debut against Matlock on 6th October 1894.

Appearances: FL: 5 apps 0 gls Total: 5 apps 0 gls

COX, William 'Billy'

Centre-forward
5' 9"   11st 11lbs
Born: Falkirk, 22nd October 1897
Died: Eastwood, Glasgow, 14th November 1965
Debut v West Bromwich Albion (h) 3.3.23, lost 0-4
CAREER: Govan Y.M.C.A. Renfrew Juniors. Whiteinch Glenbuck. Clydebank 1916.
Cardiff City September 1919. Newport County (loan) December 1920. Vale of Leven April 1922. Workington August 1922. **FOREST 23rd February 1923, fee £500.** Workington.
Said to have been a prolific scorer for Workington, and often showing excellent form in Forest Reserves, Billy Cox played in just one first team match and failed to shine in a 0-4 home defeat against West Bromwich Albion. Earlier, he assisted Cardiff City in the Southern League and was a Welsh Cup winner before making his Football League bow whilst on loan at Newport County, for whom he scored twice in six League matches.

Appearances: FL: 1 app 0 gls Total: 1 app 0 gls
Honours: (Cardiff City) Welsh Cup winners.

CRAGGS, John Owens

Outside-right
5' 8½" 11st 10lbs
Born: Trimdon Grange, County Durham, July quarter 1880
Debut v Sheffield United (a) 3.12.04, lost 0-4
CAREER: Trimdon Grange F.C. Sunderland March 1900. Reading May 1902. Sunderland August 1903. **FOREST 16th November 1904**. Sutton Town (loan) December 1906. Houghton Rovers June 1907. West Stanley September 1907.

After a slow start to his Sunderland career, John Craggs moved to Reading and regular first team football. He did so well that the Roker management persuaded him to return, and for one season was first choice at outside-right and a frequent scorer. He was a member of the Sunderland X1 who won at the City Ground a few weeks before his signing, but he failed to realise expectations in his first season with Forest, but missed only two matches in 1905-06 scoring eight goals in 40 League and Cup matches. He then lost his place after eight matches in the Division Two championship side and was loaned to Sutton United until the end of the season.
Appearances: FL: 52 apps 7 gls FAC: 4 apps 1 gl
Total: 56 apps 8 gls

CRAIG, Charles Thomson

Full-back 6' 2" 12st 4lbs
Born: Dundee, 11th July 1879
Died: New Southgate, Barnet, London, 12th January 1933
Debut v Sunderland (a) 1.9.02, won 1-0
CAREER: Dundee Our Boys F.C. Thames Ironworks 19th October 1899. West Ham United July 1900. **FOREST 5th May 1902**. Bradford Park Avenue 5th June 1907. Bradford City 18th April 1908. Norwich City 28th November 1908. Southend United August 1910. Merthyr Town June 1912, retired 1914.

For five years a stalwart in the ranks of the Forest defence Charlie Craig earned an enviable reputation in Southern League circles before joining Forest in May 1902. At over 6ft in height and with a weight to match he was no featherweight to come up against; he was also excellent in headwork and a strong and vigorous tackler. As the 'Stevens Handbook' put it: "His feet seem invariably to get into other folk's way." Eventually losing out to the emerging 'Ginger' Maltby in the 1906-07 promotion season, he did little with either Bradford Park Avenue or Bradford City but performed admirably for

Norwich City (58 matches), Southend United (23 matches) and finally Merthyr Town (59 matches.)
Appearances: FL: 136 apps 2 gls FAC: 11 apps 0 gls
Total: 147 apps 2 gls

CRAWFORD, John

Half-back 5' 9½" 11st 6lbs
Born: Renton, Dunbartonshire, 23rd February 1880
Died: Millburn, January 1934
Debut v Sheffield Wednesday (a) 28.2.03, lost 0-1
CAREER: West Calder F.C. Bonhill. Dumbarton. Renton 1897. Lincoln City 24th August 1900. **FOREST 20th February 1903 to May 1906, fee £400.**

Financial reasons led Lincoln City to accept Forest's offer of £400 for centre-half John Crawford, who had served the Imps well for the best part of three seasons, accumulating 85 appearances and scoring one goal. Stepping up a Division on joining Forest, Crawford was tried in all three half-back positions without winning a regular first team place and was released at the close of the 1905-06 season.
Appearances: FL: 13 apps 0 gls Total: 13 apps 0 gls

CRAWSHAW, Harold William Stanley

Centre-forward
5' 11½" 11st 10lbs
Born: Prestwich, near Manchester, 18th February 1912
Died: Plymouth, 17th February 1975
Debut v Plymouth Argyle (a) 31.8.38, lost 0-3
CAREER: Newton Heath Loco. Northwich Victoria (trial) August 1930. Ashington August 1932. Ashton National July 1933. Newton Heath Athletic 1934. Portsmouth February 1935. Mansfield Town July 1937, fee £225. **FOREST 6th July 1938, fee £1,750 plus Charlie Gardiner**. Hurst November 1939. (Wartime guest player with Oldham Athletic October-November 1943 and Blackburn Rovers.).

A younger brother of Richard Leigh Crawshaw, an inside-left who won a Third Division North championship medal with Nelson in 1923. Harold, an engineer's pattern maker, commenced with Newton Heath Loco, made a single appearance for Portsmouth, before hitting the headlines with Mansfield Town. Despite being handed the seemingly thankless task of succeeding 55-goal Teddy Harston (transferred to Liverpool),

Crawshaw began with a hat trick on his debut in a 4-1 win against Northampton Town. For the second successive season, a Mansfield Town player headed the Third Division South goal scoring list, Harold Crawford heading the table with 25 goals. The Stags also won the County Cup, beating Forest 2-1 in the final at the City Ground. In the following June, Forest obtained the signature of last season's leading scorer for a fee of £1,750 with Scottish forward Charlie Gardiner moving to Field Mill as part of the deal. After scoring five goals in as many matches in September 1938, the goals dried up for a Forest side that continued to struggle in Division Two. In March a change of manager saw Harry Wightman replaced by Billy Walker, and Harold Crawshaw ended his season in the reserves and was placed on the transfer list in May 1939.
Appearances: FL: 22 apps 9 gls Total: 22 apps 9 gls

CROSS, J.
Right full-back
Born: Circa 1871
Debut v Newton Heath (h) 7.4.94, won 2-0
CAREER: Albion Rovers (Coatbridge). **FOREST 23rd March 1894**
*A late season signing in March 1894, full-back Cross commenced in the same month with a debut in a goalless encounter at Sheffield United in a United Counties League fixture on 31st March. A run out in the League side followed, but it was back to the UC League for his final outing, a 0-2 home defeat by Derby County. His name did not appear in the following season's retained list.
Note: Football League registration documents do not reveal a forename for this player.*
Appearances: FL: 1 app 0 gls Total: 1 app 0 gls

DAFT, Harry Butler

Outside-left
5' 9½" 11st 0lbs
Born: Radcliffe-on-Trent, 5th April 1866
Died: High Cross, Herts, 12th January 1945
Debut v Derby County (h) 28.1.93, won 1-0
CAREER: Trent College. Notts County amateur March 1885, professional 1890. **FOREST 17th January 1893.** Notts County August 1893. Newark Town amateur January 1895 (Also assisted Corinthians 1887-90 and Nottinghamshire in representative matches)
The youngest son of Richard Daft (Nottinghamshire C.C.C. 1858-91), brother of Richard Parr Daft (Nottinghamshire C.C.C. 1886), nephew of Charles Frederick Daft (Nottinghamshire C.C.C. 1862-64) and cousin to H.C. Daft, the champion hurdle racer. For genuine all-round sporting ability, however, the star of this remarkable family was Harry Butler Daft. In addition to his England football caps, he played in 190 matches for Nottinghamshire C.C.C. and represented the Gentlemen against the Players. Additionally, he was no mean exponent of the game of lacrosse, having represented the North against the South, and was reserve for England at twenty years of age. As a footballer he was noted for his great speed, clever centres and ability as a goalscorer. An invaluable servant to the Notts County club with an overall record of 81 goals in 179 appearances, there was a parting of the ways in January 1893 when he was sensationally dismissed after he had declined to travel to Scotland for the New Year tour on account of a foot injury. He was quickly snapped up by Forest, but donned the red jersey on only four occasions, one of his appearances being against his former colleagues on 25th February 1893, on the Town Ground, Forest winning 3-1. Much to the relief of the Trent Bridge faithful, the rift was healed in the close season and Daft returned to the Magpies. He was later a cricket and sports outfitter and a licensee at the Trent Bridge Hotel.
Appearances: FL: 4 apps 1 gl Total: 4 apps 1 gl
Honours: England International, 5 caps 1889-92.
FL representative, 2 apps 1891-92. (Notts County)
FA Cup winners 1894, finalists 1891.

DAVIES, Robert Griffith
Centre half-back 5' 11" 12st 0lbs
Born: Blaenau Ffestiniog, North Wales, 19th October 1913
Died: Nottingham, 10th May 1978
Debut v Bradford Park Avenue (h) 6.3.37, won 3-2
CAREER: Blaenau Ffestiniog F.C. July 1932. **FOREST amateur 21st July, professional 2nd December 1936, fee £55 plus the proceeds of a match.** (Wartime guest player with Blackpool, Leicester City. Rochdale and Wrexham). **FOREST Reserve team coach 1947-54. Later physiotherapist to 1974.** Walsall physiotherapist to his death
A central defender with few frills in his play, Bob Davies was a strapping figure who kicked like a horse – according to the' Post Football Guide' – who also considered that he should; "Lie further up the field, the third back game can be carried to excess." Despite operating in the shadow of star centre-half Tommy Graham, Davies proved a sound deputy, able to occupy both wing-half berths as required. He was one of several Forest unfortunates who succumbed to cartilage problems, an operation restricting his activities in his final season.
Appearances: FL: 55 apps 0 gls FAC: 4 apps 0 gls
Total: 59 apps 0 gls

DAVIES, Thomas Osborne

Outside-right 5' 6½" 11st 0lbs
Born: Swindon, 27th March 1882
Died: Swindon, December 1967, age 85`
Debut v Wolverhampton Wanderers (a) 26.9.03, lost 2-3
CAREER: Swindon Thistle. Swindon Town amateur 3rd September 1899, professional 4th January 1901. **FOREST 27th April 1903.** Reading August 1906. Salisbury City 23rd October 1907. Southampton (trial) 26th April 1909, professional August 1909, retired due to injury May 1910.

Forest's signing of Tom Davies in April 1903 brought the total of ex-Swindon Town players on the books to four – Morris, Henderson, Jones and Davies. It was hoped that Davies would satisfactorily fill the outside-right position that had been a weak spot in the team in the previous season. The small but stiffly built winger held his place in the side for much of his first season at the City Ground but it was a case of diminishing returns, as he played only twice in his last season when relegation from Division One resulted. A season with Reading followed, and Forest, who retained his registration, had him on their transfer list at £300. Following a meeting of the Football League committee in October 1907, Forest agreed to reduce his fee to £30. A brother A.S. 'Bertie' Davies was also a Swindon Town player. Mainly from outside-left, and in two separate spells, he totalled 278 matches and scored 34 goals in all competitions for the Railwaymen.
Appearances: FL: 40 apps 1 gl FAC: 4 apps 0 gls
Total: 44 apps 1 gl

DAVIS, Herbert Alfred 'Bertie'

Inside-forward 5' 9" 11st 4lbs.
Born: Arnold, Nottingham, 30th March 1897
Died: Arnold, Nottingham, 26th September 1973
Debut v Hull City (a) 18.10.19, lost 0-2
CAREER: Arnold St. Mary's July 1914. Basford United. **FOREST amateur 4th professional 24th October 1919.** Boston Town August 1921. Reading August 1923. Mansfield Town May 1925 to cs 1926. Arnold Wesleyans February 1928.

First appearing in local league football at the age of 17 for Arnold St. Mary's, Bertie Davis moved quickly on to Basford United. Described at this point as: "A dashing right wing or centre-forward player, with a partiality for the role of opportunist, although able to play the combination game well." World War One intervened, and he was taken prisoner of war by the Germans in 1917. Thankfully able to resume his playing career in 1919, he scored twice for Forest Reserves against his former club, Basford United, and within days was signed as a professional. In the month of November he scored four goals in three matches, and seven in 14 during the season in which he lost his first team place when Jack Spaven was signed from Scunthorpe & Lindsey United. After a season with Boston United, Davis returned to League football with Reading, for whom he scored eight goals in 34 League and Cup matches. In a season with Mansfield Town, he assisted the Stags to runners-up position in the Midland League. He was also a Notts Senior Cup winner, scoring one of six goals by which Player's Athletic were beaten in the final.
Appearances: FL: 20 apps 7 gls Total: 20 apps 7 gls

DEAN, Alfred

Outside-right
5' 5" 11st 0lbs
Born: Willenhall, 2nd January 1877
Died: New Cross, 21st January 1959
Debut v Everton (a) 2.3.01, lost 1-4
CAREER: Tantany Rovers. West Bromwich Standard. Walsall Town Swifts September 1895. West Bromwich Albion September 1896. Walsall September 1898. **FOREST 20th February 1901, fee £120.** Grimsby Town May 1901. Bristol City May 1902. Swindon Town June 1905. Millwall May 1906. Dundee May 1907. Millwall June 1908. Wellington Town July 1909. Udley F.C. September 1911. Halmerend F.C. February 1913. Kidsgrove. Wellington October 1913. Alsagers Bank Athletic January 1914. Halmerend F.C. June 1914. Podmore Hall August 1919.

In a career not lacking variety, Alf Dean's reputation was made with Walsall (36 goals in 72 matches). At the time of his transfer to the Forest he had scored 11 Football League goals and six in FA Cup-ties – including five against Wellington Town. Sadly, on joining Forest, despite being tried at centre-forward and on the right wing, he was considered a "dead failure" by the local press and was quickly released to join Grimsby Town. When Forest played at Grimsby early in the following season, the 'Nottingham Evening Post' reported that "The form of Dean was something of an 'eye-opener' the old Walsall and Forest forward seems to be suited by the Lincolnshire Coast surroundings." Subsequently, Dean scored 35 League goals in 84 matches for Bristol City and 23 goals in 87 matches for Millwall, covering all competitions.
Appearances: FL: 7 apps 0 gls Total: 7 apps 0 gls

DENNIS, George Thomas
Outside-left 5' 9½" 11st 0lbs
Born: Moira, Leics. 12th September 1897
Died: Burton-on-Trent, 13th October 1969
Debut v Cardiff City (h) 26.2.21, lost 1-2
CAREER: Gresley Rovers. Coalville Swifts.
(Wartime guest player with Leicester Fosse January
1917.) Newhall Swifts September 1920. **FOREST
23rd February 1921.** Luton Town May 1924.
Norwich City May 1929. Bristol Rovers May 1930 to
May 1931. Gresley Rovers August 1932. Burton
Town.
*George Dennis assisted Newhall Swifts to reach
the top of the Burton & District League in season
1920-21. Playing at either inside or outside-left, he
scored 45 goals between September and February
when he signed with Forest, forestalling
Sunderland and Birmingham. On the day that he
signed for Forest he had earlier scored a hat trick
against Burton All Saints. Introduced into the
Forest attack at the expense of the former Bury
wingman Jack Lythgoe, Dennis scored in his
second appearance in a 5-1 win against Fulham at
the City Ground, and held his place for the
remainder of the season. In the following Second
Division championship campaign, Forest
commenced with the newly signed Noah Burton at
outside-left, restricting Dennis to just ten League
matches and two goals, insufficient to qualify him
for a championship medal. On joining Luton Town
of Division 3 South, he finished his first season as
joint leading scorer with 12 goals in 41 League
matches. In a five-year stay with the Hatters he
scored 44 League and Cup goals in 150
appearances. Subsequently, he appeared just once
for Norwich City and concluded with 3 goals in 27
League appearances for Bristol City.*
Appearances: FL: 30 apps 3 gls FAC: 3 apps 1 gl
Total: 33 apps 4 gls

DENNISON, Robert Smith 'Bob'

Centre or Inside-
forward
6' 0" 11st 4lbs
Born: Ambleside,
Northumberland,
6th March 1912
Died: Gillingham,
Kent, 19th June 1996
Debut v Newcastle
United (h) 25.8.34,
won 5-1
CAREER:
Radcliffe Welfare
United Juniors.
Newcastle United
May 1929.
**FOREST 26th May
1934.** Fulham June 1935. Northampton Town May
1939. (Wartime guest player with Fulham 1939-40.)
Northampton Town manager March 1949.

Middlesbrough manager July 1954 to January 1963.
Hereford United manager December 1963 to
December 1967. Coventry City scout, appointed
assistant-manager December 1967 and in
numerous other roles including a spell as caretaker-
manager March to June 1972, retired in 1978.
*Hailing from a family of ten, Bob Dennison was a
tall and strongly built centre or inside forward
who joined Newcastle United as a youngster and
waited almost four years before making his
League debut against Sheffield United in February
1933. In the following year, he must have
thoroughly enjoyed his Forest debut, a 5-1 victory
against his former employers at the City Ground.
Unable to win a regular place with the Reds, he
moved on to Fulham where he was employed
mainly in defensive roles in the course of 34
League and Cup appearances. He joined
Northampton Town just prior to the outbreak of
war and served the Cobblers both as player and
manager (246 appearances including wartime
matches.) He was next in charge of
Middlesbrough, and after four years in charge of
Hereford United he was associated with Coventry
City in numerous roles, including a spell as
caretaker-manager before retiring in 1978.*
Appearances: FL: 15 apps 5 gls FAC: 1 app 1 gl
Total: 16 apps 6 gls

DENT, John George 'Johnny'

Centre-forward
5' 10" 13st 0lbs
Born
Spennymoor,
31st January
1903
Died
Nottingham, 6th
November 1979
CAREER:
Spennymoor
Rangers.
Tudhoe United.
Thornley
Albion. Durham
City amateur
December 1923.
Tow Law Town
February 1925.
Durham City
amateur September 1925. Huddersfield Town June
1926. **FOREST 3rd October 1929, fee £1,500.**
Kidderminster Harriers August 1937 to 1939.
Debut v Bradford Park Avenue (h) 3.10.29, drawn
1-1
*Johnny Dent was once described as: "A strong,
bustling attack leader without embroidery, and a
fine shot", another appraisal considered him "A
whole hearted player and one of the most difficult
to knock off the ball". His promise first became
evident in the ranks of Durham City, his deadly*

left-foot shooting netting him 29 goals in 50 League and Cup matches. His dream move to Huddersfield Town was well earned and he celebrated his debut against Arsenal at Highbury by scoring both goals in a 2-0 win. He was a member of the first team squad in 1927-28 when Town finished as runners-up for the League championship and the FA Cup, but he did not appear at Wembley despite having featured in the two replays that were necessary to defeat Sheffield United in the semi-final. He was transferred for a then sizeable fee to Nottingham Forest. In seven seasons at the City Ground he was an unqualified success, netting 119 goals in 196 Second Division matches, and three in 10 FA Cup-ties. Highlights included his 27 goals in 35 League matches in 1933-34, an outstanding contribution in a season when Forest came close to relegation into the Third Division. In the following season he scored two hat tricks within the space of seven days in successive 5-0 wins against Oldham Athletic and Burnley. At the age of 34 he joined Kidderminster Harriers, and then served in the RAF during the Second World War. At the end of hostilities he settled in West Bridgford and was a keen amateur cricketer with his local Baptists C.C.

Appearances: FL: 196 apps 119 gls FAC: 10 apps 3 gls Total: 206 apps 122 gls

DERRICK, John Henry

Inside-forward 5' 6½" 9st 7lbs
Born: Nottingham, 8th December 1891
Died: Nottingham, 19th April 1938
Debut v Everton (a) 2.4.10, won 4-0 (scored two goals)
CAREER: Christ Church F.C. **FOREST amateur 17th September 1909, professional 28th October 1909**. Aberavon January 1920. Aberaman June 1920. Loughborough Corinthians. Stamford Town (trial) October 1925. Gedling Colliery Welfare November 1928. Nottingham East End Thursday October 1929.
One of any number of talented locally produced footballers to assist Forest over the years, John Derrick's 49 goals for Christ Church F.C., runners-up in the Notts Sunday School League in 1908-09, earned him his chance with the Forest. This was seized with alacrity when he netted two goals in a 4-0 victory at Everton on his debut. Later in the same month he scored twice against Liverpool at Anfield, but on this occasion, Forest were beaten 7-3. At one point, his height and weight was given as 5' 6½" and 8st 12lbs so it was not surprising that the 'Post Football Guide' for 1912-13 had this to say: " With a bit more size he would be a first-class forward in any of the inside positions. He is indisputably clever with the ball and well ahead of

the useful class." John Derrick served in the Leicestershire Regiment during the Great War, but played in only eight League matches with the Forest in 1919-20 before departing into non-League football.
Appearances: FL: 139 apps 35 gls FAC: 8 apps 1 gl Total: 147 apps 36 gls

DEWEY, Joseph

Outside-right
Born: Burton-on-Trent, October quarter 1873
Died: Burton-on-Trent, 17th November 1926
Debut v Preston North End (a) 7.11.96, lost 2-3
CAREER: Burton Swifts 13th August 1892. Loughborough cs 1894. **FOREST 23rd October 1896**. Burton Swifts 27th November 1896. Reading 21st May 1897. Hugglescote Robin Hoods 11th October 1898. Hinckley Town 11th July 1899. Coalville Town 4th October 1900. Stanton F.C. 24th August 1901. Trent Rovers 27th September 1904.
Between spells with Loughborough, and a Midland League championship win, and the briefest of associations with Forest, Joe Devey scored 21 Division Two goals for Burton Swifts in his first spell, and five in 17 matches in his second. A season in the Southern League with Reading followed, where he scored four goals in 12 matches. He then returned to Burton and local non-League football. In 1901 he was working as a fitter's labourer, but ten years later was working as a brakeman for Burton Corporation Tramways. He died at the age of 53, following an operation in Burton Infirmary.
Appearances: FL: 1 app 0 gls Total: 1 app 0 gls
Honours: (Loughborough) Midland League champions 1895.

DEXTER, Arthur

Goalkeeper
6' 0" 11st 0lbs
Born: Basford, Nottingham, 11th January 1905
Died: Rustington, Sussex, 10th February 1997
Debut v Everton (h) 1.9.23, won 1-0
CAREER: Highbury Vale Methodists. Bulwell St. Albans. Vernon Athletic. Stapleford Brookhill F.C. **FOREST amateur 21st October 1921,**

professional 8th May 1923, retired May 1937.

Nottingham-born goalkeeper Arthur Dexter was only 16 years old when he appeared in three matches for Forest Reserves, and was reported to have given complete satisfaction. He had, however, a very lengthy spell as understudy to Len Langford before being given his first extended run in the side in season 1927-28. A goalkeeper of sound judgment and wonderful anticipation, he was awarded a benefit in April 1930 and qualified for a second before retiring in 1937. Strongly challenged in later seasons by Percy Ashton, critics were divided on the question of who was the better of the two, but certainly Forest were fortunate to have such outstanding candidates for their last line of defence. Arthur Dexter was employed in the printing trade, and later ran his own business.
Appearances: FL: 256 apps 0 gls FAC: 18 apps 0 gls
Total: 274 apps 0 gls

DICKINSON, William 'Billy'

Inside-left
5' 9½" 11st 12lbs
Born: Tophock, 18th February 1904
Died: Newark, Notts. 17th August 1968
CAREER: New Springs FC. Tophock. Wigan Borough amateur April 1922, and again September 1924, professional February 1926. **FOREST 8th June 1928, fee £350.** Rotherham United August 1934. Southend United May 1936. Hull City May 1938 to 1939.
Debut v Swansea Town (a) 15.9.28, won 5-3 (scored two goals)

Billy Dickinson made the breakthrough into regular first-team football following a 5-0 win against Accrington Stanley on 5th December 1925, in which he scored two of Wigan Borough's goals. He finished the season with 20 goals in 30 League and Cup matches and headed the scoring list for the season. He repeated the feat in both 1926-27 (28 goals in 42 matches) and in 1927-28 (17 in 38 matches). He twice scored four goals in a match and had three hat tricks to his credit. His form attracted any number of bigger clubs and he moved on to Nottingham Forest in June 1928. Despite scoring twice on his debut against Swansea Town he did not feature regularly in Division Two until his third season at the City Ground. Some explanation was contained in a press comment in 1930: "Forest are fortunate to have a reserve centre-forward of the calibre of William Dickinson. This sprightly young man from Wigan may be wanting in certain essentials of leadership, but if he is not an expert in holding his line together he must be marked as dangerous as his record with both Forest and Wigan Borough proves." From season 1930-31 onwards he earned a regular place in the Forest side and despite lengthy spells at outside-right finished his six seasons at the City Ground with 73 goals in 143 League and Cup matches. He continued to score regularly during the rest of his career; with Rotherham United (43 goals in 70 matches), Southend United (26 goals in 59 matches) and finally with Hull City where he scored a hat trick in the Tiger's biggest League win, an 11-1 drubbing of Carlisle United on 14th January 1939. His career aggregate figures reveal a very healthy ratio of a goal every other game – 385 League appearances and 203 goals.
Appearances: FL: 136 apps 68 gls FAC: 7 apps 5 gls
Total: 143 apps 73 gls

DODSON, Albert
Right half-back
Born: Bingham, Notts. 31st March 1891
Died: Mansfield, January quarter 1966, age 74
Debut v Bradford Park Avenue (a) 20.4.12, lost 1-2
CAREER: FOREST 19th October 1911.
*A reserve wing half-back who joined Forest from
junior ranks in the season following relegation
from the top flight in 1911. With Forest stalwarts
Alf Fisher and Bert Armstrong sharing first team
duties at right half-back, Bert Dodson was
restricted to a single League appearance in the
penultimate Division Two game of the season
which carried Forest's dismal run of consecutive
defeats to seven matches.*
Appearances: FL: 1 app 0 gls Total: 1 app 0 gls

DONOVEN, Alfred Ernest 'Dickie'
Inside-left   5' 7"   11st 2lbs
Born: Bulwell, Notts. 20th June 1900
Died: Southend, October 1978
Debut v Leicester City (h) 12.2.21, lost 1-2
**CAREER: Bulwell Rangers F.C. FOREST 18th
August 1920.** Mansfield Town May 1922.
Southend United May 1925 to May 1935, fee £500.
Gas Light (Southend) July 1936.
*At the end of a pre-season trial match, Forest
signed 'Dickie' Donoven who had given a very
promising display at inside-left. He had just
reached his 20th birthday and had played in the
previous season for Bulwell Rangers, appearing in
every match and scoring plenty of goals. After
spending his second season at the City Ground
without a first team outing he made the short
journey to Mansfield to join the Stags. In his first
season he scored 14 goals, and followed with 36 in
1923-24 when the championship of the Midland
League was won. The Stags won the League for a
second time in 1924-25 with Donoven scoring 27
goals and 10 in subsidiary competitions. In
January 1925 he reached a milestone when he
netted his 100th goal for the club against
Gainsborough Trinity. He was transferred, along
with Dickie Bayliss, to Southend United for a
combined fee of £900 and scored 55 goals in 318
Football League matches and three in 14 FA Cup-
ties before retiring in May 1935, having played at
left half-back from 1930-31 onwards. A talented
musician, he could play almost any instrument. He
also enjoyed a game of cricket, golf and tennis.*
Appearances: FL: 3 apps 0 gls Total: 3 apps 0 gls

DRABBLE, Frank

Goalkeeper
5' 10½" 12st 0lbs
Born: Salford,
8th July 1888
Died: Staines,
29th July 1964
Debut v Sunderland (h)
18.2.11, lost 1-3
CAREER: Blowick
Wesleyans. Southport
Y.M.C.A. Tottenham
Hotspur (trial) May 1909,
professional October 1909. **FOREST February
1911.** Burnley December 1911. Bradford Park
Avenue June 1913. (Wartime guest player with
Brentford, Fulham and Southport Central.) Bolton
Wanderers August 1919. Southport June 1921 to
1922. Queen's Park Rangers February 1924.
*After just one League appearance for Tottenham
Hotspur, goalkeeper Frank Drabble did slightly
better in terms of League action with Forest. He
replaced Jack Smith on his debut against
Sunderland, a match that also featured another
new player, James Ridley, from Newcastle United.
The new signings were unable to lift an ailing
Forest side that won only one of their last 13
League matches and were relegated from Division
One. Drastic measures in the close season saw 12
players released, including a clean sweep of
goalkeepers, Hassell and Smith joining Frank
Drabble in the exodus. His best subsequent spells
came with Bradford Park Avenue (32
appearances) and Bolton Wanderers (29
appearances). During World War One he served in
the Royal Navy Air Service, and in civilian life
worked variously as a schoolmaster, bookmaker
and as an estate agent.*
Appearances: FL: 8 apps 0 gls Total: 8 apps 0 gls

DUDLEY, Walter William

Full-back 5' 8"   11st 12lbs
Born: Wath-upon-Dearn,
6th April 1882
Debut v Sheffield United (h)
27.12.02, drawn 2-2
**CAREER: FOREST 6th
November 1900.** Mansfield
Mechanics July 1914. Doncaster
Rovers January 1915.
*Popularly known as 'Dud', but
anything but a 'dud' at full-back, Walter Dudley
was born near to Rotherham but was bred in Old
Lenton. A most fearless type of back who never
spared himself in efforts to win the ball, he spent
his first two seasons in the reserve side, but he took
his chance in 1904-05 when deputising for the
injured Jim Iremonger. A switch from left to right
full-back eventually teamed him with 'Ginger'
Maltby and their effective partnership served
Forest well for seven seasons. Still capable of a 40-*

yards sprint in even time in 1913, his lengthy service had not impaired his speed, but a dreadful start to the 1913-14 campaign led to his replacement after seven early season matches. He was to appear only once more, in an 8-0 defeat at Leeds City, leaving him one short of 300 career appearances for the Reds.

Appearances: FL: 278 apps 0 gls FAC: 21 apps 0 gls
Total: 299 apps 0 gls
Honours: (**FOREST**) FL Division 2 champions 1907

DULSON, Joseph
Inside-forward 5' 9" 11st 0lbs
Born: Basford, Notts, 31st January 1913
Died: Arnold, Notts, 27th January 1990
Debut v Swansea Town (h) 23.4.32, won 6-1 (scored two goals)
CAREER: Newstead Colliery. Accrington Stanley (trial). **FOREST amateur 4th March 1932, professional 29th April 1932.** Accrington Stanley August 1933. Sutton Town August 1934. Grantham November 1934. Bournemouth & Boscombe Athletic (trial) August 1935. Newark Town June 1937.

A matter of weeks after leading the attack of Newstead Colliery, Joe Dulson was signed as an amateur, made his Football League debut and scored twice, and was quickly signed as a professional. Despite his whirlwind start, Forest did not give the youthful centre-forward another chance at senior level and he was transferred to Accrington Stanley. Sadly, a fractured ankle sustained in a reserve team match at Rochdale on Christmas Day brought a premature end to his season at Peel Park after he had scored once in 11 League matches. A subsequent trial with Bournemouth & Boscombe Athletic did not lead to a permanent engagement.

Appearances: FL: 1 app 2 gls Total: 1 app 2 gls

DYSON, James

Inside-forward
5' 6" 10st 0lbs
Born: Middleton, Lancs, 4th March 1906
Died: Oldham, 4th January 2000
Debut v Newcastle United (a) 19.2.38, lost 1-3
CAREER: Parkfield School (Middleton). Park Villa F.C. British Dyestuffs (I.C.I.). Northwich Victoria 1926-27. Oldham Athletic amateur February 1928, professional March 1928, fee £20. Grimsby Town March 1932, fee £2,350. **FOREST 18th February 1938 to May 1939.** Boston United August to November 1939.

(Wartime guest player with Accrington Stanley and Oldham Athletic in season 1939-40). Post-war managed Chadderton F.C.

Oldham Athletic made a donation of £20 to Northwich Victoria after Jimmy Dyson had signed a professional contract with the Latics. He proved an excellent capture, scoring 40 goals in 126 League and Cup matches. Reluctantly sold in the midst of a financial crisis in March 1932, he made 147 League and Cup appearances for Grimsby Town before joining Forest on the eve of the Second World War. He had hardly had time to get into his stride before he enlisted in the Royal Marines, serving in Egypt, Sicily and Ceylon. After the war he had a long association with the Chadderton club, whilst working as a window cleaner. He was thought to be Oldham Athletic's oldest surviving player, prior to his death at the age of 93.

Appearances: FL: 15 apps 0 gls FAC: 1 app 0 gls
Total: 16 apps 0 gls
Honours: (Grimsby Town) FL Division 2 champions 1934

EARP, Martin John 'Jack'

Right full-back
5' 9" 11st 12lbs
Born: Sherwood, Nottingham, 6th September 1872
Died: Unconfirmed, but thought to have died in South Africa when serving with Major-General Baden Powell's Police Force.
Debut v Derby Midland, FAC 1 (a) 18.1.1890, lost 0-3
CAREER: Sherwood Foresters. **FOREST amateur September 1889**. Everton amateur November 1891. **FOREST registered for FL matches 21st July 1892**. The Corinthians amateur. Sheffield Wednesday professional September 1893. Stockport County player-coach 28th July 1900 to January 1901.

Jack Earp played his early football as an amateur and it included two spells with Forest, his hometown club. He left briefly to join Everton during the course of the 1891-92 Alliance championship season but was back in time to appear in Forest's first Football League fixture, a 2-2 draw against Everton. He moved on at the end of the season to join Sheffield Wednesday and in a lengthy association captained his team in the 1896 FA Cup Final win against Wolverhampton Wanderers. After appearing in 174 League and Cup matches and scoring eight goals, he was released in April 1900. Joining Stockport County as player-coach, he captained County in their first-ever Football League match but made only 17 appearances before leaving in January 1901. He emigrated to South Africa in the same year to join Major Baden-Powell's Police Force and in December of the same year he was reported to be lying dangerously ill with enteric fever in a Bloemfontein hospital. Happily, he must have made a full recovery as he was later reported to be still serving in August 1910.

Appearances: FL: 13 apps 0 gls FAC: 8 apps 0 gls
Total: 21 apps 0 gls
Honours: FL representative, 1 app v Irish League 1898. (Sheffield Wednesday) FA Cup winners 1896.

EDGAR, Daniel

Right full-back
5' 11" 12st 0lbs
Born: Jarrow,
3rd April 1910
Died: Jarrow,
23rd March 1991
Debut v Bury (h) 31st
August 1935, drawn
2-2
CAREER: Jarrow
St. Bede's.
Sunderland amateur
May, professional
August 1930.
(Walsall loan
November 1930 to

May 1931). **FOREST 8th June 1935 to May 1939.**
Restricted to 46 League and Cup appearances during five seasons with Sunderland, Dan Edgar was tried in various positions for the Reds, before an extended trial at full-back revealed him as a defender of class, coolness and courage. Quick off the mark but with the experience to use brains to save his feet, he was ever-present in season 1936-37, but became one one of many unfortunates in the following term, when he finished up in Harlow Hospital with cartilage trouble. He was operated upon but never regained his first team place, leading to an untimely retiral. He had originally been a shipyard worker.
Appearances: FL: 100 apps 1 gl FAC: 4 apps 0 gls
Total: 104 apps 1 gl

ELLIOTT, Thomas William

Centre or Inside-
forward 5' 7" 11st 0lbs
Born Annfield Plain,
6th April 1888
Died Ryton-on-Tyne,
4th May 1955
CAREER: Annfield
Plain. West Stanley
1907. Gainsborough
Trinity May 1910. West
Stanley cs 1911.
Huddersfield Town May

1912 (Wartime guest player with Manchester City March 1918). Grimsby Town December 1919. **FOREST 3rd June 1920.** Brentford August 1921. Durham City September 1923. Crewe Alexandra February 1924. Annfield Plain September 1925; appointed trainer June 1927. Crawcrook Albion. Newcastle Tramways October 1934.
Debut v Stoke (h) 28.8.20, drawn 2-2
A prolific scorer in his second spell with West Stanley (63 goals in two seasons) Tom Elliott earned a second opportunity in League football with Huddersfield Town after an earlier undistinguished spell with Gainsborough Trinity. A goal on his debut on the opening day of the 1912-13 season kicked-off a promising start to his Leeds Road career. Comfortable in all three inside-forward berths, Elliott missed very few matches in his first two seasons, but appeared in only ten matches without scoring in his final term. He took some time to get into his stride after the Great War when a number of rapid moves took in Grimsby Town (No League appearances), Nottingham Forest (28 appearances and seven goals), and Brentford (49 appearances and eight goals). Crewe Alexandra was his last League club, where he rounded off with 18 appearances and four goals. He later became a licensee at West Stanley, where his son, John, played for the local team. Tom's elder brother, Hugh Bell Elliott, was a right full-back who appeared in 50 League and Cup matches for Durham City between 1922-25.
Appearances: FL: 28 apps 7 gls Total: 28 apps 7 gls

FALCONER, Fleming
Right half-back
Born: Hutchesontown, Glasgow, 24th May 1899
Died: Glasgow, 26th April 1991, age 91
Debut v Manchester City (a) 13.2.24, won 3-1
CAREER: Glasgow Eastern. Glasgow Ashfield.
FOREST 15th August 1923. Providence
Clamdiggers F.C. July 1924. Bo'ness F.C September 1924. Northampton Town (trial) October 1924. J & P Coates (Rhode Island) October 1927. New Bedford Whalers November 1927. Bristol Rovers February 1928. King's Park August 1929. Linlithgow Rose June to December 1931. Armadale to August 1932.
After representing the Glasgow League and winning representative honours when he played versus Ireland in a junior international in season 1922-23, Fleming Falconer appeared to have the right credentials for a career in senior football. He did not come up to expectations in his season at the City Ground, but after spells back in Scotland and in the U.S.A. he made 20 League appearances for Bristol Rovers before returning north of the border. Initially with King's Park, a Scottish Division Two side, his final club, Armadale, were expelled from Scottish Division Two a matter of months after his departure, for failing to meet match guarantees.

Appearances: FL: 2 apps 0 gls Total: 2 apps 0 gls
Honours: Scotland Junior International v Ireland
1922-23. Glasgow League representative v Irish
League.

FARMER, Alexander

Left half-back
5' 11" 11st 4lbs
Born: Lochgelly,
Fife, 9th October
1908
Died: May 1986
Debut v Stoke City
(h) 15.9.30, won
3-0
CAREER:
Thornton Hibs.
Kettering Town
June 1929.
**FOREST 14th
April 1930, fee
£50.** (Trials with
Leicester City and Newcastle United in August
1932.) Yeovil & Petters United September 1932.
Queen's Park Rangers January 1934 to 1944,
subsequently appointed assistant trainer. (Wartime
guest player with Brighton & Hove Albion, Chelsea,
Crystal Palace, Fulham, Watford and Charlton
Athletic.)
*Signed as a potential successor to Irish
international Bob Wallace, Alec Farmer created a
very good impression in the Midland League side
and took over first team duties at left-half in mid
September. An immediate upturn followed, the
defence tightened after the first four Division Two
matches of the season had seen 13 goals conceded.
Farmer held his place in the side until the end of
November, but following a 6-1 home defeat
against West Bromwich Albion he was left out.
Several other players were tried throughout the
remainder of the season, but finding an adequate
replacement for Bob Wallace was proving
extremely difficult. Farmer's best subsequent spell
came with Queen's Park Rangers whom he
assisted both before and during the war period,
scoring 11 goals in 164 competitive matches and
continuing as club assistant trainer into the 1950s.*
Appearances: FL: 16 apps 0 gls Total: 16 apps 0 gls

FIELDING A. Ross

Outside-right
Born: Stoke-on-Trent, 1881
Died: Stoke-on-Trent, 15th
February 1947
Debut v Grimsby Town (a)
9.9.02, won 1-0
CAREER: Stoke Priory F.C.
Stoke December 1901. **FOREST
9th September 1902.** Stoke
March 1903. West Bromwich
Albion June 1908. Stoke June

1909. Burton United October 1909, retired during
the World War One period.
*Ross Fielding, a lightweight but talented outside-
right enjoyed three spells with his hometown club,
scoring an overall total of 11 goals in101 League
appearances. During his fairly brief spell with
Forest he demonstrated a fair turn of speed and
accurate centring, but his failing was said to be an
inability to finish strongly, especially if challenged
by the full-backs.*
Appearances: FL: 10 apps 0 gls Total: 10 apps 0 gls

FIRTH, Robert Edwin 'Bob'

Outside-right
5'9 ½"11st 7lbs
Born: Hanley,
Stoke-on-
Trent, 20th
February 1887
Died: Derby,
July quarter
1966
Debut v
Burnley (a)
7.10.11,
lost 0-2
CAREER:
Gower Street
School.
Birmingham
Corporation
Transport. Golder's Green F.C. Birmingham April
1909. Wellington Town April 1911. **FOREST 5th
October 1911**. Port Vale June 1921. Southend
United July 1922 to May 1923. Santander (Spain)
coach by 1931.
*Former tram conductor Bob Firth scored twice in
25 League matches for Birmingham before being
released to join Wellington Town where his
outstanding form led to a quick return to League
action with Forest. Aside from an absence for some
weeks in the 1912-13 season due to illness, he
dominated the outside-right position. Fast and
clever and with any amount of determination he
was always a difficult winger for opposing
defences to contain. He was second highest scorer
in 1913-14 when he was described as: "The best
and most consistent outside-right the Forest have
had for years." Just when matters at the club were
beginning to assume a brighter look, the outbreak
of war caused the prospects of the club to become
anything but reassuring. Bob Firth, along with
Jack Bell and Tommy Fiske, who were all on the
reserve strength of the army, were recalled to the
colours. After service with the 6th Battery, Royal
Field Artillery, Firth was demobilised in the
summer of 1919 and returned to the City Ground
for a further two seasons. He then assisted Port
Vale for a season (5 goals in 39 League matches),
and followed with a season at Southend United
(one goal in 37 matches.)*

Appearances: FL: 141 apps 14 gls FAC: 5 apps 0 gls
Total: 146 apps 14 gls

FISHER, Alfred

Wing half-back
5' 8½" 11st 4lbs
Born: Nottingham,
circa 1888
Debut v Preston North
End (h) 25.3.10, drawn
0-0
CAREER: Notts.
Olympic. **FOREST 4th
May 1909 to
September 1915.**
*As the 'Post Football
Guide' put it: "Fisher is
one of the useful sort,
sturdy and with a good kick." A local recruited
from Notts Olympic he scored his first, and only
League goal at Sheffield Wednesday on 3rd
December 1910. It was not until the following
season that he was given an extended run in the
first team, appearing in 21 matches at right half-
back. He was first tried at full-back in March 1913,
and thereafter was able to fill either flank as
required. He was at right full-back in the final
fixture of the 1914-15 season, the match against
Arsenal marking his 100th League appearance for
the Reds. Unfortunately, the Gunners spoilt his
day, winning 7-0!*
Appearances: FL: 100 apps 1 gl FAC: 5 apps 0 gls
Total: 105 apps 1 gl

FISKE, William 'Tommy'

Goalkeeper
5' 10" 12st 12lbs
Born: Beccles, near
Lowestoft, 7th August 1885
Died: K.I.A. Marne, France,
27th May 1918
Debut v Derby County (h)
25.12.14, drawn 2-2
CAREER: Beccles F.C.
Suffolk County Amateurs.
Bungay F.C. Norwich City
17th October 1906. Blackpool
23rd May 1907. **FOREST 27th May 1914, fee
£250.**
*After about half a season with Norwich City
Tommy Fiske moved to Blackpool where he
appeared in 212 League appearances and seven
FA Cup-ties. Differing with the Seasiders on the
question of terms, he was placed on the transfer
list, and he cost Forest £250, the fee fixed by the
Football League Management Committee. In the
previous season, Forest had conceded 76 goals and
finished 20th in Division Two, the lowest point in
their history. Fiske's signing was expected to bring
some much- needed efficiency in goal. In the event,
he enlisted in the army on 21st August 1914, before*

*Forest's season had kicked off. He was on leave
from France when he made his five appearances,
commencing with a Christmas Day debut at the
City Ground.
He was serving as a sergeant at the time of his
death, and his body was not found. His name is
carved on the Soissons Memorial.*
Appearances: FL: 5 apps 0 gls FAC: 1 app 0 gls
Total: 6 apps 0 gls

FLETCHER, Stuart **Ernest**
Centre half-back
Born: *Circa* 1892
Debut v Bury (a) 26.9.14, lost 2-4
**CAREER: FOREST amateur 27th August 1914
to September 1915.**
*Centre-half Stuart Fletcher was signed on amateur
forms after playing exceptionally well in the pre-
season practice matches at the City Ground. He
was still in the unpaid ranks when he was given a
trial in the League side, deputising for regular
pivot Joe Mercer. Forest lost 2-4 at Bury, and it
was not until 13th January that they recorded their
first, and only, win on their travels, beating Bristol
City 2-1.*
Appearances: FL: 1 app 0 gls Total: 1 app 0 gls

FLOOD, Charles William

Inside-forward
6' 1" 12st 2lbs
Born: Newport, Isle of
Wight, 18th July 1896
Died: Cottingham, 14th
November 1978
Debut v Arsenal (ho 3.2.23,
won 2-1 (scored one)
CAREER: Army football
(R.G.A.) Plymouth Argyle
(trial) April, amateur
October, professional
December 1919. Hull City
August 1920. Bolton
Wanderers May 1922. **FOREST 30th January
1923.** York City August 1926. Swindon Town
February 1927 to August 1928.
*Charlie Flood was first discovered by Mr Robert
Jack, the Plymouth Argyle manager, whilst
playing in the Royal Garrison Artillery team, for
whom he scored 30 goals in seven matches. He
then joined Hull City, scoring 25 goals in 45
League matches. Moving on to Bolton Wanderers,
the fine form of Joe Smith, their regular inside-left,
kept him out of the side, restricting him to eight
matches and two goals. He joined a Forest side
struggling for points and did admirable work in
all three inside forward positions, and was more
than useful in the last two matches, when he filled
a vacancy at centre-forward, a position that he did
not really care for. He continued to play excellent
football until injured at Preston on 15th November
1924, and was unable to return before 14th*

February 1925. The unfortunate injury to one of their most reliable players had much to do with the Red's ultimate downfall and relegation to Division Two. After a final season spent with Forest in Division Two he joined York City, scoring 17 goals in 15 matches. Swindon Town was his last port of call, and he signed off with three goals in eight matches. As a batsman/wicket-keeper Charlie Food was associated with both Nottinghamshire and Devon County cricket clubs. Later he played for Hull Cricket Club and was appointed their coach in 1963

Appearances: FL: 97 apps 21 gls FAC: 3 apps 0 gls
Total: 100 apps 21 gls
Honours: Central League v Southern League, January 1923.

FORD, Joseph Bertram

Outside-left
5' 9½" 10st 6lbs
Born: Northwich, 7th May 1886
Died: Manchester, April quarter 1959, age 73
Debut v Preston North End (a) 1.9.10, won 2-0 (scored one)
CAREER: Witton Albion. Crewe Alexandra 1905. Manchester United 17th October 1907. **FOREST 11th June 1910**. Goole Town July 1914.

A former apprentice fitter and turner, Joe Ford was a slim and sprightly outside-left who moved from Crewe Alexandra to Manchester United as a 21 year-old. As understudy to England's George Wall at Old Trafford he found little opportunity and after appearing in only five League matches in three seasons he joined Forest in search of first team football. He made an excellent start, scoring on his Forest debut, but his season ended in disappointment as only one point was gained from the final 13 League matches and relegation from Division One ensued. For four seasons, Joe Ford was a familiar figure on Forest's left wing, appearing in excess of a century of League matches. He was, however, part of a struggling side and when he left the City Ground at the close of the 1913-14 season, Forest were faced with a re-election application, having finished at the foot of Division Two.

Appearances: FL: 102 apps 12 gls FAC: 2 apps 0 gls
Total: 104 apps 12 gls

FORMAN, Frank

Half-back
Born: Aston-upon-Trent, Notts. 23rd May 1875
Died: West Bridgford, Notts. 4th December 1961
Debut v Bolton Wanderers (h) 16.3.95, drawn 3-3
CAREER: Aston-upon-Trent F.C. Beeston Town. Derby County March 1894. **FOREST 25th February 1895, in exchange for T.P. Shrewsbury; retired May 1905. (Forest committee member 1903-61)**

Frank Forman played in only eight League matches for Derby County before joining his brother Fred at Forest. A right or centre-half back with great leadership qualities, he was a mainstay of the Forest defence in many a keen struggle, remaining calm and composed in the most difficult of situations. He won his first England cap in March 1898 and very shortly afterwards was an FA Cup winner against his former club, Derby County. In 1903 he announced his intention to retire, and the Forest directors decided, in view of the fact that he had not been awarded a benefit match, to present him with a substantial cheque and an expensively mounted rose bowl in appreciation of his long and valued service to the club. Forman stated that he would hold himself in readiness to once again don the red shirt if required, but would accept no payment for doing so. He did in fact make a further 14 appearances before finally hanging up his boots in 1905. Frank Forman was later in business in West Bridgford as a building contractor, in partnership with his brother-in-law Harry Linacre (q.v.) He also served for over half a century on the Forest committee, and lived long enough to celebrate Forest's 1959 FA Cup Final win against Luton Town.

Appearances: FL: 219 apps 23 gls FAC: 33 apps 5 gls Total: 252 apps 28 gls
Honours: England International, 9 caps 1898-1903. Forest FA Cup winners 1898.

FORMAN, Frederick Ralph

Inside-forward or Half-back
5' 11"
11st 6lbs
Born: Aston-upon-Trent, Notts.
8th November 1873
Died: Skegness, 14th June 1910
Debut v Everton (h) 22.9.94, lost 2-3

CAREER: Aston-upon-Trent F.C. Beeston Town. Derby County July 1893. **FOREST July 1894, retired May 1903. (Forest committee member 1903-10)**

Like his brother Frank (q.v.) Fred Forman spent little time with Derby County and was anxious to leave, first appealing to the Football League to grant his transfer to Forest in January 1894. The former Beeston amateur had an unfortunate start to his Forest career, being injured on his debut at Everton and being restricted to just 13 appearances in his first season. His career peaked in 1898-99 when he was pressed into action on the left wing, following injuries to both McInnes and Spouncer. He did so well that he was called up by his country and played his three International matches alongside his brother Frank. Fred's debut was a memorable one, as England beat Ireland 13-2 and he scored two of the goals, brother Frank netting one. At the time, Fred's selection for England gave rise to a great deal of adverse comment in the national press who considered it extraordinary to find him capped for England when it was remembered that for a long time he was not worth a place in the Forest team. This was probably justified, as he had played in only eight matches in 1897-98 and 11 in 1898-99. Subsequently he appeared in most first team matches, mainly on the right wing from which his centres were said to be: "Models of accuracy, being well timed and cleanly struck." Fred was a railway draughtsman by profession.

Appearances: FL: 155 apps 34 gls FAC: 23 apps 6 gls Total: 178 apps 40 gls
Honours: England International, 3 caps 1899

FORMAN, Thomas

Outside-left
5' 8" 11st 12lbs
Born: Basford, Notts.
26th October 1879
Died: Nottingham, March 1940
Debut v Aston Villa (h) 20.4.01, won 3-1
CAREER: Bulwell United. **FOREST 5th May 1900.** Manchester City 20th June 1904. Sutton Town 16th October 1905. Barnsley 3rd May 1907, fee £20. Tottenham Hotspur February 1911, fee £500. Sutton Junction F.C. June 1912 to 1915.

One of two local players signed from Bulwell United in May 1900- the other was a centre-forward named Dugdale who did not graduate to senior level at the City Ground. Tom Forman had the unenviable task of being understudy to Alf Spouncer for the left wing spot, hence his record of five first team appearances in four seasons. He failed to shine on moving to Manchester City but finally prospered with Barnsley, making 136 League and Cup appearances and scoring 16 goals. Recognised as one of the fastest wingers in the Second Division, he joined Tottenham Hotspur within a year of appearing in the FA Cup Final, but his scoring debut was followed by a serious injury in his second appearance, and he departed White Hart Lane after just nine League and Cup appearances.

Appearances: FL: 5 apps 0 gls Total: 5 apps 0 gls
Honours: Barnsley, FA Cup finalists 1910

FORREST, John Reid

Outside-right 5' 9" 11st 9lbs
Born: Tranent near Edinburgh, 3rd May 1908
Died: Reston, Berwickshire, 3rd May 1947
Debut v Everton (a) 21.2.31, lost 0-2
CAREER: Dalkeith Thistle. Rosewell Rosedale F.C. **FOREST 17th February 1931 to May 1933.** Belfast Distillery November 1933. Chirnside United 1935. Reston player/secretary June 1936.

After an early debut against Everton, the champions-elect, it was back to the Midland League football for John Forrest. The former Scottish junior, hitherto an inside-right, was tried on the right wing against Manchester United on 19th September 1931 and following a two-game absence, was next selected for the local 'Derby' against Notts County on 3rd October, in which he netted the winner in Forest's 2-1 victory. A winless run in November and December saw him deposed and replaced by Billy Dickinson. Forrest departed to try his luck in Ireland and spent two seasons with Belfast Distillery, runners-up for the Irish Cup in 1933. He was later a publican in Reston.

Appearances: FL: 14 apps 2 gls Total: 14 apps 2 gls

FRYER, John Leavy 'Jack'

Inside-forward
5' 10½" 12st 7lbs
Born: Widnes, 23rd September 1911
Died: Untraced, but known to have emigrated to New York in September 1952.
Debut v Burnley (a) 3.9.38, lost 1-2 (scored)
CAREER: Runcorn. Everton amateur May 1930, professional May 1931. Wrexham May 1933. Hull City May 1937. **FOREST 2nd June 1938 to September 1939.**

A go-ahead type of player with a deadly shot, Jack Fryer learned the rudiments of the game in the Everton nursery. He had scored 14 goals in 21 Central League matches for Everton Reserves when he was signed by Wrexham manager Ernie Blackburn in May 1933. In a stay of four years at the Racecourse he netted 28 League and Cup goals in 82 appearances before following his manager to Hull City. After scoring twice on his debut, he went on to total 23 goals in 40 League matches for The Tigers, form that attracted the scouts, Forest obtaining his signature in June 1938. In his one season prior to the outbreak of war, he scored on his Forest debut, but it was not until late season that he showed the marksmanship that enabled the Reds to avoid relegation by the narrowest of margins – on goal average ahead of Norwich City who accompanied Tranmere Rovers through the relegation trapdoor.

Appearances: FL: 22 apps 8 gls FAC: 1 app 0 gls
Total: 23 apps 8 gls

FULLARTON, William Millwright

Centre half-back 5' 9" 12st 4lbs
Born: Tradeston, Glasgow, 20th February 1882
Debut v Notts County (a) 4.11.05, drawn 1-1
CAREER: Vale of Leven August 1901. Queen's Park 1901-02. Sunderland December 1903. **FOREST 2nd November 1905, fee £612.** Plymouth Argyle player-manager 2nd June 1906. New Brompton July 1907 to 1910.

Commencing with two of Scotland's top clubs of the day, William Fullerton made 33 League and Cup appearances for Sunderland, playing his first game for the Wearsiders against Notts County at Trent Bridge on 12th December 1903. He was elected captain of Sunderland at the beginning of the 1904-05 season before joining Forest for a then noteworthy fee. Described as: "A bustling centre-half who puts all of his energy into his play," he failed to find his best form, appearing in only 20 League matches as Forest slumped to relegation from Division One. In a report of a meeting of Forest directors it was stated that the board had ruefully admitted that Fullerton had not been very good value. Having cost £612 and seeing that he had played in only twenty matches, his services had cost the club £30 per match. Nevertheless, when Fullarton was offered the post of player-manager of Plymouth Argyle, Forest objected. The deal went through, however, but financial considerations led the Plymouth club to replace their salaried manager with an unpaid management committee after just one season, in which they had finished in 15th position in the Southern League.

Appearances: FL: 20 apps 0 gls FAC: 1 app 0 gls
Total: 21 apps 0 gls

GALLOWAY, Septimus **Randolph**

Centre-forward
5' 9½"
12st 4lbs
Born: Sunderland, 22nd December 1896
Died: Mapperley, 10th April 1964
Debut v Burnley (h) 22.11.24, drawn 0-0
CAREER: Sunderland Tramways. Shildon Athletic. Derby County October 1922. **FOREST 20th November 1924, fee £2,500.** Luton Town June 1927. Coventry City December 1927. Tottenham Hotspur (trial) July 1928, professional August 1928. Grantham September 1929. Later held numerous coaching appointments, including spells with Sporting de Gijon, Valencia, Racing Santander, Costa Rica, CA Penarol, SC JF Juventos, Sporting LP, Victoria SC, Montevideo and Royal Ordnance.

Randolph Galloway began as a schoolboy full-back and was selected to represent the North of England in an international trial. He joined Derby County from Sunderland Tramways having first played at centre-forward during service with the Yorkshire Regiment in 1918, he won several medals while in India and joined the Rams and was soon among the goals, scoring 30 in 76 League and Cup matches. A forceful leader of the opportunist type, he cost Forest a then record fee but he failed to shine in his first season, scoring twice in 11 League matches as Forest crashed out of Division One. He did little better in Division Two and his Forest spell ended in suspension during the final month of the campaign. He played in little first team football after leaving the City ground, his career winding up after three appearances and two goals for the Spurs in a season marred by injuries.

Appearances: FL: 39 apps 8 gls FAC: 4 apps 0 gls
Total: 43 apps 8 gls

GARA, Andrew
Centre-forward 5' 9" 12st 2lbs
Born: Roscommon, 15th August 1878
Debut v Sunderland (a) 1.9.02, won 1-0
CAREER: Temple Bar Juniors (Belfast). Ashton-in-Makerfield 2nd October 1895. Wigan County 26th May 1897. Preston North End 22nd February 1899. **FOREST 24th April 1902.** Bristol City 1st November 1902. Earlestown F.C. July 1903. Ashton Town 2nd May 1904.
Forest were said to have paid 'a pretty substantial' fee for Irish international inside-forward Andrew Gara. In the season that he moved to the City ground he had represented his country against Wales, Scotland and England, and had registered a hat trick on his debut in Ireland's 3-0 win against Wales at Cardiff on 22nd February 1902. International recognition had come late in his three-year spell with Preston North End, for whom he scored 27 goals in 66 League matches. Sadly, he failed to reproduce such form with Forest, departing after the briefest of stays to join Bristol City, for whom he scored six goals in 18 League matches.
Appearances: FL: 6 apps 1 gl Total: 6 apps 1 gl
Honours: N. Ireland International, three caps, 1902.

GARDINER, Charles
Centre or Inside-forward 5' 6" 10st 11lbs
Born: Perth, 7th April 1915
Died: Perth, 24th January 1973
Debut v West Ham United (a) 7.9.35, lost 2-5 (scored one)
CAREER: Cherrybank Boys' Club. Roslea F.C. **FOREST 22nd August 1935.** Mansfield Town July 1938, in part exchange for Harold Crawshaw plus a fee of £1,500. Montrose June 1939. (Wartime guest player with **FOREST**, Leicester City, Bournemouth & Boscombe Athletic, Derby County and Greenock Morton.)
One described as: "A real warrior, but handicapped by lack of inches," the Scotsman was small, but good, and although his first team opportunities were limited, he appeared in all three inside positions, and never let the side down. Charlie Gardiner left the City Ground in July 1938 to join Mansfield Town as part of the deal that brought Harold Crawshaw to the Forest. He remained for a season at Field Mill, scoring four goals in 27 League matches.
Appearances: FL: 38 apps 8 gls FAC: 3 apps 0 gls
Total: 41 apps 8 gls

GEARY, George
Outside-left 5' 6" 12st. 0lbs.
Born: Hyson Green, 1st March 1876
Died: Mapperley, 11th August 1970
Debut v Aston Villa (a) 14.4.94, lost 1-3 (scored)
CAREER: Notts Rangers. **FOREST 9th August 1893.** Long Eaton Rangers July 1895. Chesterfield Town May 1899 to May 1902.
A younger brother of Fred Geary the England international forward who began with Notts County without reaching League level, but the who scored 78 goals in 91 matches for Liverpool and 14 in 39 matches for Everton in the 1890s. George's career was modest by comparison, but he was valued by Forest who refused his request for a transfer in July 1894. He did move on in the following year, and following a lengthy spell with Long Eaton Rangers he returned to League action with Chesterfield Town, scoring 12 goals in 59 League appearances.
Appearances: FL: 7 apps 3 gls Total: 7 apps 3 gls

GERMAN, Arthur **Clive** Johnson

Centre-forward
6' 1" 13st 3lbs
Born: Ashby-de-la-Zouch, Leics.
28th June 1905
Died: Nottingham, 2nd February 1968
Debut v Notts County (a) 22.2.28, won 2-1 (scored one)
CAREER: An amateur throughout with Rawden F.C. (Ashby). Repton School. Oxford University (Brasenose College). The Corinthians August 1924. Blackpool (trial) 1926. **FOREST 13th January 1928.** The Corinthians April to September 1931. Yorkshire Amateurs.
A hefty centre-forward from Ashby-de-la-Zouch who was articled to a Nottingham firm of solicitors during the time that he spent as an amateur on Forest's books. He had earlier appeared in three Varsity matches between 1924-27 and scored Oxford's winner in the 1-0 victory in season 1926-27. Associated with several of the top amateur clubs of his day. Tall, weighty and mobile, German could match most opponents in the air and his dash and persistence made him a dangerous raider, not afraid to commit defenders by heading for goal by the shortest route.
Appearances: FL: 25 apps 10 gls FAC: 7 apps 0 gls
Total: 32 apps 10 gls

GETTY, John

Outside-right
5' 9" 10st 0lbs
Born: Bonhill, 23rd April 1918
Debut v Blackburn Rovers (h)
5.12.36, won 2-0
CAREER: Vale of Leven
Academy. Alexandria Boys'
Brigade. Bonhill Union.
Milngavie F.C. Glasgow Ashfield
F.C. **FOREST 8th June 1936**.
Dumbarton July 1939.

*Very much the 'baby' of the team, Jack Getty was
an 18 year-old stripling when he joined the Forest,
who teetered on the brink of relegation in each of
the three seasons that he spent at the City Ground.
His main rival for the right wing berth was
another youthful performer, Arthur Betts, the
outstanding local product, whose cartilage
operation in season 1938-39 opened the way for
Getty to appear in 11 League matches in which he
scored two goals. Shortly after the appointment of
Billy Walker as Forest manager in succession to
Harry Wightman, Jack Getty was placed on the
transfer list and was signed by Dumbarton on the
eve of World War Two.*
Appearances: FL: 18 apps 2 gls Total: 18 apps 2 gls

GIBSON, Sydney George

Outside-right
5' 7½" 11st 0lbs
Born: Walgrave, near
Kettering, Northants.
20th May 1899
Died: West Ham,
5th July 1938
Debut v West Ham
United (a) 22.10.21, lost
0-1
CAREER: Walgrave
Amber. Kettering Town.
**FOREST 6th October
1921, fee £500**. Sheffield United 15th September
1928 to May 1932, fee £5,000. Southend United
coach November 1933, assistant-manager January
1935. West Ham United chief scout 1937-38.
*Aston Villa, Everton and two or three other League
clubs were all anxious to secure the services of Syd
Gibson, who had made his presence unmistakably
felt in Central Alliance football with Kettering
Town. Exceptionally fast, tricky, and with a good
shot, the fair-haired outside-right made his Forest
debut in the unaccustomed position of centre-
forward. It was asking a raw recruit a big
question, but the smiling stripling showed an
ability beyond his years, leading the 'Topical
Times' correspondent to label him 'The real goods.'
He became a regular on Forest's right wing for six
seasons, but was allowed to leave after five
matches of the 1928-29 season, Sheffield United
paying £5,000 for his services, a record fee for*
both clubs. *After 113 League and Cup matches and
26 goals, knee injuries enforced his retirement. He
was 33 years old at the time and received
compensation from the Football League
amounting to £350. He did, however, play in a
number of charity and local games along with his
famous manager, Mr David Jack. An exceptionally
clever pianist and church organist, in 1925 he was
said to be able to play, without sheet music, any
popular melody of the time.*
Appearances: FL: 252 apps 53 gls FAC: 24 apps 2
gls Total: 276 apps 55 gls
Honours: (**FOREST**), FL Division 2 champions
1922

GIBSON, Thomas

Full-back
5' 10" 12st 0lbs
Born: Maxwelltown,
23rd October 1889
Died: Nottingham,
February 1967
Debut v Aston Villa
(a) 25.12.07, lost 0-4
CAREER:
Maxwelltown
Volunteers. Morton.
**FOREST 15th June
1907**. (Wartime guest
player with Heart of
Midlothian November
1916.) Notts County
December 1919, fee
'over £1,000.' Southend United June 1923; retired
May 1924.

*Tom Gibson spent a lengthy period in reserve as
the long running Dudley/Maltby partnership
continued as Forest's last line of defence, but he
was firmly established by 1911-12. In the following
season he was a surprise selection at centre-
forward, a move that was considered in some
quarters to be the one successful experiment that
Forest made that season. He certainly took to the
role in fine style, his 18 goals making him leading
scorer for the season, his total including four
against Burnley at Turf Moor and a hat trick
against Leicester Fosse at the City Ground. After
five matches of the following season had all ended
in defeat, Gibson was reinstated in his old position
of left-back. He held the position until he followed
the lead given by Joe Mercer and joined the
Footballers' Battalion. He served throughout the
war, rising to the rank of Regimental Sergeant
Major. He crossed the Trent to join Notts County
midway through the 1919-20 season in which the
Magpies were relegated from Division One. They
were promoted in his final season, but by this
point he was approaching the veteran stage and
played in only four matches.*
Appearances: FL: 186 apps 32 gls FAC: 7 apps 3 gls
Total: 193 apps 35 gls

GOODCHILD, George
Inside-right
Born: New Seaham, County Durham, January
quarter 1875
Died: Durham, October quarter 1927, age 52
Debut v Sheffield Wednesday (a) 5.4.96, lost 0-3
CAREER: Ryhope Colliery. Sunderland 28th
September 1894. Derby County 5th June 1896.
FOREST 23rd March 1897. Burton Swifts
October 1897. Jarrow F.C. July 1899. Whitburn
September 1900. South Shields Athletic July 1901.
Ashington July 1904.
*George Goodchild's modest career in senior
football commenced with one appearance for
Sunderland at Sheffield United on 9th March 1895.
Two appearances for Derby County followed
before his move to the Forest, for whom he
appeared in the final three fixtures of season 1896-
97, and the opening fixture of the following season,
at home to Notts County. In the following month
he departed to Burton Swifts and scored once in
nine matches before returning to the North-East in
the close season.*
Appearances: FL: 4 apps 0 gls Total: 4 apps 0 gls

GORDON, Leslie William

Left half-back
5' 9½" 11st 4lbs
Born: Barking,
Essex,
13th July 1903
Died: Grimsby
April quarter
1941, age 37
Debut v Hull
City (a) 1.10.27,
lost 0-2
CAREER:
Grimsby
Rovers.
Sheffield
United May
1923. Crystal
Palace August
1925. Shirebrook July 1926. **FOREST 10th May
1927.** Shirebrook March 1928. Brighton & Hove
Albion August 1928, retired following an injury
sustained in December 1929.
*A good season with Shirebrook of the Midland
League attracted a lot of attention, and Les
Gordon was given another opportunity in League
football, having drawn blanks with both Sheffield
United and Crystal Palace. Billed as an inside-left
or left half-back on arrival at the City Ground, his
two League appearances were made in the middle
line as deputy to club captain Bob Wallace. Gordon
was released prior to the close of the season and
returned to Shirebrook. His final League club was
Brighton & Hove Albion, where his career was
terminated by a broken leg injury after he had
made 18 League appearances. His name*

*reappeared some years later, in October 1936,
when he applied for a permit to play for
Cleethorpes Buses works' team.*
Appearances: FL: 2 apps 0 gls Total: 2 apps 0 gls

GOUCHER, George Henry

Left full-back
5' 9" 11st 9lbs
Born: Whaley Thorns,
Derbyshire, 18th May
1902
Died: Mansfield,
January 1987
Debut v Barnsley (h)
6.10.28, lost 1-3
CAREER: Whaley
Thorns School.
Hawthorn Exchange.
Norwood Rangers.
Shirebrook F.C. May
1926. Notts County November 1926, fee £200.
FOREST 29th June 1928, fee £100. Torquay
United August 1929. Shirebrook F.C. August 1930.
Sutton Town November 1931. Ilkeston United
August 1934.
*George Goucher cost Notts County £200 when
signed from Shirebrook, but it was not until the
final match of the season that he turned out for the
first team, recording his solitary League
appearance in a 0-5 defeat at Blackpool. He fared
little better after crossing the Trent, at half of the
fee originally paid for him. A season in the south
with Torquay United featured six first team
matches. In the last of these he finally collected a
winning bonus, Torquay rounding off their season
with a 2-1 win against their next-door neighbours,
Exeter City. He later worked as a driver for the
cottage department of Glapwell Colliery.*
Appearances: FL: 1 app 0 gls Total: 1 app 0 gls

GRAHAM, James Arthur

Centre-forward
5' 10½" 12st 0lbs
Born: Cottingham, Corby,
Northants. 13th January
1911
Died: Bath, 28th November
1987
Debut v Fulham (a)
24.12.32, won 1-0
CAREER: Corby British
Legion. Desborough Town.
**FOREST 10th December
1932.** York City July 1935. Hartlepools United
October 1935. Southend United May 1936. Clapton
Orient May 1937. Yeovil & Petters United June
1938. (Wartime guest player with Charlton Athletic
& Leicester City.)
*The former Desborough Town centre-forward was
handed his League debut by Forest at Fulham on
Christmas Eve 1932, and was never absent for the*

remainder of the season. Strongly built Jimmy Graham was said to have a lot to learn, but was not lacking in thrustfulness and marksmanship. Despite reservations, he did well enough to keep ace marksman Johnny Dent out of the team for several months, but his form evaporated thereafter and despite several subsequent moves in League circles he failed to reproduce his earliest form. His final career figures amounting to 19 League goals in 70 matches for his five clubs.

Appearances: FL: 32 apps 13 gls FAC: 2 apps 1 gl
Total: 34 apps 14 gls

GRAHAM, Thomas

Centre half-back 5' 9" 11st 4lbs
Born: Hamsterley, County Durham, 12th March 1905
Died: West Bridgford, 29th March 1983
Debut v Bristol City (a) 7.4.28, drawn 0-0
CAREER: Blackhill Mill Schoolboys. Derwentside Blues. Chopwell Institute. Newcastle United (trial). Hamsterley Swifts August 1922. Consett Celtic October 1926. **FOREST (trial) May 1927, professional 26th January 1928, fee £50. Retired from playing in 1944 and then appointed trainer to January 1961, then scout to July 1970.**
Tommy Graham was signed as a youthful left-half from Consett Celtic, who had won promotion to the First Division of the North Eastern League in 1926-27, and were runners-up in the North West Charity and Newcastle Infirmary Cups. He

became a regular first team player in his second season, initially at left-half, but when Percy Barratt was injured, he filled the vacant left-back position with equal faculty. He moved seamlessly into the centre-half role following the transfer of Albert Harrison to Leicester City. An outstanding utility player with speed, good ball control and with an untiring work rate, in emergency he was even called upon to lead the attack. An injury in 1931-32 prevented him from playing in an England trial match but he won two International caps against France and Ireland. He was unfortunate in season 1934-35 when he fractured a bone in his leg after scoring in a 3-3 draw at Norwich City on Boxing Day and was out for much of the remainder of the season. At the end of the 1938-39 season the club promised Graham a second benefit, the match to be played early in 1939-40. The outbreak of war prevented the club from keeping their promise, but in July 1943 a sum of £200 in account was presented to him. In various capacities Tommy Graham served the Forest club for a period in excess of fifty years, a truly remarkable achievement by the ultimate clubman.

Appearances: FL: 372 apps 7 gls FAC: 18 apps 0 gls
Total: 390 apps 7 gls
Honours: England International, 2 caps 1931. FL representative, 2 apps. 1931.

GREEN, Arthur William

Centre-forward
5' 10½" 12st 4lbs
Born: Aberystwyth, 24th April 1881
Died: Nottingham, 24th September 1966
Debut v Burnley (h) 19.1.07, won 2-0
CAREER: Aberystwyth Town August 1897. Swindon Town 1899. Aston Villa 30th August 1900. Ebbw Vale. Walsall September 1901. Notts County 12th May 1902. **FOREST 18th January 1907, fee £350.**
Stockport County May 1909. Brierley Hill Alliance 1911-12.
One of the first footballers to be transferred between Notts County and Forest, Welsh international centre-forward Arthur Green was once described as: "Broad, strong and tall, a capable dribbler and a sticker when he gets on the ball. He is a very accurate shooter, and something of a man of moods, at times apt to slow down a bit, but at his best, one of the best." He had scored 59 goals in 142 League and Cup appearances for Notts but relations between club and player had deteriorated after he had been dropped from the side, suspended, and placed on the transfer list. After joining Forest, the 'Post Guide' considered

that Green had retained some of his old attributes, but had slowed the game down too much. That said, his six goals in 13 matches in his first season assisted Forest to win the championship of Division Two. He netted 10 goals in 20 First Division matches in the following campaign, but was sparingly used in his final season. Aside from football, Arthur Green represented Nottinghamshire County at tennis and was an eight-handicap golfer. For many years, up to his retirement in 1949, he was a representative for Critall's, the window manufacturers. A qualified draughtsman, he was a prominent member of the Nottingham Mechanics Institution.

Appearances: FL: 38 apps 19 gls Total: 38 apps 19 gls

Honours: Wales International, 8 caps 1901-08.

FOREST FL Division 2 champions 1907.
Aberystwyth Town Welsh Cup winners 1900.

GREEN, Harold 'Harry'

Right half-back
5' 11½" 12st 6lbs
Born: Sedgley,
3rd August 1904
Died: Wolverhampton,
October quarter 1975
Debut v Port Vale (a)
27.8.27, drawn 2-2
CAREER: Cosely
Amateurs. Redditch
United. Sheffield United
March 1925, fee £150.
**FOREST 18th May 1927,
fee £100.** Halifax Town
July 1928. Hereford Town August 1929.
Kidderminster Harriers July 1930. Droitwich
Comrades & W.M.C. October 1931. Droitwich Old
Boys October 1934.

Harry Green's form with Redditch United, the Birmingham League club, led to his upward move to Sheffield United in March 1925. He had a year to wait before making his League debut, against Bolton Wanderers in April 1926, but this was his only first team involvement in a two-year stay at Bramall Lane. He did little better in a season at the City Ground, his four early season appearances ending after a 4-0 defeat at Leeds United on 10th September. Off the field, he was awarded a Royal Humane Society certificate for his action in saving a boy from drowning in the river Trent.

Appearances: FL: 4 apps 0 gls Total: 4 apps 0 gls

GREEN, John

Outside-right
5' 9½" 11st 8lbs
Born: Blackburn, July
quarter 1896
Died: Victoria, Canada, 13th
December 1960, age 64
Debut v Leeds United
6.5.22, drawn 0-0
CAREER: Army football
(Grenadier Guards).
Blackburn Rovers May
1919; free transfer 3rd February 1922. Fleetwood cs
1921. **FOREST 7th February 1922.** Luton Town
June 1923. Southend United (trial) 1924. Lancaster
Town November 1924. Emigrated to Canada April
1926 to join Montreal Carsted, later with
Providence Clamdiggers from September 1926 to
June 1929. Montreal CNR to *circa* 1937.

John Green's career received an early setback when he seriously injured knee ligaments when playing for Blackburn Rovers Reserves against Stalybridge Celtic at Ewood Park on 1st September 1919. The promising local product was reported to be 'recovering from a badly damaged knee' at the start of the 1920-21 season, but he was released in February of the same campaign, and joined Fleetwood in the close season. It was when he joined Forest that Blackburn Rovers contested the transfer, but the Football League management Committee decided that the Rovers no longer had any title to the player, and the move was sanctioned. Green's debut came in the final fixture of season 1921-22 when Forest celebrated their promotion to the top flight. Tried at outside-right and centre-forward without establishing a regular place in the starting line-up, he was released in the close season. A season in the Third Division South with Luton Town provided more opportunities – 26 League matches and five goals – he also scored against Arsenal in the 1st round of the FA Cup at Highbury, but the Gunners won 4-1. After a spell in non-League football, Green emigrated to Canada. In August 1927 he was the victim in a hit-and-run accident that almost cost him his life. Thankfully, he recovered to continue his career and 1929 he assisted Montreal CNR to win the Canada FA Trophy. In the following year they were runners-up in the same competition, losing to Westminster Royals.

Appearances: FL: 11 apps 2 gls FAC: 3 apps 1 gl
Total: 14 apps 3 gls

GRIFFITHS, Henry 'Harry'
Inside-left   5' 7"   11st 0lbs
Born: Aston, Birmingham, 29th November 1875
Died: Birmingham, 23rd December 1950
Debut v Blackburn Rovers (h) 19.9.03, lost 0-1
CAREER: Leamansley. Redditch Excelsior. Burton Swifts 7th May 1898. Bristol Rovers 3rd May 1900. Reading 2nd May 1901. **FOREST 5th May 1903**. Bristol Rovers 3rd May 1904. Millwall Athletic 6th October 1905. Kidderminster Harriers 9th December 1905.
Leading goal scorer for Burton Swifts in his two seasons with the Brewers (27 goals in 76 League and Cup matches), he repeated the feat in two seasons with Reading for whom he netted 38 Southern League goals in two seasons. Griffiths distinguished himself when opposed to Forest in the FA Cup competition of season 1902-03. He assisted Reading to hold the Reds to a 0-0 draw at the City Ground, and was a scorer in the replay, although he finished on the losing side, Forest winning 6-3. Despite being able to play in any forward position, Griffiths did not get a run in Forest's first team until late in the season, his only goal coming in the 5-1 win against Derby County on 12th March 1904. Early in the following campaign he returned to Southern League circles for a second spell with Bristol Rovers. His final senior club was Millwall Athletic, but made only three appearances in a brief stay before returning to the Midlands to assist Kidderminster Harriers.
Appearances: FL: 8 apps 1 gl Total: 8 apps 1 gl

HADLEY, Harry

Half-back   5' 9½"   12st 7lbs
Born: King's Norton, April quarter 1875
Died: West Bromwich, 3rd October 1942
Debut v Woolwich Arsenal (a) 2.4.06, lost 1-3
CAREER: Cradley Heath Schools. Colley Gate United. Halesowen September 1895. West Bromwich Albion 8th April 1898. Aston Villa 1st March 1905. **FOREST 26th March 1906**. Southampton May 1907. Croydon Common May 1908. Halesowen February 1910. Merthyr Town player-manager May to August 1919, then manager to April 1922. Chesterfield manager April to August 1922. Aberdare manager November 1927 to April 1928. Merthyr Town manager April to November 1928 and August 1930 to September 1931. Gillingham manager. Bangor City manager July 1935 to April 1936.
One of two half-backs signed by Forest, within the space of two days, in March 1906. Harry Hadley followed Teddy Hughes, the Wrexham half-back, to the City Ground. It was hoped that the signings would get Forest out of difficulties at the wrong end of Division One, but sadly they did not succeed and relegation to Division Two ensued. In earlier days, Hadley quickly established himself as a regular with West Bromwich Albion, and it was not long before he was considered one of the best half-backs in the game. In 1903 he was awarded his England cap against Ireland to add to his Division Two championship medal, won in the previous season. After appearing in 181 League and Cup matches he departed the Hawthorns to join Aston Villa. Ironically, he had sustained a serious injury when opposed to the Villa in a Birmingham Cup-tie and this had kept him out of action for a considerable time. He made little impact with the Villa and was unable to hold a first team place at the City Ground. He did rather better with Southampton, appearing in 30 Southern League matches before moving into non-League football. He subsequently enjoyed a lengthy, and largely successful career, as a manager with a variety of clubs in the lower divisions.
Appearances: FL: 12 apps 1 gl Total: 12 apps 1 gl
Honours: England International v Ireland in 1903. (West Bromwich Albion) FL Division 2 champions 1902.

HAGUE, Eric Montague

Outside-left
5' 7½"   11st 10lbs
Born: Sheffield, 21st July 1901
Died: Dinnington, 10th July 1976
Debut v Bradford Park Avenue (h) 8.9.28, won 3-2
CAREER: Birmingham 1924. Blackpool May 1925. Swindon Town May 1926. Darlington September 1927. Gainsborough Trinity November 1927. **FOREST 10th May 1928**. West Ham United (trial) April 1929. Walsall April 1929. Crewe Alexandra October 1930 to January 1931.
Despite his association with a number of Football League clubs, Eric Hague had yet to make a first team appearance when he arrived at the City Ground. Billed as a speedy and tricky winger, he had assisted Gainsborough Trinity to attain the Midland League championship in 1927-28, but it was ex-Barnsley winger Bobby Morton who dominated the outside-left berth during 1928-29 and Hague was released to take a trial with West Ham United which did not lead to a permanent engagement. He subsequently made eight appearances for Walsall and two for Crewe Alexandra. Outside of the game he was employed as a monumental mason.
Appearances: FL: 4 apps 0 gls Total: 4 apps 0 gls

HALES, Herbert 'Smiler'
Outside-left   5' 7"   10st 10lbs
Born: Kettering, 21st November 1908
Died: Gainsborough, October quarter 1982
Debut v Millwall (a) 9.3.28, drawn 1-1
CAREER: Desborough Hotspur. Desborough
Town June 1927. **FOREST 12th January 1929.**
Northampton Town (trial). Peterborough & Fletton
United June 1929. Stoke City April 1930, fee £200.
Preston North End May 1931, fee £200.
Chesterfield June 1933, fee £650. Stockport County
December 1934, fee £225. Rochdale July 1935.
Burton Town July 1936. Kidderminster Harriers
May 1937. Cheltenham Town January 1938.
Forest's own version of the yet to be introduced
'January transfer window' saw them recruit four
new players within the space of three days in
January 1929. 'Smiler' Hales, the genial outside-
left, was one of the quartet and he launched his
senior career with Forest, but it was not until he
reached Preston North End that his fortunes took
an upturn, scoring 10 goals in 57 League matches.
He later gave good service to Chesterfield,
runners-up in the Third Division North in 1933-34,
Stockport County and Rochdale, accumulating
career figures of 24 League goals in 157
appearances.
Appearances: FL: 3 apps 0 gls Total: 3 apps 0 gls

HAMILTON, Alexander McCline

Goalkeeper   6' 0"   12st 0lbs
Born: Bulwell, 26th
December 1890
Died: Nottingham, July
quarter 1971
Debut v Fulham (a)
23.12.11, lost 0-2
CAREER: Bestwood F.C.
Assisted FOREST
Reserves as an amateur
November 1908 to
March 1909. Bestwood
F.C. **FOREST amateur 22nd December 1911 to**
May 1913.
Understudy to Irish international goalkeeper Jack
Hanna, local custodian and coal miner Alex
Hamilton was called upon to deputise on six
occasions in 1911-12. Despite stepping up from
local football he did not look out of place in
Division Two, although he was criticised for a
tendency to parry shots, rather than field them
and clear promptly.
Appearances: FL: 7 apps 0 gls Total: 7 apps 0 gls

HAMILTON, Thomas
Right half-back   5' 6"   10st 3lbs
Born: Ayrshire
Debut v West Bromwich Albion, FA Cup semi-final
(at Wolverhampton) 5.3.1892, drawn 0-0
CAREER: Hurlford. **FOREST August 1891,**
registered for FL matches 30th May 1892 to
May 1893.
At the time of his selection for Scotland (March
1891), Hamilton was considered to be the best half-
back in Ayrshire. Although physically small, this
did not hamper him in either attack or defence,
and he certainly had an excellent first season with
Forest, with an Alliance championship medal won,
and an appearance in the FA Cup semi-final. He
did less well when Forest were elevated to the First
Division of the Football League, and was the only
player released at the end of the season. To take
his place, Alex Stewart of Everton was signed.
Appearances: FL: 7 apps 0 gls FAC: 2 apps 0 gls
Total: 9 apps 0 gls
Honours: Scotland International, 1 cap v N. Ireland
1891. **(FOREST)** Football Alliance champions
1892.

HANCOCK, John Burns
Inside-right
Born: Chesterfield, July quarter 1871
Died: Sheffield, April quarter 1925, age 53
Debut v Bolton Wanderers (h) 16.3.95, drawn 3-3
CAREER: FOREST 15th September 1892
John Hancock had a lengthy wait before making
his senior debut that came after he had scored the
first goal in a 6-2 win against Sheffield United in a
United Counties League match on 11th March 1895.
His Football League debut followed within a
matter of days, but it proved to be final outing.
Note: *There was another player named Hancock*
on Forest's books, initials W.T., who was signed on
1st September 1892. He did not appear at senior
level, and it is not know whether the pair were
related.
Appearances: FL: 1 app 0 gls Total: 1 app 0 gls

HANNA, A. John 'Jack'

Goalkeeper
5' 11" 11st 7lbs
Born: Corkrely,
Ballymoney,
3rd April 1888
Debut v Leeds City (h)
2.9.11, won 2-1
CAREER: Pottinger
F.C. (Belfast). Linfield
Athletic. **FOREST 25th
May 1911.** Scunthorpe
& Lindsey United July
1919 to May 1921.
*Forest's Irish
goalkeeper, Jack
Hanna, had attracted
much attention
following excellent
displays for Linfield Athletic FC, Belfast. He had
only had 13 goals registered against him in fifteen
Irish League matches, and was rewarded with an
appearance for the Irish League against Southern
League at West Ham. Before joining Linfield he
was with Pottinger FC, one of the smaller Belfast
clubs. He was expected to fill a gap in the side and
bring some stability to the important role of
goalkeeper that had been a problem since the
departure of Harry Linacre at the close of the
1908-09 season. Happily, he came through his first
season with flying colours, fully upholding the
high reputation that accompanied him from
Ireland. First choice throughout his stay at the City
Ground, his outstanding displays were rewarded
by the award of two full caps for his country,
against Scotland and Wales in 1912.*
Appearances: FL: 97 apps 0 gls FAC: 5 apps 0 gls
Total: 102 apps 0 gls
Honours: N. Ireland International, 2 caps 1912.
Irish League representative v Southern League
March 1911

HARDSTAFF, Joseph

Inside-right
Born: Nuncargate,
Notts.
9th November 1882
Died: Nuncargate,
Notts. 2nd April 1947
Debut v Sunderland
(a) 2.1.05, lost 0-1
**CAREER: FOREST
2nd November
1904-06.** Sutton
1906-07.
*Joe Hardstaff, who
was much better
known as a cricketer,
was born at
Nuncargate and later lived at Kirkby-in-Ashfield.
He played for Nottinghamshire between 1902-24,*

*appearing in 340 matches. He was one of six new
players tried by Notts in his debut season, but only
two, Hardstaff and George Gunn were destined to
become regular members of the team. Although
somewhat short in stature, he was a great
cricketer, a plucky batsman and a fine fielder. He
toured Australia with A.O. Jones' team in 1907-08
and played in all five Test matches (he was still on
Forest's transfer list at the time.) On his return
from Australia he was chief guest at a banquet in
his honour by local residents at Kirkby, and was
presented with an illuminated address. He hit
1,000 runs in a season seven times and scored one
double century – 213* against Sussex at Hove in
1914. He later became a first-class umpire and
officiated in Test Matches. His son, Joseph junior,
was also a Notts and England batsman, with 408
matches for the County between 1930-55 and in 23
Test Matches 1935-48. Joe senior had complained
of chest pains but had not sought medical advice in
the week before his death at the age of 58.*
Appearances: FL: 12 apps 1 gl FAC: 1 app 0 gls
Total: 13 apps 1 gl

HARDY, Sam

Goalkeeper
5' 9½" 12st 0lbs
Born: Newbold,
Chesterfield, 26th
August 1882
Died: 24th October
1966
Debut v Crystal
Palace (a) 27.8.21,
lost 1-4
CAREER:
Newbold White
Star 1899.
Chesterfield Town
amateur cs 1902,
professional April
1903. Liverpool
May 1905, fee
£340. Aston Villa May 1912. (Wartime guest player
with **FOREST**). **FOREST 22nd August 1921,
retired May 1925, fee £1,000.**
*Once described as "The Prince of Goalkeepers,"
Sam Hardy assisted Forest to their first wartime
championship, and in 1922-23 had the supreme
satisfaction of assisting them to win the honour
again, and with it promotion to the First Division.
Blessed with great powers of anticipation, he was
always unspectacular and made goalkeeping look
easy, he also maintained his form and fitness and
was still at the top of his game when he turned 40.
In terms of League appearances alone, his
impressive totals were: 71 for Chesterfield Town;
219 for Liverpool; 159 for Aston Villa, and 102 for
Forest. In February 1922, when he was the
popular host of the Gardeners' Arms, Chesterfield,
a reporter from the 'Topical Times' visited his*

hostelry, and reported as follows: "Although Sam Hardy is the least egotistical player I have ever come across, the famous goalkeeper has been persuaded by his friends to have all his trophies on display in a cabinet in the smoking room. There are 26 caps, Cup medals, League medals, Inter-League medals, and I don't know what else, one of the most wonderful collections I have ever set eyes upon."

Appearances: FL: 102 apps 0 gls FAC: 7 apps 0 gls
Total: 109 apps 0 gls
Honours: England International, 21 caps 1907-20. FL representative, 10 apps. England 'Victory' International, 3 apps 1919. (Liverpool) FL Division 1 champions 1906. (Aston Villa) FA Cup winners 1913 and 1920. (**FOREST**) FL Division 2 champions 1922.

HARDY, William Henry

Inside-right   5' 8"   11st 0lbs
Born: Denaby, 25th October 1915
Died: Gainsborough, July 1990
Debut v Leicester City (a) 24.4.37, lost 1-2
CAREER: Swinton W.M.C. Rotherham United September 1935. **FOREST 15th February 1937**. Gainsborough Trinity June 1938. Grantham May 1947.
Commencing with Rotherham United as a 19 year-old inside-right, Bill Hardy made steady progress and, at the time of his transfer to the City Ground, had scored 11 goals in 46 Third Division North matches. Sadly, he was unable to establish himself in Division Two, his debut at Leicester City being followed by reserve team football throughout the following campaign.
Appearances: FL: 1 app 0 gls Total: 1 app 0 gls

HARRIS, Fred Mawson

Centre-forward/Outside-right   5' 8½"   11st 0lbs
Born: Rothwell, Northants. 11th October 1892
Died: Rothwell, Northants. 6th July 1962
Debut v Huddersfield Town (a) 7.2.14, drawn 1-1 (scored)
CAREER: Rothwell Congs. Burton Swifts. Desborough Town. Northampton Town. Kettering Town November 1913. English Wanderers 1914. **FOREST amateur 6th February 1914**. South Shields 1919. Swansea Town July 1919. Kettering Town June 1920. Southend United July 1921. Kettering Town June 1922. Rothwell Town cs 1925. Kettering Town July 1926.
A fast and determined amateur centre-forward and occasional outside-right, Fred Harris was a keen opportunist who combined football with his work as chief clerk in a shoe factory. The 'Post Guide' for 1914-15 considered that the fast and determined centre-forward would be capable of scoring ' a hatful of goals' if operating between two inside-forwards who 'tumbled' to his style. Unfortunately, Harris played most of his matches on the right wing in 1914-15, and Forest managed

to score only 43 goals in 38 League matches. In late December 1914, Harris and J.H. Lockton accepted an invitation to play in the English Wanderers team against Queen's Park in Glasgow on New Year' Day. They were just about back in time to line up in the Forest side that lost 0-4 at Grimsby Town on 2nd January! Harris served in the Royal Flying Corps during World War One and apart from one season with Southend United operated in non-League football, finally returning to one of his former clubs, Kettering Town.
Appearances: FL: 48 apps 12 gls FAC: 1 app 0 gls
Total: 49 apps 12 gls

HARRISON, Albert

Centre half-back 5' 11" 11st 0lbs
Born: Leigh, Lancashire, 15 February 1904
Debut v Port Vale (a) 27.8.27, drawn 2-2
CAREER: West Leigh FC. Wigan Road Villa. Wigan Borough amateur May, professional October 1922. Atherton Collieries September 1923. Chorley December 1924.
FOREST 1st April 1927, fee £350. Leicester City December 1929. Dundalk May 1931. Drumcondra August 1932. Wigan Athletic July 1933. Lugano (Switzerland) player-coach December 1933.
Tall and blond-haired, Albert Harrison rejoiced in the nickname 'Snowy.' He made his first-team debut with Wigan Borough at the age of eighteen and proved a capable deputy for Frank Whitfield in the 1-0 win at Halifax Town. Despite his undoubted potential he lacked opportunities with the Borough, but they eventually netted a useful fee when he joined Nottingham Forest in March 1927. He began with the Reds at Port Vale on 27th August 1927 in a 2-2 draw. Forest won their next two home matches by wide margins (7-0 v Fulham and 7-2 v South Shields), but throughout his time at the City Ground, during which he made 81 League and Cup appearances and scored five goals, Forest remained a mid-table Second Division side. Taking the short move to join First Division Leicester City he made 33 League and Cup appearances and scored one goal before losing his place to Roger Heywood. Spells in Ireland and a sojourn with the fledgling Wigan Athletic club preceded his mid-season move to Lugano, whom he assisted to third place in the newly formed Swiss National League.
Appearances: FL: 77 apps 5 gls FAC: 4 apps 0 gls
Total: 81 apps 5 gls
Honours: FA Tour to South Africa in 1930.

HARROLD, Sidney

Outside-left or right 5' 8" 10st 12lbs
Born: Stourbridge, 5th June 1895
Debut v Stoke (h) 28.8.20, drawn 2-2
CAREER: Willenhall Swifts. Stourbridge F.C.
1914-15. Wednesbury F.C. Leicester Fosse February
1919. **FOREST 7th May 1920.** Accrington Stanley
June 1922, retired due to injury January 1923.
*A clever and speedy outside-left who commenced
his career with three seasons in the Birmingham &
District League. Sid Harrold joined Leicester Fosse
in the final season of football played under
wartime conditions, making his first appearance
at the City Ground on 11th January 1919 in a 1-1
draw. When normal League football resumed, he
made 18 appearances and scored two goals before
joining Forest in May 1920. Appearing on either
wing, he enjoyed a good first season, being second
highest scorer with eight goals in 37 League
matches. In the Division Two promotion season
that followed he made 13 appearances, losing out
when Syd Gibson was signed from Kettering
Town. He was then recommended to Accrington
Stanley by Pat Nellis, the former Stanley and
Forest centre-forward. Sadly, Sid Harrold's career
was tragically cut short when he suffered a badly
broken and dislocated ankle in a game against
Durham City in September 1922. A benefit match
was played for him in May 1922. About 3,000
spectators attended the game that featured a*
*Lancashire & Yorkshire X1 versus a Nottingham
Forest & Leicester City X1. Harrold's injury did not
prevent him from resuming his cricket career as
professional with Newtown Wednesbury, and he
was later a licensee in Wednesbury.*
Appearances: FL: 50 apps 8 gls FAC: 2 apps 0 gls
Total: 52 apps 8 gls
Honours: **(FOREST)** FL Division 2 champions
1922

HART, Horace Alfred
Inside-right 5' 9½" 12st 4lbs
Born: Nottingham, 16th August 1894
Died: Nottingham, 7th June 1975
Debut v Stoke (a) 24.1.20, won 2-0
CAREER: New Hucknall Colliery. Stalybridge
Celtic. **FOREST amateur 24th, professional
26th January 1920.**
*Commencing with New Hucknall Colliery in the
Central Alliance League, Horace Hart scored four
goals in as many matches and was quickly
snapped up by Stalybridge Celtic, where he netted
seven goals in five matches. His elevation
continued when he made his Forest debut at Stoke,
replacing Bertie Davis. In the following month he
scored his only Football League goal in a 2-0 win
against Grimsby Town at the City Ground. There
then followed a winless run of eight matches that
included Hart's final appearance, an 8-0 defeat at
Birmingham.*
Appearances: FL: 6 apps 1 gl Total: 6 apps 1 gl

HASSELL, Albert Arthur 'Bert'

Goalkeeper
6' 0" 12st 6lbs
Born: St. George,
Bristol, 5th May
1885
Died: Montpelier,
Bristol, 3rd March
1955
Debut v Aston Villa
(a) 1.1.10, lost 1-4
CAREER:
Eastville
Wednesday. Bolton
Wanderers 4th May
1906.
Middlesbrough 31st July 1907. **FOREST 24th
December 1909.** Plymouth Argyle November
1911. Swindon Town June 1912, fee £10. (Wartime
guest player with Notts County December 1918.)
*A reserve goalkeeper with both Bolton Wanderers
and Middlesbrough, Bert Hassell was a tall
goalkeeper whose height gave him a fine reach,
and coupled with his natural agility, he enjoyed
lengthy spells of first team football with the Forest.
He was, however, operating behind a leaky
defence and when the Reds were relegated at the
close of the 1910-11 season he, along with the other
two goalkeepers on the books (Smith and Drabble)*

were all released. On retiring he worked at a chocolate factory in Bristol.
Appearances: FL: 34 apps 0 gls FAC: 4 apps 0 gls Total: 38 apps 0 gls

HEATHCOCK, Joseph **Berty**

Centre-forward
5' 8½" 11st 0lbs
Born: Cradley Heath, 5th December 1903
Died: Cradley Heath, 21st May 1990
Debut v Barnsley (h) 6.10.28, lost 1-3
CAREER: Cradley Heath. Leamington Town September 1923. Leicester City October 1923. **FOREST 5th June 1928, fee £150.** Cradley Heath June 1930. Hereford United September 1931. Nuneaton Town August 1932. Cradley Heath November 1932. Vono Sports (Tipton) September 1933.
Berty Heathcock led the Forest attack regularly in the closing stages of season 1928-29, and got well amongst the goals – eight in five matches including a hat trick against Preston North End. In earlier days he joined Leicester City from Birmingham Combination football, but with star centre-forward Arthur Chandler as competition, Heathcock was restricted to just one Football League appearance, in which he scored two goals.
Appearances: FL: 20 apps 15 gls Total: 20 apps 15 gls

HENDERSON, George
Half-back 5' 7½" 12st 0lbs
Born: High Blantyre, Lanarkshire, 15th December 1873
Debut v Wolverhampton Wanderers (a) 2.9.01, lost 0-2
CAREER: Coatbridge St. Patrick's. Burnbank Swifts. Motherwell December 1893. Airdrieonians 22nd June 1895. Preston North End 20th May 1897. Swindon Town 13th May 1898. Millwall Athletic 4th May 1900. **FOREST 8th June 1901.** Hamilton Academical 21st March 1906. Girvan Athletic (loan) March 1907. Hamilton Academical March 1907.
One of 26 players fielded by Preston North End in season 1897-98, George Henderson made his debut in the opening day defeat by Wolverhampton Wanderers at Molineux but added only one further first team appearance. North End finished in a disappointing 12th place in Division One – at that time there were only 16 clubs in the Division – and Henderson departed to spend the next three years playing in the Southern League with Swindon Town and Millwall Athletic. It took a month of negotiations between Preston North End, who held his Football League registration, and the Forest before the sturdy Scottish half-back became a Red. Suited to any position in the middle line, he spent

the best part of five seasons at the City Ground, leaving in the late stages of the 1905-06 relegation season to join Hamilton Academical. In all League competitions – including Scottish and Southern League – he appeared in 221 matches. He scored a total of 24 goals, mainly from successful penalty kick conversions.
Appearances: FL: 103 apps 6 gls FAC: 10 apps 0 gls Total: 113 apps 6 gls

HESLOP, Robert

Inside-left 5' 7" 10st 10lbs
Born: Rowlands Gill, 5th February 1907
Died: Rowlands Gill, July quarter 1969
Debut v Millwall (h) 27.10.28, lost 0-4
CAREER: South Pontop Villa. Annfield Plain F.C. Burnley amateur February 1928. Annfield Plain. **FOREST 24th October 1928.** Bishop Auckland (trial) August 1934. Annfield Plain August 1934. Gateshead June 1935. Bedlington United February 1939. (Wartime guest player with Consett March 1940.)
As the 'Post Football Guide' observed in 1930: "The only thing this player lacks are height and weight. Heslop's ball control is excellent, and he is equally at home at either inside-right or left." He was out of action for much of season 1930-31 with cartilage trouble but recovered to enjoy his best campaign in 1932-33, scoring 11 goals in 28 League matches to assist Forest to 5th position in Division Two. The former steelworks labourer returned to the North-East in the summer of 1934, and later enjoyed a three-year spell in the Third Division North with Gateshead, scoring 13 goals in 95 League appearances.
Appearances: 92 apps 23 gls FAC: 2 apps 0 gls Total: 94 apps 23 gls

HEWITT, Arthur Harper
Left full-back 5' 8" 11st 0lbs
Born: Beeston, Notts. 10th January 1900
Debut v Notts County (h) 24.1.25, drawn 0-0
CAREER: Ilkeston Town. **FOREST amateur 7th November 1923, professional 1st February 1924.** Watford August 1925 to April 1926. Cossall St. Cathrine August 1928.
After a lengthy wait in reserve, Arthur Hewitt made the first of his four League appearances in the local 'Derby' against Notts County as deputy for the emerging Percy Barrett. Forest suffered relegation from the top flight in the same season, and Hewitt was amongst the players released. He was quickly fixed up with Watford, but did not appear for them at the senior level
Appearances: FL: 4 apps 0 gls FAC: 1 app 0 gls Total: 5 apps 0 gls

HICKS, Thomas Chester

Left full-back
5' 11"   11st 6lbs.
Born: Trehaford, 1st March 1902
Died: St. Austell, July quarter 1961
Debut v Fulham (a) 15.9.27, lost 0-2
CAREER: Trehaford. Pontypridd July 1923. Preston North End July 1924. **FOREST 9th June 1927, fee £300.**
Northampton Town May 1928. Chester August 1929. Connah's Quay & Shotton December 1929.
Tom Hicks commenced with Preston North End and made an early debut in a 2-0 defeat against Burnley at Deepdale on 6th September 1924. He made only one other appearance in the season that ended in relegation from the First Division. Never more than a reserve, he made just nine League appearances in three seasons before joining Forest. An early season injury to Bill Thompson provided Hicks with his chance, and he held his place for six matches before Thompson recovered to take his usual place alongside Percy Barratt. After just two more first team appearances – the last a 5-0 defeat against his former team Preston North End – Hicks was released. He joined Northampton Town but made only five first team appearances in the Cobblers' side that finished third in the Third Division South.
Appearances: FL: 8 apps 0 gls Total: 8 apps 0 gls

HIGGINS, Alexander 'Sandy' M.M.

Inside-left   5' 8"   11st 4lbs
Born: Kilmarnock, 4th November 1885
Died: Newcastle-on-Tyne, 15th March 1939
Debut v Stoke (h) 28.8.20, drawn 2-2 (scored one)
CAREER: Belle Vue Juniors. Kilmarnock 1904. Newcastle United June 1905, fee £250. (Wartime guest player with Houghton Rovers, Hull City and Clydebank).
Kilmarnock August 1919. **FOREST 3rd August 1920.** Jarrow player-manager September 1921. Norwich City November 1921. Wallsend December 1922. Workington June 1923. F.C. Berne (Switzerland) trainer 1925. Preston Colliery player-coach November 1926 to 1927.
As the 'Post Football Guide for 1920-21' observed: "The signing of Alec Higgins from Newcastle United links up present day Forest football with that of the past. Alec is the son of the famous 'Sandy' Higgins, one of the most brilliant players

ever to wear the Garibaldi." Alec signed for Newcastle United as a teenager and remained at St. James' Park until he joined the Durham Light Infantry and was awarded the Military Medal and a citation during service in World War One. After demobilisation he joined Kilmarnock and stayed with them for a season. He was awarded a Scottish Cup Final winners' medal in 1920 although he did not play in the final, due to the sad death of his father Alexander (q.v.) on the day of the match. Billed as a clever and resourceful forward, able to take any of the inside positions, he did much to preserve Forest's place in Division Two in a disappointing season that finished with the Reds only one point ahead of the two clubs at the foot of the table. Recognised as one of the best forwards in the game in the Edwardian era, he made 150 League and Cup appearances for Newcastle United, scoring 41 goals. After retiring from the game he returned to Tyneside where he ran a grocer's business in Byker.
Appearances: FL: 33 apps 7 gls FAC: 2 apps 0 gls
Total: 35 apps 7 gls
Honours: Scotland International 4 caps 1910-11 (Newcastle United) FL Division 1 champions 1909. FA Cup winners 1910, finalists 1911.

HIGGINS, Alexander 'Sandy'

Centre-forward
5' 9½"   11st 7lbs
Born: Kilmarnock, 7th November 1863
Died: Kilmarnock, 17th April 1920
FL Debut v Everton (a) 3.9.92, drawn 2-2 (scored both goals)
CAREER: Kilmarnock 1882. Derby County August 1888. **FOREST July 1890, for FL matches 9th August 1892, released April 1894.** Kilmarnock 1894.
Forest's first goal scorer in the Football League, Alex 'Sandy' Higgins was already a local celebrity, having scored five goals against Clapton in an FA Cup-tie in January 1891, and followed by scoring 26 goals in 20 matches in Forest's Alliance championship winning side of 1891-92. He had earlier been capped by his country, and scored four goals in an 8-2 win against Ireland. Doubtless, he would have won further caps, but Scottish selectors of the time were loath to pick players who were operating in England. Known as: "The demon dribbler", he began in League football with Derby County, and was their leading scorer for two seasons before joining Forest.
Appearances: FL: 47 apps 18 gls FAC: 17 apps 18 gls
Total: 64 apps 36 gls
Honours: Scotland International, 1 cap 1885 (FOREST) Football Alliance champions 1892.

HINDLEY, Frank Charles

Centre-forward
5' 10" 12st 0lbs
Born: Worksop, 2nd
November 1914
Died: Worksop, 13th
March 2003
Debut v Millwall (a)
19.11.38, lost 0-5
CAREER: Netherton
United. **FOREST 23rd
December 1937.**
Brighton & Hove Albion
May 1939 to May 1947.
(Wartime guest player with **FOREST** and
Mansfield Town.)

*On joining Forest Frank Hindley was quickly
getting goals for the Reserves. Well-built, and one
of the speediest players on the books, he had a
powerful shot but his ball control was that of an
immature player. He was at his best with inside
partners who could make the most of his
outstanding speed by launching long passes up the
middle. The value of his speed was most apparent
in the game against Sheffield United at Bramall
Lane on Boxing Day 1938, when he nipped in to
intercept a back pass and scored a goal that gave
Forest the points. The outbreak of World War Two
interrupted his fledgling career, and he enlisted in
the Sherwood Foresters and suffered a bullet
wound to his shoulder in North Africa in 1940.
Resuming his career after the war, Hindley scored
five goals in 11 League and Cup matches for
Brighton & Hove Albion. Frank Hindley was the
father of Peter, the Forest full-back with over 400
appearances for the Reds in a career stretching
between 1962 and 1974.*
Appearances: FL: 6 apps 3 gls FAC: 2 apps 0 gls
Total: 8 apps 3 gls

HITCH, Alfred

Right half-back 5' 8" 11st 4lbs
Born: Walsall,
28th December 1876
Died: Uxbridge, Middlesex,
April quarter 1962
Debut v Wolverhampton
Wanderers (a) 2.9.01, lost 0-2
CAREER: Walsall Unity.
Walsall F.C. 19th November
1897. Wellington Town 14th
January 1898. Thames Iron
Works 16th September 1898.
Grays United 16th January 1898. Queen's Park
Rangers August 1899. **FOREST 17th April 1901.**
Queen's Park Rangers 5th May 1902. Watford 10th
May 1906 to May 1908.

*After commencing with two Football League
appearances for Walsall, Hitch spent much of his
subsequent career in Southern League circles,
most notably with Queen's Park Rangers, for
whom he clocked up 183 appearances in two
separate spells. Outstanding in headwork, despite
his relatively short stature; at either wing half or
in the centre he linked defence with attack by his
constructive use of the ball. He endured a mixed
season with the Forest, his first team involvement
ending after a 1-0 defeat at Blackburn Rovers on
New Year's Day 1902. Said to be clever, if
inconsistent, he had proved to be better in attack
than defence, his most memorable moment coming
on Boxing Day, when his goal gave Forest the
points against local rivals Notts County at the City
Ground. A former collier, he spent his final two
seasons with Watford, during which time he
opened a tobacconists shop in the town.*
Appearances: FL: 13 apps 2 gls Total: 13 apps 2 gls

HODGKINSON, Vincent Arthur

Inside-right 5' 9" 10st 8lbs
Born: Wollaton, Notts. 1st November 1906
Died: Scunthorpe, 28th June 1990
Debut v Chelsea (h) 31.8.25, lost 1-5
CAREER: Nottingham High School. Magdala
Amateurs. **FOREST amateur 5th March 1924,
signing professional 28th August 1925.**
Blackpool May 1927. Grantham September 1928.
Loughborough Corinthians August 1931. Lincoln
City (trial) September-October 1933. Lysaght's
Sports July 1935 to September 1939.

*On leaving Nottingham High School at the age of
16 Vince Hodgkinson played many fine games for
Magdala Amateurs in the Midland Amateur
Alliance before becoming a regular in the ranks of
Forest Reserves. Also a talented cricketer, he had
trials with Nottinghamshire C.C.C. and was on the
club's groundstaff at the age of 20. He was later to
spend a lengthy spell with Lincolnshire C.C.C.,
appearing in 44 Minor Counties matches between
1936 and 1952, taking 162 wickets. Rather less
successful as a footballer, aside from his nine
appearances for the Forest, he made just one more
senior appearance for Lincoln City against
Plymouth Argyle on 21st October 1933.*
Appearances: FL: 9 apps 1 gl Total: 9 apps 1 gl

HOLDSTOCK, Herbert Frederick.

Left half-back 6' 1" 12st 10lbs
Born: St. Albans 29th October 1879
Died: Bedford, October quarter 1965
Debut v Newcastle United (a) 8.4.05, lost 1-5
CAREER: Luton Star F.C. Luton Town 18th May
1900. **FOREST 11th May 1904 to May 1905.**
Hitchen Town 16th October 1905.

*The 'Cricket & Football Field' newspaper,
reporting on the prospects for the Forest club for
season 1904-05, advised that the club was
burdened with debt, but had a new grandstand to
replace the one burnt down. Annual subscriptions
had been increased from 12s.6d. to 15s. Transfer
activity had been relatively modest and included
Holdstock (Luton Town half-back), Niblo (Aston*

Villa centre-forward) and Peter Robinson (Dundee half-back.) Of the trio, only Niblo played with any regularity. Holdstock, largely a reserve team player during four years with Luton Town (13 appearances and one goal), continued in a similar role with the Forest. Peter Robertson, the Scottish international, appeared in the opening five matches before a reoccurrence of knee trouble sidelined him for much of the remainder of the season.
Appearances: FL: 1 app 0 gls Total: 1 app 0 gls

HOLLIS, Joshua Norris
Outside-right
Born: Bradford, 6th May 1875
Died: Nottingham, July quarter 1944
Debut v Burnley (h) 24.10.96, won 4-1 (scored one)
CAREER: FOREST 22nd August 1895. Sheppey United 21st May 1897.
As understudy to Fred Forman for the outside-berth, Hollis was restricted to a single first team appearance. He might have felt aggrieved at not receiving a further call up, considering that he had marked his senior debut with a goal. It was, however, back to reserve team football until his transfer in May 1897 to Sheppey United, whom he assisted to the runners-up position in the Second Division of the Southern League in his first season.
Appearances: FL: 1 app 1 gl Total: 1 app 1 gl

HOLMES, George **Albert**

Outside-left
5' 7½" 10st 0lbs
Born: Mansfield, July quarter 1885
Debut v Blackburn Rovers (a) 2.12.05, drawn 1-1
**CAREER: Grantham.
FOREST 6th May 1905-07**
Signed from Grantham to understudy Alf Spouncer in the outside-left role, Albert Holmes found few opportunities operating in the shadow of Forest's star wingman who dominated the left wing position for the best part of 13 seasons. He did, however, travel as twelfth man on Forest's 1905 tour to Argentine and Uruguay, which embarked on May 19th and arrived home on August 2nd. Forest won all eight matches that they played, scoring 56 goals and conceding only three.
Appearances: FL: 5 apps 0 gls FAC: 1 app 1 gl Total: 6 apps 1 gl

HOOD, Clarence
Outside-right 5' 10½" 10st 2lbs
Born: Mansfield, 28th April 1912
Died: Mansfield, January quarter 1977
Debut v Port Vale (h) 1.12.34, won 2-0
CAREER: Bilsthorpe Colliery. Mansfield Invicta. Mansfield Town amateur November 1932.
FOREST amateur 9th, professional 28th

November 1934 to May 1935. Ollerton Colliery September 1936.
Clarence Hood commenced with Bilsthorpe Colliery and signed his first professional form with the Forest, having failed to appear in League football with Mansfield Town. Having signed on the dotted line, he was given an early opportunity, replacing Arthur Masters at outside-right for the visit of Port Vale. The tall and willowy wingman held his place for three matches, and considering the fact that all three resulted in wins, he could have felt disappointed in not getting another opportunity.
Appearances: FL: 3 apps 0 gls Total: 3 apps 0 gls

HOOPER, William George

Outside-right
5'5" 10st 6lbs
Born: Lewisham, 20th February 1884
Died: Southport, 3rd September 1952
Debut v Clapton Orient (a) 23.2.07, won 1-0
CAREER: Catford South End F.C. Army football (R.A.S.C.) Grimsby Town August 1905. **FOREST 21st February 1907.** Notts County August 1912. Barrow June 1913. Gillingham May 1914. (Wartime guest player with Southport Vulcan December 1916.) Southport 1919-20. Lancaster Town 1920-21.
Bill Hooper caught the eye of Forest officials in matches for Grimsby Town against the Reds' Reserves in a Midland League match on 17th November 1907, and again against the first team on 29th December. In the latter, his sensational display in the Mariners' 3-0 win at the City Ground led to his joining Forest early in the New Year. He proved to be a very popular personality in the team and with the crowd who would loudly demand: "Give it to Hooper." The pocket-sized wingman was described as a perfect athlete in miniature, and his searing turn of speed that had carried him to victory in numerous spring handicaps, was fully utilised in dashes down the touchline. Playing in the final thirteen matches of season 1906-07, he scored against Hull City and Glossop as the Division Two title was secured, with a record of eleven wins and two draws in the final thirteen matches. After leaving Forest he was relegated with Notts County in 1912-13 and did not appear again in League football. He served for a second time with the Army Service Corps during the First World War.
Appearances: FL: 147 apps 22 gls FAC: 9 apps 2 gls Total: 156 apps 24 gls
Honours: **(FOREST)** FL Division 2 champions 1907.

HORROCKS, John James

Outside-right 5' 5" 10st 8lbs
Born: Castleton, near Rochdale, 22nd March 1887
Died: Castleton, near Rochdale, June 1957, age 70
Debut v Newcastle United (a) 11.9.09, won 2-1
CAREER: Seedfield F.C. (Bury and District
League). Bury St. Thomas's. Stand All Saints.
Ramsbottom. Atherton 15th June 1907. Lancaster
Town 28th October 1907. Stockport County 4th May
1908. **FOREST 7th May 1909.** Bury 11th July 1911
to cs 1912.

*In August 1911 the Athletic News reported that
John Horrocks, a cotton warehouseman, was a
well-known figure in local cricketing circles,
playing for Bury St. Thomas's in the local Amateur
League. With a batting average of 33 runs per
innings he was expected to carry off the league's
batting prize. He did less well in his season at Gigg
Lane when the Shakers were relegated from the
top flight, finishing at the foot of the table, twelve
points adrift of Preston North End the other
relegated club. In earlier days, Horrocks joined
Stockport County, who fielded many newcomers in
season 1908-09. Former Bury and Everton star
Jimmy Settle was Horrocks' inside partner on the
left wing, and the diminutive wingman enjoyed a
good season, scoring five goals in 34 League and
Cup matches. Two seasons with Nottingham
Forest followed in which he made 16 League
appearances in his first season, but only four in
1910-11 when Forest lost their top flight status,
gathering just one point from their final 13 fixtures
of the season.*
Appearances: FL: 22 apps 0 gls Total: 22 apps 0 gls

HOWIE, Charles

Outside-right 5' 8" 10st 6lbs
Born: Larbert, Stirling, 29th April 1906
Died: Falkirk, 25th December 1940
Debut v Millwall (h) 27.10.28, lost 0-4
CAREER: Old Plean Amateurs. Stenhousemuir.
FOREST 19th October 1928. Stenhousemuir
May 1931.

*One month after transferring Syd Gibson to
Sheffield United for £5,000, Forest signed Charlie
Howie from Stenhousemuir of the Scottish League
Division Two. At the time of his signing, Forest had
seven of their players either sick or injured, so
Howie was quickly introduced, and made 16
Division Two appearances in his first season,
scoring his first League goal against the Wolves in
a 3-2 win on Christmas Day. In his final Forest
appearance he scored at Reading on Boxing Day
1930, but finished on the losing side, the Reds
going down by five goals to two. Released at the
end of the season, Howie returned to Scotland and
signed for a second time with Stenhousemuir.*
Appearances: 23 apps 2 gls FAC: 1 app 0 gls Total:
24 apps 2 gls

HOWLETT, Harry William Alfred

Centre-forward/Outside-left 5' 9½" 11st 7lbs
Born: Auckland, County Durham, 23rd June 1910
Died: Havant, 12th October 1989
Debut v Plymouth Argyle (h) 1.10.32, drawn 1-1
CAREER: Evenwood Town. Cockfield F.C. Shildon
F.C. September 1927. Bishop Auckland. Rochdale
amateur August 1928. Cockfield F.C. Crook Town
May 1929. Bishop Auckland. Cockfield F.C.
September 1930. Portsmouth amateur July,
Professional August 1931. **FOREST 8th October
1932.** Crook Town October 1932. Poole Town
December 1932. Bournemouth & Boscombe
Athletic June 1933.

*Harry Howlett became Rochdale's youngest
Football League player when he made his sole
appearance against Wrexham on Boxing Day
1928. Later on trial with Forest, he doubled his
tally of League appearances before returning to
his native North-East. Harry's elder brother,
Charlie, a wing half-back, played in League
football with Durham City, Rochdale and Halifax
Town*
Appearances: FL: 1 app 0 gls Total: 1 app 0 gls

HUGHES, Edwin 'Teddy'

Right half-back
5' 7" 10st 10lbs
Born: Wrexham,
18th October 1886
Died: Montgomery,
17th April 1949
Debut v Sheffield Wednesday
(h) 16.4.06, lost 3-4
CAREER: Wrexham St.
Giles'. Wrexham Victoria.
Wrexham F.C. 1903-06.
FOREST 24th March 1906,
fee £200. Wrexham F.C. April 1911. Manchester
City October 1912. Aberdare Athletic June 1920.
Colwyn Bay United. Llandudno Town player-coach
August 1923.

*Teddy Hughes made his Forest debut at the age of
twenty, and in his first full season he appeared in
36 League matches and collected a Second
Division championship medal. Hard-working and
stylish, he was rarely absent from the right-half
berth for four seasons, his consistent displays soon
catching the eye of the Welsh selectors, who
awarded him 16 caps, nine while on Forest's books.
He was not retained after relegation from Division
One in 1910-11, but he subsequently added over a
century of League appearances with Manchester
City (77 and two goals) and Aberdare Athletic (32
and one goal).*
Appearances: FL: 163 apps 5 gls FAC: 12 apps 1 gl
Total: 175 apps 6 gls
Honours: Wales International, 16 caps 1906-14.
(FOREST) FL Division 2 champions 1907.
(Wrexham) Welsh Cup winners 1905. (Wrexham
Victoria) Welsh Amateur Cup winners 1903.

HUNT, Arthur
Left full-back
Debut v Burnley (h) 7.3.96, won 2-1
CAREER: FOREST 22nd August 1895 to 1896.
At Forest's Annual General Meeting in late June 1895 it was announced that eight local players had been signed. Not all were registered to play in Football League matches, but Arthur Hunt was. With the full-back berths dominated by Ritchie and Scott, Hunt was restricted to just one senior outing, with the emerging Jim Iremonger the favoured deputy.
Appearances: FL: 1 app 0 gls Total: 1 app 0 gls

HUNT, Ashley Kenneth

Goalkeeper 6' 0" 11st 0lbs
Born: Kirkby-in-Ashfield, 24th November 1921
Died: Holme Pierrepont, 3rd November 1940
Debut v Tranmere Rovers (h) 4.2.39, drawn 2-2
CAREER: Hawley's Athletic. **FOREST amateur 18th August 1937, professional November 1938.** (Wartime guest player with Mansfield Town 1939-40.)
Signed by Forest as a promising 17 year-old, Kenneth Hunt played in several matches with the Reds' reserve, and twice for the League side, before the outbreak of the Second World War. He was serving as an Army Lance Corporal at the time of his tragic death at the age of just 18 years of age. As recently as the previous Saturday he had appeared in goal for Mansfield Town against Walsall, having been loaned to The Stags by Forest at the commencement of wartime season 1939-40. The young soldier/goalkeeper was found shot at Home Pierrepont. His home was at 38, Fox-Grove, Old Basford. He was interred at Bulwell on November 7th 1940.
Appearances: FL: 2 apps 0 gls Total: 2 apps 0 gls

HUNT, Joseph Frederick
Inside-right
Born: Dublin South, 5th February 1913
Died: Bedford, December 1982
Debut v Bradford City (h) 4.5.35, won 2-0
CAREER: Bray Unknowns. **FOREST March to May 1935.** Bray Unknowns August 1936. St. James' Gate November 1937.
Briefly associated with the Forest at either side of spells with the quaintly named Bray Unknowns of the Irish Free State League. In 1932-33 they had remained undefeated at home throughout the season, but in 1934 they had been required to apply for re-election. In his one first team outing at the City Ground Hunt finished on the winning side, but he was not considered up to the standard required for Second Division football, and he returned to Ireland.
Appearances: FL: 1 app 0 gls Total: 1 app 0 gls

INNES, Robert

Right half-back
5' 9" 11st 0lbs
Born: Lanark, 23rd July 1878
Died: Swindon, 3rd March 1959.
Debut v Bury (a) 12.9.03, drawn 2-2
CAREER: Linton Villa. Strathclyde. Royal Ordnance Factory (Woolwich) 16th October 1895. Gravesend United 23rd May 1896. New Brompton 7th May 1898. Notts County 14th May 1901. **FOREST 25th September 1903.** Brighton & Hove Albion 2nd May 1905. Swindon Town 23rd June 1906 to May 1910. Swindon Victoria cs 1914.
Having crossed the border to find work, Bob Innes commenced his football career in the Royal Ordnance Factories League side. In the same competition he also assisted Gravesend United and New Brompton, before stepping up to First Division football with Notts County. After appearing regularly for two seasons (51 League and Cup appearances) he crossed the Trent to join Forest. He was on Notts' transfer list at £200, but the 'Nottingham Evening Post' reported that "Forest have paid nothing like that sum for him." After just 23 appearances in two seasons he departed, his career ending, as it had commenced, in Southern League football with Brighton & Hove Albion (29 appearances) and Swindon Town (33 appearances.)
Appearances: FL: 23 apps 0 gls Total: 23 apps 0 gls
Honours: Southern League representative v London F.A. at Millwall, February 1899

IREMONGER, Harold 'Harry'
Goalkeeper 6' 0" 11st 0lbs
Born: Wilford, Notts. 30th December 1893
Died: Nottingham General Hospital, 27th February 1957
Debut v Stockport County (a) 25.4.14, lost 1-2
CAREER: Sherwood Institute. **FOREST amateur 22nd April, professional 14th August 1914.**
Brother of James (q.v.) and Albert, the famous Notts County goalkeeper and record appearance holder, with 601 League and Cup outings that included 222 consecutive appearances, a total only ended by suspension in October 1912. Harry, who was said to be a goalkeeper of excellent promise, certainly possessed the family aptitude for the game, initially exemplified with the Sherwood Institute club. Sadly, his potential was never fully realised, as, after appearing in the first nine matches of the 1914-15 season, he enlisted into the Footballers' Battalion and made just one more appearance before the Football League suspended operations for the duration.
Appearances: FL: 11 apps 0 gls Total: 11 apps 0 gls

IREMONGER, James 'Jimmy'

Full-back/
goalkeeper
6' 1" 13st 7lbs
Born: Norton,
West Yorkshire,
5th March 1876
Died: West
Bridgford,
Nottingham, 25th
March 1956
Debut v Stoke (a)
21.3.96, lost 0-1
CAREER: Wilford
F.C. Nottingham
Jardines Athletic.
FOREST 7th
March 1896 -
May 1910. Notts
County trainer cs
1919 to May 1927.

One of eight local players engaged for the reserve
team in 1895, Jimmy Iremonger was by far the
most successful, quickly establishing himself as a
member of the back division and at the same time
embarking on a successful career as a County
cricketer. Born at Norton in West Yorkshire but
brought up in Wilford, an early success came
against his native county when he took 8 wickets
for 34 runs for Notts Colts against Yorkshire Colts
at Barnsley in May 1899. On the football field, he
became fully established following the retirement
of Archie Ritchie and Adam Scott, and his excellent
displays led to his selection for England in 1901
and 1902. Like his famous brother Albert, the Notts
County goalkeeper, Jimmy was also a fine
goalkeeper, and late in his career he took over as
deputy to Harry Linacre. Described as being "Cool
as a cucumber, and able to take all kinds of
shots with equal faculty." He stepped into a very wide
breach in late season 1908-09, when one of his
appearances was made in the record 12-0 defeat of
Leicester Fosse, in which three Forest players
performed the hat trick. His cricket career
spanned 15 years and 315 matches for Notts C.C.C.
He also toured Australia with the MCC in 1911-12.
He scored 16,622 runs at an average of 35.06, with
a highest score of 272 against Kent at Trent Bridge
in 1904. He also took 619 wickets at an average
cost of 22.97. He was later coach at Trent Bridge
from 1921 to 1938.
Appearances: FL: 276 apps 2 gls FAC: 26 apps 1 gl
Total: 302 apps 3 gls
HONOURS: England International, 2 caps 1901-02.
FL representative 4 appearances, 1901-03 .

JEACOCK, Thomas

Right half-back
Born: Hinckley, October quarter 1866
Debut v Linfield Athletic, FAC 1 (h) 2.2.1889,
drawn 2-2
CAREER: Mellor's F.C. **FOREST (debut)**
February 1889, registered for FL matches cs
1892. Burton Swifts January 1893 (along with
William Mason). **FOREST 1894.**
A Forest regular at left half-back in the first two
seasons of Alliance football, Thomas Jeacock then
lost his place in the side that won the
championship of the competition in season 1891-
92. He moved on to Burton Swifts, along with
another Forest reserve, William Mason, in
January of the Reds' first season as a Football
League club. He made his debut against Walsall
Town Swifts in February 1893, and played just
once more before being released. On returning to
Nottingham, he assisted the Forest just once,
appearing at outside-right in a 2-3 home defeat
against Everton in September 1894. Note:
Another player of the same name – E.A. Jeacock –
played for Forest Reserves and joined Swindon
Town in August 1901. He was born at Leicester on
29th November 1876, but it is not known whether
he was a relative of the Forest player.
Appearances: FL: 1 app 0 gls FAC: 8 apps 0 gls
Total: 9 apps 0 gls

JENNINGS, Samuel

Centre-forward
5' 11" 11st 4lbs
Born: Cinderhill,
Nottingham, 26th
December 1898
Died: Robertsbridge,
Sussex, 26th August 1944
Debut v Stoke (h) 25.8.28,
lost 1-5
CAREER: Highbury Vale
Methodists. Basford
United. 5th Reserve
Battalion Coldstream
Guards, Basford National

Ordnance Factory (Wartime guest player with Notts
County and Tottenham Hotspur.) Norwich City
May 1919. Middlesbrough April 1920, fee £2,500.
Reading (loan) April, professional June 1921. West
Ham United June 1924. Brighton & Hove Albion
March 1925, fee £650. **FOREST 11th May 1928.**
Port Vale May 1929. Stockport County September
1931. Burnley January to May 1932. Olympique
Marseille (France) coach September 1932. Club
Frances 1933-34. Scarborough July 1934. Wisbech
Town player, then secretary-coach August 1935.
Coached in Switzerland 1935-36. Glentoran coach
June 1936. Rochdale manager October 1937 to
September 1938.

Sam Jennings, brother of Billy Jennings, the Notts County centre-half, was bought by Middlesbrough for £2,250 from Norwich City in his first season of senior football. He scored on his debut against Everton but did little to justify his hefty transfer fee thereafter, the former Coldstream Guardsman moving on after scoring two goals in 10 League matches. Happily, he did much better subsequently. With Reading he netted 45 goals in 110 Third Division matches, form that earned him an upward move to West Ham United. Again scoring on his debut, he had scored three goals in nine matches when Brighton & Hove Albion paid a club record fee for his transfer later in the same season. Leading scorer at the Goldstone Ground in consecutive seasons 1925-27, he netted 61 goals in 110 League matches before joining Forest in May 1928. After a bright start that included a hat trick in a 5-3 win at Swansea Town in September, he was out of the side throughout January and February, as Bert Heathcock was introduced and netted 14 goals in 16 matches. Released after a season, his wandering path took a marked decline after he had scored 42 goals in 63 League matches for Port Vale. His final goal in senior football – for Burnley in a 1-5 defeat at Manchester United on 17th February 1932 – took his overall career record to a very impressive 172 goals in 349 League matches.
Appearances: FL: 27 apps 15 gls FAC: 1 app 1 gl
Total: 28 apps 16 gls

JOHNSON, Joseph

Goalkeeper
6' 0½" 13st 0lbs
Born: Tibshelf, Derbyshire, 23rd June 1882
Debut v Rotherham County (a) 30.8.19, lost 0-2
CAREER: Tibshelf Church. Newton F.C. Ripley Athletic May 1904. Aston Villa January 1905. Plymouth Argyle May 1906. Crystal Palace April 1908. (Wartime guest player with **FOREST** and Rotherham County.) **FOREST June 1919.** Clay Cross Town August 1921. Sutton Town May 1922.

Joe Johnson was sixteen years of age and already stood 6' 0½" when he commenced with Tibshelf Church. A spell with Newton F.C. preceded his move to Ripley Athletic, a club that became famous for its goalkeepers that included Harry Maskrey (Derby County and England) and Harry Bailey (Luton Town, Exeter City, Brentford & Thames). From Ripley he went to Aston Villa and next down to Plymouth, but it was with Crystal Palace that he made his name, appearing in 274 Southern League appearances and 19 FA Cup-ties. He was first associated with Forest as a guest player. When the great Sam Hardy was serving in the Navy in 1917-18, Johnson made 31 appearances, missing only three matches. He was Forest's regular goalkeeper in post war football until former wartime guest Sam Hardy had signed permanently in August 1921. Joe Johnson, who was a lay preacher, served in the Royal Corps of Signals during the First World War.
Appearances: FL: 53 apps 0 gls FAC: 1 app 0 gls
Total: 54 apps 0 gls
Honours: Southern League representative, 3 apps.

JONES, Albert Thomas

Full-back 5' 10" 12st 4lbs
Born: Talgarth, 6th February 1883
Died: Belper, 28th July 1963
Debut v Sunderland (h) 10.10.03, won 3-0
CAREER: Builth Juniors. Builth Town. Talgarth. Harbone Lynwood. Aston Villa (trial) July/August 1902. Swindon Town November 1902. **FOREST 27th April 1903.** Notts County 6th December 1905. Norwich City May 1907. Wellington Town September 1908. Swansea Town amateur 1913.

A young Welshman who was signed along with Tom Davies from Swindon Town, Albert Jones did not win a regular place in the League side, although many critics felt that he was worth it. His fortunes took an upturn after leaving the City Ground, although he won his first cap while on Forest's books. The son of a Builth chemist, both Albert and his younger brother Gordon each won two Wales caps. Sadly, an injury when playing against England halted Albert's progress, but when fit he was described as: "A dashing tackler with a beautiful kick in either foot." Much later, he made a surprise return to the game as a reinstated amateur and was still a potent force, being capped by Wales at that level. Following in his father's footsteps, he qualified as a Pharmacist in 1931 and worked for Boots in Treochy. Later he set up in business on his own account in Llantwit Vardre, Pontypridd.
Appearances: FL: 10 apps 0 gls FAC: 3 apps 0 gls
Total: 13 apps 0 gls
Honours: Wales International, 2 caps 1905-06. Wales Amateur International.

JONES, Charles

Outside-left
5' 7" 11st 9lbs
Born: Troedyrhiw, near Merthyr Tydfil, 12th December 1900
Died: Liverpool, 8th June 1969
Debut v Derby County (h) 26.9.25, lost 1-2
CAREER: Cardiff City August 1919. Stockport County May 1921. Oldham Athletic March 1923, fee £1,000. **FOREST 25th September 1925, fee £750**. Arsenal 18th May 1928, fee £4,800. Notts County manager May to December 1934. Crittall's Athletic secretary-manager March 1935 to 1939.

Stockport County were the first winners of the championship of the Third Division North in 1921-22, and their newly signed wingman Charlie Jones made a major contribution with nine goals in 34 matches. He joined Oldham Athletic in the late stages of the following term, but was unable to halt the team's relegation from the top flight. After 58 League and Cup matches and five goals, he joined Forest and his career took an immediate upturn. Hardly as fast as some wingers but with wily ball control, he was selected to play for Wales against England on 1st March 1926, and although appearing at inside-left instead of his usual position on the wing, he was a big success. It was in the inside berth that he established his reputation with the Reds. He had won four Wales caps at the time of his signing by Arsenal, and at Highbury he was used with great success at left half-back, from which position he was the driving force for the Gunners' domination of the First Division in the early 1930s. Sadly, he was unable to carry his success into the role of manager of Notts County, who won only one in 17 matches before he was sacked, after only seven months at Meadow Lane. He later ran a hairdressing business in London.

Appearances: FL: 100 apps 22 gls FAC: 10 apps 0 gls Total: 110 apps 22 gls
Honours: Wales International, 8 caps 1926-33. (Arsenal) FL Division 1 champions 1931, 1933, 1934. FA Cup finalists 1932. (Stockport County) FL Division 3 North champions 1922.

JONES, George William

Centre half-back
Born: Cinderhill, Nottingham, 30th November 1896
Died: Nottingham, 24th August 1965
Debut v Bury (h) 30.10.20, won 4-2
CAREER: Carlton Swifts. **FOREST amateur 4th March, professional 23rd October 1920**. Mansfield Town May 1921. Grantham July 1922 to February 1924.

Signed by Forest as cover for Fred Parker for the centre-half position, George Jones was released at the close of the relegation season 1920-21. This despite the fact that in his eight consecutive first team appearances he had played a full part in one of the best spells of the season that included back-to-back wins against Bury and South Shields, and Hull City in home and away matches. Jones was quickly fixed up with Mansfield Town, competing for the first time in the Midland League. The Stags finished 8th in the table and reached the 6th Qualifying Round of the FA Cup before going out, after a replay, against Walsall. Before departing to join Grantham, George Jones picked up a winners' medal in the Notts Charity Cup, after beating Worksop Town 1-0 in the final at Field Mill.

Appearances: FL: 8 apps 0 gls Total: 8 apps 0 gls

JONES, Harry

Full-back
5' 9½" 12st 7lbs
Born: Blackwell, Derbyshire, 24th March 1891
Died: Derby, May 1947
Debut v Glossop (h) 5.10.12, won 3-2
CAREER: Blackwell Boys' Brigade. Blackwell Wesley Guild. Blackwell Colliery. **FOREST 28th October 1910 to May 1924**. Sutton Town December 1924 to April 1925. Ollerton Colliery.

Harry Jones commenced his football career at the tender age of eleven with Blackwell Boys' Brigade and graduated with his local Colliery side. He was nineteen years old when he joined Forest, and created a highly favourable impression by his displays in the reserve team. His senior career was threatened when he suffered a broken leg at Lincoln City on 14th February 1914, but he recovered to take his place in the side from October 1914, and he later assisted Forest to win the championship of the 1918-19 Midland Section Tournament. A defender with any amount of dash and courage, he matured into one of the best full-backs in the country. After assisting Forest to the Second Division championship in 1922, he was awarded his lone England cap, a matter of weeks before his 32nd birthday, in a 4-1 win against France. In the following year he was in the

Football League X1 who beat the Irish League at Windsor Park, Belfast, by 6-2. His full-back partner in the match was William Ashurst of Notts County.
Appearances: FL: 224 apps 7 gls FAC: 15 apps 3 gls
Total: 239 apps 10 gls
Honours: England International, 1 cap 1923. FL representative, 1 appearance, 1924. (**FOREST**) FL Division 2 champions 1922.

JONES, Thomas Daniel
Inside-left 5' 7" 10st 0lbs
Born: Aberaman, Glamorgan, June 1884
Died: Porthcawl, Glamorgan, 8th February 1958
Debut v Middlesbrough (h) 23.4.04, drawn 1-1
CAREER: Aberaman Athletic 1900. Aberdare Town 1903. **FOREST amateur 28th March 1904, professional 11th May 1904.** Aberdare Town April 1908 to August 1910. Grantham. Merthyr Town secretary manager 1923-24. Cardiff City scout to 1930.
Capped by Wales at both full and amateur level, Tommy Jones joined Forest as a young but promising inside-left after starring with Aberdare Town, finalists in the Welsh Cup in successive seasons 1903-04. Although he made little headway at the City Ground, he won international recognition after returning to Aberdare in 1908. The son of an Aberaman grocer, he qualified as a solicitor in 1913, and following army service, practiced in Aberdare for many years.
Appearances: FL: 3 apps 0 gls Total: 3 apps 0 gls
Honours: Wales International, 1 cap 1908. Wales Amateur International 1908. (Aberdare Town) Welsh Cup finalists 1903 and 1904.

KEETON, William Walter

Inside-right
Born: Shirebrook, Derbyshire, 30th April 1905
Died: Forest Town, Mansfield, 10th October 1980
Debut v Bradford Park Avenue (a) 24.9.32, lost 1-3
CAREER: Mansfield Colliery Boys' Brigade. Mansfield Shoe Company. Watford 'A'. Notts County 'A'. Mansfield Colliery 1925. Grantham amateur October 1926, professional February 1927. Sunderland October 1930 to December 1931, fee £450.
FOREST 20th September 1932. Loughborough Corinthians January 1933. Grantham October 1933.
A useful inside-right whose spell with Sunderland ended when he asked to be placed on the transfer list, as he wished to return south because of his wife's ill-health. On returning to Nottingham he was expected to join Loughborough Corinthians, but was persuaded to assist Forest. Walter Keeton

was much better known as the Notts and England cricketer, who played in two Test Matches (against Australia in 1934 and the West Indies in 1939.) He first played for Nottinghamshire in 1926, becoming a regular team member in 1931, starring as an attractive opening right-handed batsman and brilliant deep field. Despite illness and injuries – the most serious when he was involved in a road accident, being knocked down from behind by a lorry in 1935 – his cricket career lasted until 1952. Keeton made 54 centuries, scored 1,000 runs in a season 12 times (on six occasions exceeding 2,000) and scored a century against every county. His highest score was 312 not out v Middlesex in 1939, and he hit six other double centuries. After retiring he ran a sports shop, later working for the National Coal Board.
Appearances: FL: 5 apps 0 gls Total: 5 apps 0 gls

KENT, Thomas William
Outside-right
Born: Foleshill, Coventry 14th January 1872
Died: Nottingham, July quarter 1951
Debut v Derby County (a) 20.4.98, lost 0-2
CAREER: Carrington F.C. **FOREST 25th May 1898.** Stanton Hill August 1900.
Tom Kent's only first team experience came in the final two fixtures of the 1898-99 season. Two days on from his debut at Derby County he appeared again on the right wing against West Bromwich Albion at the City Ground. Forest rounded off their season with an emphatic 3-0 victory, Kent's inside partner Fred Forman scoring a hat trick.
Appearances: FL: 2 apps 0 gls Total: 2 apps 0 gls

KERR, Neil
Centre-forward
Born: Bowling, Dunbartonshire, 13th April 1871
Died: December 1901
Debut v Everton (a) 7.9.95, lost 2-6
CAREER: Cowlairs F.C. Rangers May 1890. Liverpool June 1894. **FOREST 31st August 1895**. Clyde 11th February 1896. Falkirk 28th November 1896. Rangers 4th September 1897. Falkirk 31st May 1898.
Neil Kerr was ever present in 1890-91, the very first season of the Scottish League when Rangers shared the championship with Dumbarton, each side with 29 points from 18 matches. Normally an inside-right or centre-forward, Liverpool fielded him at outside-right in his season at Anfield, in which he scored three goals in 12 League matches. On moving to the Forest, a report on his first appearance in a pre-season practice match considered him: "Well-built for the game and clever on the ball, but lacking dash and judgment and overall somewhat of a disappointment." The early assessment was confirmed when he was said to have failed entirely at centre-forward on his debut in the 2-6 defeat at Everton. His display was blamed in some measure for the total

disorganisation of the side. Kerr was not given a second opportunity and returned to Scotland before the close of the season.
Appearances: FL: 1 app 0 gls Total: 1 app 0 gls
Honours: (Rangers) Scottish League joint champions 1891.

KIRRAGE, Frank Bernard
Inside-right   5' 9½"   10st 12lbs
Born: Bromley, Kent, 3rd March 1893
Died: Fiskerton, Notts. 25th January 1933
Debut v Stockport County (h) 27.9.19, drawn 1-1
CAREER: Nottingham High Pavement Secondary School. Lenton Church. Mapperley F.C. Bulwell F.C. **FOREST September 1917**. (Wartime guest with Leicester Fosse 1918-19.) Ilkeston United August 1920. Newark Town. Newark YMCA to 1929.
All round sportsman Frank Kirrage was a useful footballer in the lower grades of professional football. Additionally, he played cricket for Newark C.C. and took a keen interest in rugby and hockey. As a youngster he picked up his first trophy when his team, Lenton Church, won the Notts and Derby Church Cup. In season 1918-19, the final season of football played under wartime conditions, he made two guest appearances for Leicester Fosse and scored one goal on his debut in a 2-4 defeat at Leeds City on 25th January 1919. He was later a licensee at the Old Elm Tree Inn at Hoveringham.
Appearances: FL: 1 app 0 gls Total: 1 app 0 gls

LANGFORD, Leonard

Goalkeeper
6' 0½"   12st 9lbs
Born: Alfreton, 30th May 1899
Died: Stockport, 26th December 1973
Debut v Sheffield United (h) 14.2.25, lost 2-3
CAREER: Sheffield Schoolboys. Attercliffe Victory 1923. Rossington Colliery. **FOREST 19th November 1924**. Manchester City June 1930. Manchester United June 1934 to May 1937. Manchester University coach. Goslings F.C.
Born in Alfreton, and brought up in Sheffield, where he kept goal for Sheffield Schoolboys in the English Schools Charity Shield; incidentally, Len Langford's father kept goal for Newstead Byron in the late 1890s. He became a soldier at the age of 15 and served throughout the war with the 2nd Coldstream Guards. After leaving the army in 1923 he joined Attercliffe Victory. Obtaining work
at Rossington Colliery he played in goal for the colliery club, and it was after a remarkable performance at Sincil Bank against Lincoln City that Forest secured his services. Very much an all-round sportsman, Langford won the middleweight boxing championship of the Household Brigade for three successive years, and the championship of the Aldershot Command on one occasion. In addition, he won several prizes for high jumping and was a wicketkeeper of more than average ability. Succeeding Arthur Bennett as Forest's first-choice goalkeeper, he missed only two League matches in as many seasons between 1925-27. He was seriously injured in season 1927-28 but made a fine recovery, and remained at the City Ground until June 1930 when he joined Manchester City. He won an FA Cup finalists' medal in 1933, but lost his place to the emerging Frank Swift in 1934, thus missing out when City returned to Wembley and were successful against Portsmouth. In the close season Langford moved across Manchester to join the United, sharing senior goalkeeping duties with England international Jack Hacking in his first season.
Appearances: FL: 136 apps 0 gls FAC: 8 apps 0 gls
Total: 144 apps 0 gls
Honours: (Manchester City) FA Cup finalists 1933

LANGHAM, Frank
Centre half-back   6' 0"   11st 0lbs
Born: Nottingham, 12th March 1889
Died: Bodmin, October quarter 1967, age 78
Debut v Blackpool (a) 23.3.12, lost 0-2
CAREER: South Nottingham F.C. **FOREST 25th April 1912**. Northampton Town 31st August 1912. Rushden Town.
Frank Langham graduated in the ranks of South Nottingham F.C. as an amateur, and achieved something of a reputation as a centre-half. Signing a professional form with the Forest in late season 1911-12, he was given two opportunities in the first team, as deputy for Joe Mercer (father of the England international of the same name.) Without further first team involvement, Langham was signed by Northampton Town, managed at that time by Walter Bull, the former Notts County and Spurs half-back, who had taken over the post vacated by Herbert Chapman, later to manage Huddersfield Town and Arsenal with outstanding success.
Appearances: FL: 2 apps 0 gls Total: 2 apps 0 gls

LANGLEY, Ronald
Outside-left   5' 5"   10st 0lbs
Born: Basford, Notts. 8th March 1912
Died: Thanet, 25th August 1975
Debut v Bury (h) 19.11.32, lost 0-2
CAREER: Quarry Road Old Boys. **FOREST amateur 19th October, professional 15th November 1932, released April 1934.** Heanor Town October 1934.

Described by the 'Post Football Guide' as a 'pocket' outside-left and a true home product, brought up with Quarry Road Old Boys, Bulwell. After featuring as an amateur in the junior Reds at outside-left, he was signed as a professional at 20 years of age. Despite his lack of weight and inches he gained the reputation of a progressive wingman with an exceptional turn of speed. He was handed his first start in the League side in Cyril Stocks' benefit match against Bury and held his place in the side for five matches, scoring his only League goal in the 1-1 draw at Lincoln City on his second appearance.

Appearances: FL: 5 apps 1 gl Total: 5 apps 1 gl

LAWS, Joseph Minto

Outside-left
5' 3½" 10st 3lbs
Born: Cornsay Colliery, 6th July 1897
Died: Euxton, Chorley, 26th December 1952
Debut v Manchester City (h) 2.10.26, drawn 3-3 (scored one)
CAREER: Wheatley Hill School. Castleford Town (trial) August 1920.
Spennymoor United September 1920. Grimsby Town May 1921. Worksop August 1923. York City November 1924. **FOREST 30th September 1926.** Southport June 1927. Macclesfield July 1929. Ashton National October 1930. Macclesfield cs 1931. Chorley July 1932-33.
Although lacking height and weight, Joe Laws was very fast and clever with a strong shot in either foot. Introduced to League football by Grimsby Town he scored five goals in 53 League matches. He joined Forest from York City, for whom he scored 14 goals in Midland League matches in 1925-26. A scoring debut against Manchester City was an excellent start to his Forest career, but he failed to hold a place in the first team and left to join Southport in June 1927. He missed only three games in his two seasons at Haig Avenue, scoring 11 goals in 81 matches, before finishing his career in non-League football. He was later a publican in Macclesfield and Preston, and later again worked in a bleachworks in Chorley.
Appearances: FL: 7 apps 1 gl Total: 7 apps 1 gl
Honours: North-Eastern League representative v Central League.

LAWTON, James Allsop

Centre half-back 5' 11½" 12st 8lbs
Born: Ripley, Yorkshire, 27th September 1893
Died: Bognor Regis, 23rd March 1975
Debut v Wolverhampton Wanderers (a) 1.11.19, lost 0-4
CAREER: Derbyshire Schoolboys. Openwoodgate F.C. Ilkeston United. Notts County (trial). Ripley

Town. Portsmouth June 1912. Chesterfield Town (trial) November 1913. Brampton Ironworks. Chesterfield Town December 1913. Ilkeston United cs 1919. **FOREST 1st November 1919.** Ripley Town.
Forest were reported to have paid a substantial fee to Ilkeston United, and a friendly match for their benefit, for the transfer of the former England Schools international James Lawton. He had been playing at centre-forward for Ilkeston, but during four years in the army, which he left in the spring of 1919, he did very good work at centre-half. Selected for his Football League debut in place of Fred Parker, his trio of outings contained two heavy defeats, 4-0 at Wolves on his debut and 5-2 at Tottenham Hotspur on 29th November. The latter being his final involvement in the League side.
Appearances: FL: 3 apps 0 gls Total: 3 apps 0 gls
Honours: England Schoolboy International v Wales 1907

LEMOINE, Harold Meredith

Goalkeeper
Born: Bassingbourn, Cambridge, 4th October 1877
Died: Edgware, 5th September 1961
Debut v Bury (h) 14.12.12, drawn 1-1
CAREER: Shepherd's Bush. Clapton. Southend United December 1911. **FOREST amateur 13th December 1912.** Woking August 1914. Hunslet F.C.
England amateur international goalkeeper Harold Lemoine, described by one contemporary critic as: "Cool, plucky and active," served Forest well during Jack Hannah's illness at a critical period in mid season 1912-13. It was also suggested that the Shepherd's Bush amateur should have been more frequently called upon in the following season when Forest finished at the foot of Division Two with the worst defensive record in the Football League. An all round sportsman, Lemoine played in Minor Counties cricket for Hertfordshire. Outside of sporting activities, he worked as general manager for a Phonograph company.
Appearances: FL: 9 apps 0 gls Total: 9 apps 0 gls
Honours: England Amateur International.

LENNOX, William

Outside-right 5' 8" 11st 0lbs
Born: Pelaw, 15th June 1908
Died: Pelaw, January quarter 1977
Debut v Bradford Park Avenue (a) 19.1.29, drawn 1-1
CAREER: Pelaw. Shildon Colliery March 1928. **FOREST 12th January 1929.** Washington Colliery September 1929, player-manager March 1930. Spennymoor Athletic September 1930. Lochside United (Newcastle) September 1933. North Shields Collingwood February 1936. Wilson's F.C. by 1938.

The right-wing position, for so long dominated by Syd Gibson, became a problem for Forest following the former Kettering Town wingman's departure to Sheffield United in the early weeks of the 1928-29 season. In October, when the Reds' ranks were depleted with no fewer than seven players on the sick or injured list, Charlie Howie was signed from Scottish Division Two club, Stenhousemuir. A further change was deemed necessary as the side struggled at the wrong end of Division Two, leading to the arrival of Billy Lennox from Shildon Colliery in mid January. He shared the problem right-wing berth with Howie for the remainder of the season, scoring once in nine matches, but was released in April, returning to non-League football with Spennymoor United.
Appearances: FL: 9 apps 1 gl Total: 9 apps 1 gl

LESSONS, George **Frederick**

Centre-forward
5' 9½" 11st 3lbs
Born: Stockport, 3rd August 1883
Died: K.I.A. in the Eterpigne area, 7th September 1918, age 35
Debut v Preston North End (h) 6.10.04, lost 0-1
CAREER: Notts Jardines Athletic 1903. **FOREST 11th May 1904.** Northampton Town 1st May 1907.

Recruited from Notts Jardines Athletic, winners of the Notts Alliance championship in season 1903-04. Fred Lessons was an athletically built centre-forward of the go-ahead bustling type. Said to open the game out well, he was a raw talent who was given an early chance and scored the only goal of the game in his second appearance, at Preston North End on 17th December 1904. In the following season he began well but then did not come up to expectations, lacking steadiness when in sight of goal. As the 'Post Guide' for 1906-07 commented: "A centre-forward who is much too good for local football, but still needs coaching to fulfil his potential." In early July 1907, Northampton Town, who had to apply for re-election to the Southern League, signed George Lessons. In a remarkable transformation, by season 1908-09, the Cobblers won the championship of the Southern League for the first time, scoring 90 goals in 40 matches, Fred Lessons being the only ever-present player throughout the successful campaign in which he scored 23 goals. He appeared in 234 matches for the Cobblers between 1907 and 1915, scoring 75 League goals. He also acted as manager of the club from 1913 to 1915. He was later to lose his life when serving as a Lance-Corporal in the Northamptonshire Regiment

Appearances: FL: 31 apps 8 gls FAC: 3 apps 0 gls
Total: 34 apps 8 gls
Honours: (Northampton Town) Southern League Division One champions, 1909.
FA Charity Shield runners-up, 1909.

LINACRE, James Henry 'Harry'

Goalkeeper
6' 0" 11st 8lbs
Born: Aston-upon-Trent, Derbyshire, 26th March 1881
Died: Nottingham, 11th May 1957
Debut v Bury (h) 4.11.99, drawn 2-2
CAREER:
Loughborough Grammar School. Aston-upon-Trent F.C. Draycott Mills. Derby County December 1898. **FOREST 18th August 1899. Retired May 1909.**

Appearances: FL: 305 apps 0 gls FAC: 27 apps 0 gls
Total: 332 apps 0 gls

Harry Linacre started life at Aston-upon-Trent, and when fourteen years of age kept goal for Loughborough Grammar School, where he was educated. He later joined Derby County, playing mainly for the Reserves, and was signed by Forest to understudy Dennis Allsop. Nephew to the brothers Forman, Linacre was given an early opportunity, and a match report penned on his debut revealed that: "He was given plenty to do, but faced several persistent attacks with coolness and confidence, and kept out a number of shots that no one would have been surprised to see score. Altogether, Forest, with three men away, did very well to make a draw against such hard fighters as Bury." An alert goalkeeper with a long reach, his first honour was an appearance for the North versus the South, followed by Inter-League selection and a first international cap against Scotland. A custodian with no embroidery in his play, he did his work in a deliberately unassuming way, but was ever on the alert. A regular in the Forest goal for nine seasons, he departed the City Ground in 1909, the decision not to re-engage him being taken with great regret
Honours: England International, 2 caps 1905. FL representative. **(FOREST)** FL Division 2 champions 1907

LINLEY, Edward 'Ted'/'Raz'

Outside-left
5' 8" 10st 10lbs
Born: East Retford,
26th September 1894
Died: Worksop, 29th
June 1974
Debut v Reading (a)
4.9.26, lost 0-4
CAREER: Kiverton
Park. Army football
(Sherwood Rangers).
Worksop Town cs
1919. Birmingham
amateur October,
professional
December 1920, fee £800 plus another player.
FOREST 4th September 1926. Sutton Town
August 1927. Mansfield Town February 1928.
Shirebrook September 1928.
*A rather unlikely looking footballer, balding and
knock-kneed, nevertheless 'Raz' Linley could show
his heels to most full-backs, and a lengthy spell
with Birmingham spanned 118 League and Cup
appearances and 11 goals. 12 appearances and two
goals being his contribution to the Blues Division
Two championship win in season 1920-21. He
honed his skills in Army football and whilst
serving with the Sherwood Rangers was a winner
of the Palestine Army championship. Generally
first choice at outside-left during his season at the
City Ground, he formed a dangerous wing
partnership with the wily Wales international
Charlie Jones as his inside partner. Linley moved
on to Sutton Town in the close season, appeared
briefly with Mansfield Town, finishing up with the
Stags local rivals, Shirebrook.*
Appearances: FL: 29 apps 5 gls FAC: 2 apps 0 gls
Total: 31 apps 5 gls
Honours: (Birmingham) FL Division 2 champions
1921

LLOYD, Clifford John
Left half-back 5' 9" 11st 0lbs
Born: Swansea, 30th September 1902
Died: Swansea, 30th October 1975
Debut v Bury (a) 6.12.30, lost 0-1
CAREER: Swansea Town 1926. **FOREST 4th
December 1930**. Crystal Palace 31st January 1931.
Waterford. Barrow November 1932.
*Cliff Lloyd began with his hometown club,
Swansea Town, making his debut in Division Two
in a 2-0 win against Port Vale at the Vetch on 11th
February 1928. In the following season he
appeared in 24 League matches and one FA Cup-
tie – the latter against Forest at the City Ground –
and despite finishing on the losing side, he had
impressed with his work rate, hard tackling and
dexterous headwork. In the following season he
was transferred to the Forest, but after replacing
Bill Farmer at right-half for a run of four matches,*

*he was dropped following a heavy 2-5 defeat at
Reading. Within a month he was transferred to
Crystal Palace, and later to Barrow following a
spell in Ireland, but he did not appear at senior
level again.*
Appearances: FL: 4 apps 0 gls Total: 4 apps 0 gls

LOCKETT, Harry

Inside-forward
5' 8" 11st 5lbs
Born: Market Drayton,
27th December 1887
Died: Tunstall, Stoke-on-
Trent, 17th May 1959
Debut v Preston North End
(a) 1.9.10, won 2-0
CAREER: Wilmslow.
Whitchurch. Crewe
Alexandra 31st January 1906.
Market Drayton February 1908. Bolton Wanderers
March 1908. **FOREST 28th June 1910**. Exeter
City July 1911. Chesterfield 1913. Stalybridge Celtic
June 1913, retired September 1924.
*Harry Lockett's first season in League football
with Bolton Wanderers ended in disappointment,
as the Trotters crashed out of Division One. He had
made his debut in a 0-4 home defeat against
Newcastle United on 7th September 1909, but later
outlined his potential by scoring in three successive
matches against Sunderland, Everton and
Manchester United. On moving to Forest in the
close season, he played little first team football
after Christmas, and for the second successive
season suffered relegation from the top flight. He
was one of thirteen Forest players released in the
wake of relegation, but thereafter his fortunes took
an upturn in the Southern League with Exeter
City. Successfully switched from inside-forward to
left half-back, he appeared in 70 Southern League
matches and four FA Cup-ties. His League career
ended with Stalybridge Celtic, and in their two
seasons as members of the Football League, he
appeared in 70 matches and scored one goal.*
Appearances: FL: 23 apps 5 gls Total: 23 apps 5 gls

LOCKTON, John Henry
Inside-left 5' 10½" 11st 7lbs
Born: Peckham, 22nd May 1892
Died: Thornton Heath, 29th June 1972
Debut v Barnsley (a) 17.1.14, lost 0-5
CAREER: London University. Fulham amateur.
Ilford F.C. **FOREST amateur 16th January 1914
to May 1915**. Crystal Palace February 1920.
*Amateur inside-forward Johnnie Lockton was a
student at London University and on Fulham's
books when his transfer to Forest was arranged.
On New Years' Day he had played for London
Amateurs against The Southern Counties, and a
matter of days after signing for the Reds he played
for The South against The North in an amateur
international trial match at Oxford. He had also*

represented London Amateurs on three occasions. Sadly, his introduction failed to lift Forest from the foot of Division Two and a re-election application. His neat approach work in attack lacked a scoring finish, but he was not alone as Forest registered just 37 League goals in 38 matches in 1913-14. After the Great War he was a master at Dulwich College, and he did not re-appear with the Reds, joining the more conveniently located Crystal Palace in February 1920.

Appearances: FL: 20 apps 2 gls FAC: 2 apps 1 gl
Total: 22 apps 3 gls

LOCKYER, William Thomas
Goalkeeper
Born: Bristol, 15th June 1875
Died: Bristol, January quarter 1963
Debut v Preston North End (h) 2.9.99, won 3-1
CAREER: Hucknall St. John's. **FOREST 1st June 1898.** Newstead Byron 5th October 1900.

Despite the fact that Forest's long serving goalkeeper Dennis Allsop was entering his final season with the Reds, reserve custodian Tom Lockyer was restricted to a single appearance, in which he did all that was required in the opening day defeat of Preston North End at the City Ground. With Allsop's place in the first team passing to Harry Linacre, Lockyer returned to non-League football with Newstead Byron with whom he received a mention in the 'Nottingham Evening Post' in November 1901, when he was praised for an outstanding display, despite suffering an injury, in the match against Notts County Reserves at Meadow Lane.

Appearances: FL: 1 app 0 gls Total: 1 app 0 gls

LOFTUS, Joseph Leo

Inside-left 5' 9" 12st 0lbs
Born: Ferryhill, 24th January 1906
Died: Durham Central, 23rd October 1992
Debut v Hull City (a) 2.11.29, won 2-1
CAREER: Chilton Lane United. Cornforth United. Bishop Auckland. Willington. Stockport County amateur August 1925. South Shields May 1926. **FOREST 31st May 1929.** Bristol City June 1932. Gillingham August 1935. Burton Town October 1935. Barrow June 1936 to May 1937.

Leo Loftus commenced his senior career in Division Two with South Shields. When just two days away from his 20th birthday he made a winning debut against Clapton Orient at Horsley Hill. The bulk of his first team appearances were made in the following season – six goals in 25 League matches – but Shields suffered relegation and he played little in 1928-29 and joined Forest in the close season. The Reds made a dreadful start to the 1929-30 campaign, winning only one of their first twelve League matches. Loftus was introduced, along with amateur inside-forward Clive German and goalkeeper Arthur Dexter. The changes had the desired effect, form in League and Cup taking an immediate upturn. A run to round six was finally ended, after a replay, by Sheffield Wednesday who, in the same season, reached the semi-finals and also won the First Division championship. Loftus scored the two goals that knocked out Fulham in round four and netted at Rotherham United and in home ties against Sunderland and Sheffield Wednesday. He had another FA Cup adventure with his next club, Bristol City, who reached round five in season 1934-35, playing in eight matches with replays against Bury (twice), Portsmouth and Preston North End. After scoring 29 goals in 93 matches for the Robins, an unrewarding spell with Gillingham (2 appearances) preceded his move into non-League football. However, his form with Burton Town – 31 goals in season 1935-36 – earned him another opportunity of League football with Barrow. After a slow start he scored eight of his nine goals during an 18-match run from late January through to the end of the season. His final figures being nine goals in 28 League and Cup matches.

Appearances: FL: 54 apps 14 gls FAC: 7 apps 5 gls
Total: 61 apps 19 gls

LOWE, Henry Charles 'Harry'

Half-back
5' 9" 12st 0lbs
Born: Whitwell, Derbyshire, 20th March 1886
Died: Worksop, 25th October 1958
Debut v Birmingham (a) 10.3.20, lost 0-8
CAREER: Whitwell Board School. Whitwell St. Lawrence July 1906. Gainsborough Trinity May 1907. Liverpool April 1911. **(Wartime guest player with FOREST September 1915).** **FOREST 9th March 1920.** Mansfield Town May 1923 to April 1924. Newark Town May 1929. Grantham July 1931. Newark Old Scouts October 1936.

Harry Lowe's first club of note was Gainsborough Trinity, for whom he scored three goals in 106 League appearances. From there he was transferred to Liverpool, where he became captain of the side. A stalwart right half-back who tackled hard and distributed the ball accurately, he subsequently became very popular with the Forest spectators as one of the wartime helpers of the

Reds. He joined Forest on a permanent basis in March 1920,but after he had sustained an accident in training, he lost his place in the side, and was unable to regain it. Although he had assisted Forest to win the Victory Shield in 1919, he was unable to lift a poor Forest team in 1919-20. His nine appearances commenced with an emphatic 8-0 defeat at Birmingham, and concluded with four successive losses.

Appearances: FL: 9 apps 0 gls Total: 9 apps 0 gls

LYALL, Thomas
Inside-right
Born: Eckington, Derbyshire, 14th September 1899
Died: Eckington, October quarter 1978
Debut v Coventry City (h) 7.5.21, lost 0-2
CAREER: Eckington Red Rose December 1919. **FOREST amateur 20th August 1920, professional 17th May 1921.** Eckington Works F.C. August 1921. Chesterfield June 1924. Staveley Town August 1926.
Although Tom Lyall was rewarded with a professional contract after spending a season in the unpaid ranks, he quickly returned homewards to sign for Eckington Works, where he was employed as a cost accountant. He was later associated with Chesterfield, but did not appear in any of their Division Three North fixtures.
Appearances: FL: 1 app 0 gls Total: 1 app 0 gls

LYNAS, Ralph John Langtrey
Inside-left 5'8" 10st 7lbs
Born: Belfast, 28th February 1904
Died: Holywood, County Down, 24th December 1992
Debut v Darlington (a) 28.8.25, drawn 0-0
CAREER: Glenrosa. Cliftonville. **FOREST amateur 22nd, professional 28th May 1925.** Ards June 1927 to 1929. Broadway United June 1930. Carrickfergus August 1932 to May 1934.
Ralph Lynas attracted widespread attention by his clever and consistent displays for Cliftonville and several prominent clubs were chasing his signature, including Glasgow Rangers. He signed his first professional form with Forest, a step that he had deferred until the completion of his apprenticeship as a compositor. After an early debut at Darlington he was immediately dropped and did not reappear until December when two separate spells of first team action brought his total for the season to 21 League and Cup matches and two goals. He appeared only once in 1926-27 before returning to Irish League football.
Appearances: FL: 20 apps 2 gls FAC: 2 apps 0 gls Total: 22 apps 2 gls

LYTHGOE, JACK

Centre-forward
5'8" 12st 6lbs
Born: Dixon Fold, near Bolton, 3rd April 1892
Died: Little Hulton, Bolton, 5th June 1969
Debut v Rotherham County (a) 30.8.19, lost 0-2
CAREER: Newbury F.C. Walkden Central 1912. Bury amateur 27th November 1913. (Wartime guest player with Bolton Wanderers and Nottingham Forest.)
FOREST September 1918, fee £1,000. Newport County August 1921. Norwich City June 1922. Ebbw Vale October 1923. Eccles United November 1923. Chorley May 1924. Margate August 1925. Horwich R.M.I. Kearsley Celtic October 1931.
Described by the 'Post Guide' as: "A big-hearted player who works like a Trojan all through the match, sparing himself no effort." Forest paid their then record fee to secure his services, and he was leading scorer in his first season with 11 goals in 40 matches. In earlier days, he joined Bury from Lancashire Combination football, and after joining the Army in 1918 made a guest appearance for Forest while stationed in the district. Within a matter of weeks he was ordered to France where he served in both the Machine Gun and Tank Corps. His lengthy career wound up, at the age of 39, with Kearsley Celtic.
Appearances: FL: 61 apps 13 gls FAC: 3 apps 0 gls Total: 64 apps 13 gls

McCALL, Robert Henry 'Bob'

Utility 5'9½" 11st 9lbs
Born: Whitwell, 29th December 1915
Died: Worksop, 6th February 1992
Debut v Bradford Park Avenue (a) 1.2.35, won 4-1
CAREER: Worksop Town amateur October 1933. **FOREST 5th March 1935 to 1952.** (Wartime guest player with Derby County, Leicester City, Mansfield Town and Lincoln City.)
Subsequently appointed grounds man and coach to the Forest 'A' Team. Worksop Town manager July 1952.
Signed by Forest at the age of 19 after spending two seasons with Worksop Town as an amateur, Bob McCall began as a forward in Forest's Reserves, but by season 1938-39 his 30 Division Two appearances were made in roles as diverse as right-half, right-back and centre-forward. Certainly Forest's most adaptable player, he served the Reds with distinction on either side of

the Second World War, being a regular in the side until 1949-50, with a swansong at Brentford on 22nd September 1951 in the midst of an injury crisis.
Appearances: FL: 162 apps 1 gl FAC: 10 apps 0 gls
Total: 172 apps 1 gl

McCALLUM, Cornelius Joseph 'Neilly'

Forward
5' 7" 11st 6lbs
Born: Bonhill, Dunbartonshire, 3rd July 1868
Died: Glasgow, 5th November 1920
Debut v Clapton, FA Cup Round 1 (a) 17.1.1891, won 14-0 (scored two goals)
CAREER: Renton Athletic 1884. 2nd Renton 1885. Renton 1886. (Rangers loan February 1888) Celtic May 1888. Blackburn Rovers February 1890. **FOREST 1890**. Celtic January 1891. **FOREST 30th May 1892**. Newark Town 1894 Notts County June 1895. Heanor Town September 1896. Middleton F.C. September 1897. Folkestone August 1898. Gravesend October 1903. Celtic May 1905.
A famous name in Celtic's history, McCallum was the scorer of the opening goal in their very first fixture, a 5-1 win against Shettleston in September 1888. Earlier, he was capped by Scotland as a Renton player, and assisted the Renton club to victory in the Scottish Cup Final in February 1888 with a record score of 6-1 against Cambuslang. He played in the Scottish trial matches in 1889, but was so seriously injured at Cowlairs shortly afterwards that was sidelined for ten months. In his first trip across the border he appeared only twice for Blackburn Rovers, but then scored nine goals in 20 Alliance matches for Forest before returning to Celtic. He re-signed for Forest to assist them in their first season as a Football League club, but an injury sustained at Burnley on Boxing Day kept him sidelined until early March, and his second season was also disrupted by niggling injuries. He regained his best form in a season with Newark, but when Notts County signed him, it took a Football League ruling to allow the transfer, Forest claiming that he was still their registered player. He appeared in 15 League and Cup matches for the Magpies, scoring three goals. All of his appearances were made at inside-right, whereas his reputation had been made as an extreme wingman, elusive to a degree and fully warranting his nickname 'The Shadow.'
Appearances: FL: 37 apps 13 gls FAC: 5 apps 2 gls
Total: 42 apps 15 gls
Honours: Scotland International, 1 cap 1888.
Scottish League representative, 1 app. (Renton)

Scottish Cup winners 1888. (Celtic) Scottish Cup winners 1889, finalists 1892.

McCANN, Daniel

Inside-right
5' 8" 10st 7lbs
Born: Hurlford, 18th March 1888
Debut v Grimsby Town (h) 30.9.11, won 1-0
CAREER: Hurlford Thistle. Galston 15th October 1906. Nithsdale Wanderers 12th September 1907. Hurlford Athletic 25th September 1907. Dundee 13th March 1908. Celtic 6th May 1910. Ayr United (loan) March 1911. Dundee Hibernian May 1911. **FOREST (trial) 19th September 1911**. Hurlford Athletic 26th October 1911. Galston 21st March 1914. Dundee (loan) during WW1.
On his debut for Dundee, dashing young centre-forward Dan McCann scored twice in a 4-2 win against Rangers at Dens Park, and one week later was presented with the match ball, autographed by his team-mates. A dream move to Celtic brought only seven first team appearances and one goal, and his one-month trial with Forest was not extended. He was offered a trial by Liverpool in 1913, but he joined the forces in 1914 and was serving as a corporal in 1917 when he made his final appearances for Dundee, 12 appearances and one goal in season 1917-18.
Appearances: FL: 1 app 0 gls Total: 1 app 0 gls

McCRACKEN, Peter James

Left half-back 5' 9" 12st 4lbs
Born: Newton Stewart, 1870
Debut v Everton (a) 3.9.92, drawn 2-2
CAREER: Springburn F.C. Third Lanark 1886. Sunderland Albion cs 1890. **FOREST 28th May 1892**. Middlesbrough 25th August 1899. Chesterfield Town 4th August 1900.
In his first season with Sunderland Albion Peter McCracken represented the Football Alliance versus the Football League at Olive Grove, Sheffield, on 20th April 1891. In the same Alliance eleven was William 'Tich' Smith, and the pair were later to become team-mates, after McCracken joined Forest for their first season as a Football League club. Operating from left half-back, the former Third Lanark and Sunderland Albion defender missed only one first team match in his first season with the Reds, and although his appearances became fewer in later seasons, he served Forest well in a seven-year association. On

leaving, he was presented with a gift of £25 from the club, plus whatever fees were obtained for his transfer. McCracken was quickly back in harness with Middlesbrough, whom he captained in their first season as a Football League club, appearing in 33 League matches and one FA Cup-tie. He was approaching the veteran stage when he joined Chesterfield Town, but marshalled an inexperienced defence to good purpose through 52 League matches and seven FA Cup-ties.

Appearances: FL: 113 apps 0 gls FAC: 10 apps 0 gls
Total: 123 apps 0 gls
Honours: (**FOREST**) FA Cup winners 1898.

McCURDY, William

Right full-back
5' 10" 12st 0lbs
Born: Bridgeton,
4th September 1876
Debut v Everton (a) 2.3.01,
lost 1-4
CAREER: Vale of Clyde.
Luton Town 20th May 1899.
FOREST 1st February 1901. New Brompton 7th July 1902. Tottenham

Hotspur 6th May 1904. New Brompton 5th May 1905. Luton Town 10th April 1906, retired May 1910.

Bill McCurdy was a tall, broad shouldered full-back who was not short of Scottish First Division admirers in early days with Vale of Clyde. He opted to move South, however, and had appeared in 31 League matches for Luton Town before arriving at the City Ground. He took the place of Teddy Peers for seven matches on arrival, but in the following season he added only a further four outings, the rear division being shared throughout by Iremonger, F. Forman and White. After a season with New Brompton, he joined Tottenham Hotspur but appeared in only 12 Southern League matches. He then returned to New Brompton, and followed with another spell with Luton Town, whom he assisted until retirement. **Note:** An unconfirmed report suggested that he had died in Toronto, but with no date given this has been impossible to trace or confirm.

Appearances: FL: 11 apps 0 gls Total: 11 apps 0 gls

McDIARMID, George

Half back
5' 7½" 11st 10lbs
Born: Shettleston,
25th January 1880
Debut v Notts County (a)
26.12.00, lost 0-1
CAREER: Cambuslang.
FOREST 8th May 1900.
Airdrieonians 4th December 1901. Grimsby Town June 1903. Glossop 30th September

1905. Clyde July 1907. Grimsby Town 31st October 1907. Darlington 20th July 1908.

George McDiarmid's first League club was Nottingham Forest, but the young defender appeared in only four First Division matches before returning to Scotland to join Airdrieonians. He assisted the 'Onians' to promotion from Division Two in season 1902-03, but departed in the close season for the first of his two separate spells with Grimsby Town. Variously described as a successful sprinter and the best centre half in Division Two, a rather less complimentary and contradictory verdict was "A plodder all through", which was probably meant to indicate that he was more solid than showy. He gave good service in the heart of Glossop's defence until displaced by Patrick Galvin for the final two and a half months of his final season.

Appearances: FL: 4 apps 0 gls Total: 4 apps 0 gls
Honours: Airdrieonians: Scottish League Division Two champions 1903

McINNES, Thomas

Outside-left
5' 6" 10st 11lbs
Born: Glasgow,
29th August 1870
Died: December 1937
Debut v Everton (a) 2.9.92, drawn 2-2
CAREER: Dalmuir Thistle. Cowlairs. Newcastle East End. Newcastle West End. Clyde 1888.
FOREST 2nd June 1892. Bristol Rovers 9th October 1899.

Lincoln City September 1900 to May 1903. (Noted to be training with Third Lanark November 1904.) Port Glasgow Athletic January 1905.

Tom McInnes was one of the finest, and also one of the youngest, inside-forwards to cross the border, being blest with phenomenal dribbling skills. He had the faculty of keeping the ball under perfect control when at full speed, and his centres and shots were wonderfully accurate. He was, however, essentially a solo player, never able to eradicate his tendencies towards individualism, even after his fleetness of foot, which had enabled him to make his brilliant runs, had declined. His style of play left him the victim of numerous hefty challenges by unscrupulous defenders, and in later seasons his efficiency was reduced. He played little after the FA Cup Final success, an injury sustained in the match against against Newcastle United on 12th November 1898 keeping him out for the remainder of the season. In May 1899 he was placed on Forest's transfer list, and there was no shortage of clubs eager to sign him, including Notts County and Liverpool, but the fee asked was considered too much, and he signed for Bristol Rovers of the Southern League. By the following season he was back in Nottingham, and turned out at outside-left under the guise of 'T. Collins' for Forest Reserves against Heanor Town. He scored a good goal, and the 'Evening Post' correspondent noted: "He evidently has plenty of good football in him yet. Saturday's display will probably lead to his engagement by a neighbouring club." Lincoln City were the club who signed him, and he gave the Imps excellent service for three seasons, scoring 20 goals in 79 appearances. **Note**: He was not related to a player of the same name who assisted Notts County between 1889-92 and was a Scottish international.

Appearances: FL: 168 apps 45 gls FAC: 18 apps 10 gls Total: 186 apps 55 gls

Honours: Scotland International, 1 cap 1889. (**FOREST**) FA Cup winners 1898.

McKAY, Thomas Galloway

Inside-forward
5' 7" 10st 8lbs
Born: Possilpark, Glasgow, 16th July 1909
Died: Southport, 16th October 1988
Debut v Charlton Athletic (h) 25.4.31, won 4-3
CAREER: Lyon Street Church (Glasgow). Dreghorn. Glasgow Ashfield. **FOREST amateur 30th January 1931**, **professional 30th June 1931.** Yeovil & Petters United October 1932. Queen of the South May 1933. Southport July 1936 to May 1939.

Lightly built Scottish inside forward Tom McKay made a promising start at the City Ground. He was still on amateur forms when he made his debut, and he retained his place for the final match of the season, a 3-1 home win against Southampton. Signed as a professional in the close season, he then spent the remainder of his Forest days in the Midland League side, apart from just two first team outings in 1931-32. After a season in non-League football, and a return to Scotland to join Queen of the South, he returned to Football League action with Southport. When the outbreak of the Second World War suspended League football, he had scored five goals in 68 matches in a successful three-year spell at Haig Avenue. During the war years he served for four and a half years in the Navy. He later settled in Southport, where he died at the age of 78. His elder brother,

John Reid 'Jock' McKay, also an inside-forward, played for Blackburn Rovers and Middlesbrough in the inter war period, and was capped by Scotland against Wales in 1924.

Appearances: FL: 4 apps 0 gls Total: 4 apps 0 gls

McKENNAN, Hugh

Centre-forward 5' 9" 11st 2lbs
Born: Airdrie, 8th February 1905
Died: Glasgow, 19th February 1964
Debut v Stoke (h) 28.4.28, lost 0-2
CAREER: Airdrie Merchants F.C. Hamilton Academical. **FOREST 29th October 1927.** Glasgow Ashfield. St. Johnstone August 1929. Greenock Morton August 1930. Cowdenbeath August1931.

One of nine brothers and working as a labourer in a steelworks, Hugh McKennan was sought by several Scottish League clubs but elected to join Forest. Powerfully built and with dash and confidence in plenty, he was expected to develop but never looked likely to displace the likes of Noah Burton and Berty Heathcock in the League side. He did a little better on returning to Scotland, netting seven goals in 34 League appearances for his three different clubs.

Appearances: FL: 1 app 0 gls Total: 1 app 0 gls

McKINLAY, William Hodge 'Billy'

Right half-back
5' 9" 11st 7lbs
Born: Dysart, 23rd August 1904
Died: Uddingston, 4th March 1976
Debut v Wolverhampton Wanderers (a) 27.12.27, lost 0-1
CAREER: Inverkeithing Juniors. Lochgelly United. Bathgate F.C. December 1925. **FOREST 24th October 1927, fee £757, to May 1937.** Alloa Athletic (loan) September 1937. Albion Rovers (trial) August 1938. **FOREST scout 1937-48.**

Excellent in ball control, and with a rare turn of speed, Billy McKinlay was the best type of Scottish half-back, effective without being showy and an extremely clever feeder of his forwards. As the 'Post Football Guide' for 1931-32 reported: "Brain, not brawn, is Billy's chief stock in trade." A remarkably fit and consistent performer, he averaged almost 36 games per season for ten campaigns. On leaving the City Ground he was initially loaned to Alloa Athletic, for whom he had an outstanding debut at Tannadice, in the guise of 'Newman'. In the following season he was noted in a number of unsigned players who turned out in a

trial match for Albion Rovers in August 1938, when he was also actively scouting for the Reds. One of his best recommendations was that of his nephew, Bobby McKinlay who was playing as a winger for Bowhill Rovers, but it was at centre-half that he starred for Forest in 682/3 League and Cup appearances between 1951 and 1969.
Appearances: FL: 334 apps 13 gls FAC: 22 apps 0 gls Total: 356 apps 13 gls

McKNIGHT, James 'Jimmy'

Inside-forward
5' 7" 10st 7lbs
Born: Belfast,
2nd May 1892
Debut v Leicester Fosse (h) 3.9.13, lost 1-3
CAREER: Glentoran 1908. Preston North End August 1911. Glentoran October 1912. **FOREST 10th May 1913.** Belfast Celtic June 1914.
Capped by the Irish League, and with junior and full international honours for his country, great expectations surrounded Jimmy McKnight's signing by Forest. It was hoped in some measure his arrival would compensate the Reds for the irreparable loss sustained by the retirement of star inside-forward Grenville Morris. Sadly, he did little better with Forest than he had done earlier with Preston North End (11 appearances and two goals.) In nine first team appearances, he collected just one winning bonus, this for the 1-0 win against local rivals, and champions-elect, Notts County on Boxing Day. A coupon-busting result, considering that Notts topped the final Division Two table, and Forest finished at the bottom and had to apply for re-election.
Appearances: FL: 9 apps 0 gls FAC: 2 apps 1 gl
Total: 11 apps 1 gl
Honours: N. Ireland Junior International. N. Ireland International, two caps, both v Scotland in 1912 and 1913 (scored one goal in both matches) Irish League representative two apps 1911-14.

McLACHLAN, Edward Rolland

Inside-right 5' 9" 11st 0lbs
Born: Glasgow, 24th September 1903
Died: Leicester, 16th March 1970
Debut v Reading (a) 22.10.27, won 2-0 (scored one)
CAREER: Glasgow Boys' Brigade. Queen's Park September 1921. Clyde June 1922. Third Lanark July 1924. Vale of Leven May 1925. Leicester City amateur August 1926, professional January 1927. **FOREST 11th May 1927.** Mansfield Town June 1928. Northampton Town May 1930. Mansfield Town July 1931 to May 1932.

Ted McLachlan played with Vale of Leven and in the Scottish League First Division with Queen's Park and Third Lanark in his hometown of Glasgow. He moved to Leicester to take up an appointment as a draughtsman, and signed an amateur form with Leicester City, later signing as a professional. On joining Forest, he was given an early debut, taking the place of Cyril Stocks, and scored one of Forest's two goals that helped secure the points in the season's first away win. In two subsequent spells with Mansfield Town, he was prominent in the Stags' FA Cup run that took them to Highbury and a lucrative tie against the Arsenal, and in the same season they won the championship of the Midlands League. Latterly working as a commercial traveller, he was appointed Hon. Sec. of the Leicestershire Football Association in March 1935.
Appearances: FL: 8 apps 2 gls Total: 8 apps 2 gls

McMILLAN, Stuart Thomas

Inside-forward
5' 7½" 10st 7lbs
Born: Leicester, 17th September 1896
Died: Ashbourne, 27th September 1963
Debut v Wolverhampton Wanderers (h) 26.12.27, won 3-2
CAREER: Derby County December 1914. (Wartime service with the 7th Derbyshire Yeomanry.) Chelsea May 1919. Gillingham March 1921. Wolverhampton Wanderers June 1922. Bradford City May 1924. **FOREST 17th June 1927.** Clapton Orient August 1928 to May 1930. Derby County advisor 1942, then manager January 1946 to November 1953.
Born in Leicester, the son of John Stuart McMillan, who registered over a century of League goals for five different clubs and later managed Glossop and Gillingham. Stuart McMillan was an all-round sportsman who also appeared in County Cricket with Derbyshire. He represented six different League clubs without reaching the same heights as his father, but in management he led Derby County to victory in the 1946 FA Cup Final – he had played for them just once in season 1914-15. He did not appear at senior level with Chelsea, but scored twice in 30 League appearances for Gillingham – managed by his father. Relegation and promotion with the Wolves followed, and a further relegation with Bradford City preceded his move to the City Ground where he was unable to establish a regular place in the side. A final spell with Clapton Orient wound up his playing career,

his final career figures being 169 League appearances and 14 goals.
Appearances: FL: 9 apps 0 gls FAC: 1 app 0 gls
Total: 10 apps 0 gls
Honours: (Wolverhampton Wanderers) FL Division 3 North champions 1924. (As manager) Derby County FA Cup winners 1946.

McNAUGHTON, Gibson Norrie

Inside-left 5' 9½" 11st 5lbs
Born: Broughty Ferry, Dundee, 30th July 1911
Died: West Bridgford, 16th September 1991
Debut v West Ham United (h) 3.10.36, won 1-0
CAREER: Dundee Violet Juniors. Clyde September 1933. Dundee August 1934. (Loaned to East Fife and Dunfermline Athletic in 1936). **FOREST 19th May 1936**. Notts County May 1939. Ilkeston Town player-manager cs 1949 to cs 1950.

A clever schemer with delightful ball control, 'Gib' McNaughton was not related to Scottish full-back' Jock' McNaughton who had assisted Forest in the season prior to the arrival of 'Gib' from Dundee, who had granted the player a free transfer. Manager Whiteman had seen McNaughton in action for Dunfermline, for whom he made two appearances in the Rosebury Charity Tournament, and scored on each occasion. He was immediately signed up, and during three years at the City Ground he went some way towards filling the gap caused by the continued absence of Tom Peacock due to injury problems. He was not, however, nearly so effective in front of goal, his best seasonal return being seven goals in 1937-38. His move across the Trent came on the eve of the Second World War, and it marked his final involvement in senior football.
Appearances: FL: 66 apps 12 gls FAC: 4 apps 1 gl
Total: 70 apps 12 gls

McNAUGHTON, John 'Jock'

Full-back
5' 10½" 11st 6lbs
Born: Stormontfield, Perth, 19th January 1912
Died: Almondbank, Perthshire, 27th June 1986
Debut v Newcastle United (h) 25.8.34, won 5-1
CAREER: Perth Roselea. **FOREST July 1934**. Brighton & Hove Albion August 1936.

Signed as cover for full-backs Smith and Barrington, Jock McNaughton was adept on both flanks and proved a valuable emergency man on ten occasions in his first season at the City Ground. The signing of Dan Edgar from Sunderland, and a more regular employment of Billy Burton restricted McNaughton to just a single first team outing in 1935-36, and he moved on to Brighton & Hove Albion in the close season. In three seasons at the Goldstone Ground he made only six first team appearances. Enlisting in the army as a PT instructor, he was among members of the BEF who were evacuated from Dunkirk in 1940. He returned to Perth after the war and worked as a lorry driver.
Appearances: FL: 11 apps 0 gls Total: 11 apps 0 gls

MacPHERSON, John

Centre half-back
5' 7" 11st 0lbs
Born: Motherwell, 28th February 1867
Died: Canada, *circa* 1935
Debut v Aston Villa (a) 15.10.92, lost 0-1
CAREER: East of Scotland F.A. Cambuslang. Heart of Midlothian. **FOREST May 1891**. Heart of Midlothian May 1892. **FOREST 7th October 1892**.
Motherwell August 1902. Cambuslang.

At the outset of his career John McPherson captained a Lanarkshire X1 against Edinburgh. His opposing captain was David Calderhead, who also became well known in Nottingham, making over 300 appearances for Notts County. For the best part of nine seasons, McPherson was an indispensable figure in Forest's early success. He commenced with 19 appearances (in the 20-match tournament) and four goals as Forest won the championship of the Football Alliance. He returned briefly to Hearts before returning to Nottingham in October 1892, having served a four-weeks suspension, passed by the FA, for having played in the close season! When Forest lifted the FA Cup in 1898, it was McPherson's goal, scored four minutes from time, that sealed the Reds victory over Derby County by 3-1. He left the City Ground in 1902 to join Motherwell, and later emigrated to Canada.
Appearances: FL: 226 apps 25 gls FAC: 34 apps 1 gl
Total: 260 apps 26 gls
Honours: Scotland International, 1 cap 1891. (Heart of Midlothian) Scottish Cup winners 1891.
(FOREST) FA Cup winners 1898. Football Alliance champions 1892.

MACHIN, Prestwood Udall

Right full-back
5' 8½" 10st 11lbs
Born: Nottingham,
1st July 1892
Died: Nottingham, April
quarter 1948, age 55
Debut v Fulham (h)
27.4.12, drawn 1-1
CAREER: Halifax Place
Mission F.C. **FOREST
amateur 25th April
1912, signing
professional May
1912.** Notts County July 1913 to May 1914.
*Good work with Forest Reserves led to a first team
debut for Prestwood Udall, at the age of nineteen,
in the final Division Two fixture of season 1911-12.
The unusually named builder's joiner did not get
another opportunity before crossing the Trent to
join Notts County. Despite an early debut with the
Magpies he failed to break into a strong side that
won promotion back to the top flight after just one
season in Division Two.*
Appearances: FL: 1 app 0 gls Total: 1 app 0 gls

MALTBY, George Henry 'Ginger'

Left full-back
5' 7½" 10st 9lbs
Born: Long Eaton,
16th April 1887
Died: Nottingham,
October quarter 1950
Debut v Leeds City (h)
22.9.06, won 2-0
CAREER: Notts
Rangers. **FOREST
amateur 28th August
1905 and re-signed
professional 25th May
1912.** Doncaster Rovers
August 1914.
*Said to be one of the finds of the 1906-07 season,
'Ginger' Maltby had made an enviable reputation
in Notts. Junior League circles, and followed with
sterling performances in Midland League matches
with Forest Reserves. Despite his light build and
lack of inches, his efforts were neatly summarised
by the Post Football Guide as follows: " Untiring
left back who never acknowledges defeat, and
perseveres for every minute of the game, he is a
natural successor to Adam Scott." Maltby first
caught the eye of the Football League selectors
when was introduced for the match against the
Irish League at Cliftonville, Belfast, on 10th October
1908. Maltby's effective full back partnership with
Walter Dudley spanned all of seven seasons
although an injured knee, sustained at
Huddersfield in November 1911, kept him sidelined
for much of the remainder of the season. He was
similarly inactive throughout much of his final*
season, when Forest finished at the foot of Division
Two, having gained only 23 points from 38
matches.
Appearances: FL: 216 apps 3 gls FAC: 14 apps 0 gls
Total: 230 apps 3 gls
Honours: FL representative, three apps. v Irish
League October 1908 and October 1910, and v
Southern League November 1910. (**FOREST**) FL
Division 2 champions 1907

MARRISON, Thomas

Inside-forward
5' 7" 11st 7lbs
Born: Darnall, April
quarter 1881
Died: Sheffield,
21st August 1926
Debut v Blackpool (a)
24.11.06, won 2-1 (scored
one)
CAREER: Walkley School.
Sheffield Wednesday 21st
February 1902. Rotherham
Town 7th September 1906. **FOREST 22nd
November 1906.** Oldham Athletic June 1911, fee
£200 Bristol City May 1912 to May 1912.
*Commencing with Sheffield Wednesday, inside-
forward Tom Marrison appeared in only five
League and Cup matches in a stay of over four
years. A prolific scorer at reserve team level, he
nevertheless failed to progress his career and
moved on to non-League Rotherham Town in
September 1906. His career then took a decided
upturn when Forest signed him a matter of weeks
later. His scoring debut commenced a run of 25
consecutive League matches that ended with a 3-1
home win against Lincoln City, and the Reds
promoted as champions of Division Two. Deft in
footwork and polished in constructive play, he
served Forest well for five years but was amongst
13 players released in the wake of relegation from
Division One in 1911. He was quickly back in the
top flight with Oldham Athletic, but lost his place
in mid-term, following a 6-1 defeat at Aston Villa
on Boxing Day 1911. He then spent a final season
in Division Two with Bristol City, scoring four
goals in 17 matches.*
Appearances: FL: 162 apps 38 gls FAC: 9 apps 1 gl
Total: 171 apps 39 gls
Honours: (**FOREST**) FL Division 2 champions
1907

MARSDEN, Harry

Right full-back
5' 8" 11st olbs
Born: Bentley,
25th November 1901
Died: Don Valley,
July quarter 1958
Debut v
Wolverhampton
Wanderers (a) 8.2.26,
lost 0-4
CAREER: Bentley
Colliery 1919.
Doncaster Rovers
amateur March 1924.
Wombwell F.C. August
1924. **FOREST 12th May 1925.** Brighton & Hove
Albion June 1929. Gillingham July 1934. York City
(trial) August 1935. Peterborough United
September 1935.

*An excellent season with Wombwell, for whom he
appeared in practically every match, led to Harry
Marsden's signing by Forest in May 1925. The
former cinema projectionist was said to be a very
likeable personality (which is nice to know, even
ninety-odd years later!) He was said to kick a fine
length, and possessed a useful turn of speed and a
crunching tackle. He was, however, destined to
occupy a reserve role throughout most of his time
at the City Ground, but was commended for some
excellent displays towards the end of season 1925-
26 when he deputised for the injured Bill
Thompson in six matches. His move to Brighton &
Hove Albion provided many more first team
opportunities, in five seasons he accumulated a
total of 187 League and Cup appearances. His
career wound up with a season in the Midland
League with Peterborough United for whom he
appeared in 31 League matches and one FA Cup-
tie. The latter being Peterborough's first match in
the competition, which they lost 0-3 to Rushden
Town.*
Appearances: FL: 14 apps 0 gls Total: 14 apps 0 gls

MARSDEN, Joseph William

Right full-back
5' 8" 11st olbs
Born: Nottingham, April
quarter 1885
Debut v Tottenham
Hotspur (a) 25.12.09,
drawn 2-2
CAREER: Dronfield.
Stanton Hill Victoria.
**FOREST 15th April
1909 to May 1910.**
*Said not to have missed
a match during his*
connection with the Stanton Hill club, becoming a
great favourite with the local crowd, Marsden
found the step up to the top flight a difficult

*transition. After spending a season and a half in
the Midland League, his two first team outings
came as deputy for the injured Walter Dudley.
Following his Christmas Day debut against the
Spurs, his second and final outing followed in a 4-1
defeat at Bury on 3rd January 1910. He was not
retained at the end of the season.* **Note:** *Football
League registration documents list his forenames
as John William.*
Appearances: FL: 2 apps 0 gls Total: 2 app 0 gls

MARSHALL, William Henry 'Harry'/ 'Watty'

Inside-left 5' 8½" 9st 7lbs
Born: Linby Colliery, Hucknall, Notts, 16th February
1905
Died: Linby Colliery, Hucknall, Notts, 9th March
1959
Debut v Manchester City (h) 9.2.24, lost 1-2
CAREER: Hucknall Primitives. Bromley's Athletic.
**FOREST amateur 24th January, professional
24th February 1924.** Southport July 1926.
Wolverhampton Wanderers March 1928, fee
£1,500. Port Vale March 1930, fee £1,000.
Tottenham Hotspur March 1932, fee £1,200.
Kidderminster Harriers July 1933. Brierley Hill
Alliance August 1934. Rochdale August 1935.
Linfield July to October 1938.
*Fair-haired youngster Harry Marshall, the
youngest of a family of five, became a professional
at the City Ground at the age of nineteen, having
already made his debut while still on amateur
forms. The 'Football Post' described him as:
"Undeniably clever, and with a good shot." They
also added: "When he thickens out a bit and gains
a little more weight, he is likely to make his mark."
Two goals in seven matches was a promising start
in 1923-24, but as the side continued to struggle in
the top flight – they were relegated in 1925 –
Marshall failed to score in nine matches and was
released. On joining Southport, his weight was up
to 10st 8lbs, and he enjoyed two good seasons at
Haig Avenue, scoring 27 goals in 54 matches. He
commanded four-figure fees in his next three
moves, but failed to make a first team appearance
for Tottenham Hotspur. Following spells in non-
League football he returned to League action with
Rochdale, scoring 22 goals in 105 appearances.
The son of a miner, he followed his father down the
pit and he collapsed and died at the coalface at the
age of 54. His elder brother Bobby played for
Sunderland and Manchester City, making a grand
total of 560 League and Cup appearances, scoring
153 goals.*
Appearances: FL: 19 apps 3 gls Total: 19 apps 3 gls

MARTIN, David Kirker 'Davy'/'Boy'

Centre-forward
5' 7" 10st 4lbs
Born: Belfast,
1st February 1914
Died: Belfast,
10th January 1991
Debut v Burnley (a)
29.8.36, lost 0-3
CAREER: Cooke School.
Royal Ulster Rifles Boys.
Cliftonville *circa* 1930.
Belfast Celtic March 1932,
fee £5. Wolverhampton
Wanderers December
1934, fee £5,750.
**FOREST 30th June
1936, fee £3,000**. Notts
County November 1938,
fee "approximately
£3,500". Royal Ulster Rifles October 1939.
Glentoran March 1941 to April 1943, Royal Ulster
Rifles. (Wartime guest player with Watford,
Aldershot and Fulham). Derry City 1945-46.
Ballymoney United April 1946. Ballymena United
March/April 1947.
*Martin was an orphanage boy who commanded a
record fee for an Irish player when he moved to
the Wolves in December 1934. Earlier he was
bought out of the army to sign for Belfast Celtic.
His nickname 'Boy' was earned from his army
days when he served as a drummer boy in the
Royal Ulster Rifles. He saw active service in the
Second World War, was wounded at Caen in 1944,
but made a full recovery. He won his first
international cap in September 1933 and scored
against Scotland in a 1-2 defeat. Within a matter
of weeks he was snapped up by the Wolves. On
arrival at Forest, he beat Enoch West's goal
scoring record that had stood since 1907-08,
finding the net 31 times in League and Cup
matches. Ten of his goals being scored in eight
consecutive matches spanning
September/October. He was less prolific in 1937-
38, but he repaid a large slice of his transfer fee
when he charged the Barnsley goalkeeper, and the
ball, over the line in the last match of the season to
preserve Forest's Second Division status. A
relatively brief spell with Notts County followed,
and despite the lack of quality support he netted 16
goals in 29 League and Cup matches.*
Appearances: FL: 81 apps 41 gls FAC: 3 apps 5 gls
Total: 84 apps 46 gls
Honours: N. Ireland International, 10 caps 1934-
39.

MARTIN, Henry 'Harry'

Outside-left
5' 10" 12st 0lbs
Born: Selston, Notts,
5th December 1891
Died: Sandiacre, Notts,
31st December 1974
Debut v Sunderland (h)
26.8.22, won 1-0
CAREER: Selston. Sutton
Junction 1909. Sunderland
January 1912 (Wartime
guest player with **FOREST,**
Chesterfield Town and Hull
City). **FOREST 24th May 1922**. Rochdale player-
coach June 1925 to August 1928 when appointed
club trainer. York City trainer-coach August 1931.
Mansfield Town coach November 1933, manager
December 1933 to March 1935. Newport County
trainer November 1935. Swindon Town trainer cs
1936, remaining on their training staff into the
1950s.
*A star outside-left who adorned the Sunderland
team for ten years, with the exception of the war
period, when he appeared for Forest until the time
came for him to join the army. Once described as:
"One of the finest outside-lefts who ever laced a
boot." He scored on his Sunderland debut, and
gained club and international honours within little
more than two years of joining. He collected a
championship medal in 1913, and played in
Sunderland's first FA Cup Final in the same year.
His record with the Roker club amounting to 231
League and Cup appearances and 24 goals. Forest
knew all about his capabilities from a series of
wartime guest appearances, when he struck up a
brilliant wing partnership with ex-Roker team
mate Walter Tinsley. Blessed with remarkable
speed his flashing runs down the wing came with
the ability to centre with deadly accuracy on the
run. After leaving Forest he assisted Rochdale for
a time and then became their trainer and
manager. Subsequently, he was for a time trainer-
manager to York City before succeeding Mr. J.G.
Hickling as manager of Mansfield Town. His
lengthy career in the game concluded in a
remarkably lengthy stint as part of Swindon
Town's support staff.*
Appearances: FL: 107 apps 13 gls FAC: 7 apps 0 gls
Total: 114 apps 13 gls
Honours: England International, 1 cap v Ireland
1914. England 'Victory' International 1919. FL
representative, 2 apps. (Sunderland) FL Division 1
champions 1913. FA Cup finalists 1913.

MARTIN, Thomas
Goalkeeper
Born: Marlpool, Derbyshire, *circa* 1875
CAREER: Newark. FOREST 23rd April 1896-98. Ilkeston Town 30th June 1899. Stapleford Town 22nd September 1900 to 1901.
Debut v Preston North End (h) 8.4.97, drawn 0-0
One of three local players signed in the close season of 1896 – the brothers Capes were also recruited from Burton Wanderers – Tom Martin had almost a year to wait before making his League debut, with Dennis Allsop firmly established in the Division One side. Martin's next senior involvement came in a run of four consecutive matches in March and April 1898 that concluded happily with a 3-1 home win against Bury. Tom Martin departed to Ilkeston Town in June 1899 and was replaced as reserve goalkeeper by Harry Linacre, who in turn proved to be an excellent replacement for Dennis Allsop, who had dominated the position for eight seasons.
Appearances: FL: 6 apps 0 gls Total: 6 apps 0 gls

MARTINDALE, Harling Richardson
Inside-right
Born: Beeston, Notts. 20th September 1899
Died: Stirling, Scotland, 1979
Debut v Wolverhampton Wanderers (a) 1.11.19, lost 0-4
CAREER: North Staffordshire Regiment.
FOREST 1st November to 1920.
A late selection for the position of inside-right at Wolverhampton was Second-Lieutenant Harling Martindale who, three days earlier, scored three of the four goals by which his team North Staffordshire Regiment 'Present' X1 beat their 'Past' counterparts. Perhaps unsurprisingly, he found less success against the Wolves who were comfortable winners by 4-0. He was commissioned in the North Staffordshire Regiment from October 1918 and, some twenty years later, was working as buyer and manager of a homewares business in Newcastle-under-Lyme.
Appearances: FL: 1 app 0 gls Total: 1 app 0 gls

MASON, William
Outside-right
Born: In the West of Scotland, possibly at Wishaw
Debut v Preston North End (a) 17.9.92, lost 0-1
CAREER: Heart of Midlothian *circa* 1890.
FOREST cs 1891, registered for FL matches 28th May 1892. Burton Swifts February to December 1893.
A Scottish Cup winner with Hearts, who beat Dumbarton 1-0 at Second Hampden in February 1891. William Mason joined Forest in the close season and made his debut at outside-right in the Football Alliance opener against Burton Swifts, won 7-0 with Sandy Higgins the scorer of a hat trick. Undefeated in their first eleven matches, Forest went on to secure the championship, Mason
missing only four of the season's matches, scoring six goals. As Forest strengthened in preparation for their debut in the Football League in the following season, Mason found himself crowded out by several new signings, and was restricted to just five first team appearances. Moving on to Burton Swifts he made nine Division Two appearances in 1892-93, scoring two goals, both coming in a 3-3 draw against Burslem Port Vale on 18th March. He was released in mid-term of the following season, having appeared in ten matches without scoring.
Appearances: FL: 5 apps 0 gls Total: 5 apps 0 gls
Honours: (Heart of Midlothian) Scottish Cup winners 1891.**(FOREST)** Football Alliance champions 1892

MASTERS, Arthur

Outside-right
5' 7" 10st 7lbs
Born: Coppull, 17th August 1910
Died: Cardiff, 26th July 1998
Debut v Lincoln City (h) 8.4.33, drawn 2-2
CAREER: Horwich R.M.I.
FOREST 23rd February 1933. Port Vale June 1937 to cs 1939, in exchange for Alan Todd.
A late-season capture from Horwich R.M.I. of the Lancashire Combination, in his first few appearances Arthur Masters showed that he had a sound knowledge of what was required for a wing man. Rapid development into a first class winger saw him established as a first team regular for every season but his last, maintaining a very respectable scoring rate for a wide player. After four years with the Reds he was transferred to Port Vale in a player-exchange deal that brought goalkeeper Alan Todd to the City Ground. In two seasons before the outbreak of the Second World War, Masters appeared in 72 League and Cup matches and scored 15 goals.
Appearances: FL: 109 apps 24 gls FAC: 9 apps 2 gls
Total: 118 apps 26 gls

MAWSON, Joseph Spence

Inside-forward
5' 8½" 10st 9lbs
Born: Brandon Colliery, 26th October 1905
Died: Stoke-on-Trent, 10th September 1959
Debut v Bradford Park Avenue (a) 3.9.34, drawn 1-1
CAREER: Langley Park School. Washington Colliery. Crook Town September 1925. Bishop Auckland November 1926. Durham City amateur August 1927. Langley Park

December 1927. Stoke City January 1929. **FOREST 23rd May 1934.** Stockport County May 1935. Linfield November 1935. Crewe Alexandra August 1936 to May 1937. Stafford Rangers September 1937.

Joe Mawson made a scoring Football League debut with Stoke against Swansea Town in season 1928-29, but he did not become a first team regular until 1931-32 season, in which he scored 24 League and Cup goals in 39 matches. In the following season, Stoke won the championship of Division Two with Mawson leading the scoring with 16 goals in 28 League and Cup matches. He had played little for the Potters in 1933-34 and struggled at the City Ground, and also at Stockport County, for whom he made just three appearances. A spell in Ireland brought some welcome success; with Linfield he was a winner in the Jubilee and Charity Cup competitions, and a City Cup finalist in 1936. He returned to England to spend a final season of League football with Crewe Alexandra, scoring on his debut against Rochdale and netting three goals in 11 Division Three North matches. In the Welsh Cup competition he netted a hat trick against modest opponents Llay Welfare in the sixth round 9-2 win in which another two Crewe players registered hat tricks. Mawson did not play in the final, or the replay, which Crewe won 3-1 against Rhyl, after extra time.

Appearances: FL: 2 apps 0 gls FAC: 2 apps 1 gl
Total: 4 apps 1 gl
Honours: (Stoke) FL Division 2 champions 1933

MERCER, Joseph Powell

Centre half-back 6' 1" 13st 1lb
Born: Ellesmere Port, 21st July 1890
Died: Ellesmere Port, 20th May 1927
Debut v Tottenham Hotspur (h) 24.12.10, lost 1-2
CAREER: Bebington Vics. Bolton Wanderers (trial). Chester Castle. Tranmere Rovers cs 1909. Burnell's Ironworks F.C. **FOREST December 1910.** Ellesmere Port Town June 1915. Tranmere Rovers July 1919 to 1921.

Long and lithe, Joe Mercer was a splendid attacking half-back whose height and lengthy stride made him a difficult man to pass. Rarely absent from the centre of the Reds' defence throughout his stay at the City Ground, he was one of the first Forest players to join the Colours in November 1914 when he enlisted in the Footballers' Battalion. His son Joe junior was an outstanding half-back with Everton (184 League and Cup appearances) and Arsenal, with whom he won a League championship medal in 1948 and captained the Gunners side that beat Liverpool at Wembley in the 1950 FA Cup Final. A successful career in management followed, which included a temporary spell as England manager after the resignation of Don Revie in 1977.

Appearances: FL: 149 apps 6 gls FAC: 8 apps 0 gls
Total: 157 apps 6 gls

MILLER, Andrew

Outside-left 5' 6½" 10st 7lbs
Born: Bo'ness, 27th February 1899
Debut v Arsenal (h) 30.8.24, lost 0-2
CAREER: Newton Thistle. Vale of Grange. Croy Celtic. Celtic August 1920. Dumbarton Harp (loan) July 1922. Dumbarton (loan) July 1923. **FOREST 9th July 1924.** Bo'ness F.C. July 1925. Camelon Juniors 1927. Montrose October 1930.

Andrew Miller began with Celtic as an outside-left, and made his Scottish League debut in a 2-1 win against Hamilton Academical on 11th September 1920. Later in the season he scored his only goal in a 3-0 win against Hibernian, but as understudy to Adam McLean he managed only five first team appearances. He spent some time out on loan before moving to join Forest, but after appearing at inside-left in the opening three fixtures of 1924-25 – that all ended in defeat – he made only a further two appearances, on the right wing and the left, before returning to Scotland at the close of the season in which Forest were relegated from Division One.

Appearances: FL: 5 apps 0 gls Total: 5 apps 0 gls

MILLS, Joseph

Right half-back 5' 8" 10st 0lbs
Born: Cresswell, Derbyshire, 10th April 1895
Died: Doncaster, 5th April 1938
Debut v Rotherham County (a) 30.8.19, lost 0-2
CAREER: Red Row F.C. Whitwell St. Lawrence F.C. **FOREST July 1917.** Luton Town July 1924. Bentley Colliery F.C. 1925. Thorne Colliery August 1926. Selby O.C.O. August to December 1930

Once described as: "A mere stripling," Joe Mills' lightweight physique suggested that he was unfitted for the fray, but his hard work and enthusiasm carried him through. He was working as a miner when first discovered by Forest, and he played in 18 of the 30 matches in season 1918-19 when Forest won the championship of the Midland Section. He completed 27 Division Two matches in 1919-20 but failed to maintain his form and made only occasional first team appearances thereafter. A season with Luton Town in Division 3 South followed, in which he scored twice in 32 League and Cup matches.

Appearances: FL: 43 apps 0 gls FAC: 2 apps 0 gls Total: 45 apps 0 gls

MORGAN Francis **Gerald**

Centre half-back
5' 10½" 11st 9lbs
Born: Belfast,
25th July 1899
Died: St. Anne, Belfast,
3rd March 1959
Debut v Burnley (h)
11.11.22, won 1-0
CAREER: Christian
Brothers School. St.
Peter's Juniors. Army
Service with Machine
Gun Corps and Army
Service Corps. St.
Peter's Swifts.

Cliftonville amateur 1919. Linfield May 1921.
FOREST 10th November 1922. Luton Town May 1929. Grantham 1930. Cork F.C. June 1931. Ballymena United player-manager July 1933 to April 1934. Linfield Colts, coach-trainer October 1935. Northern Ireland trainer.

Gerry Morgan would certainly qualify as one of Forest's best investments in the inter-war period. Secured from Linfield in November 1922, he was first tried at wing-half, but when Fred Parker was injured, Morgan was placed at centre-half, and maintained such brilliant and consistent form there that there was never any likelihood of his being removed from that position. A great defensive player who tackled relentlessly and was rarely beaten in aerial encounters, he was with Linfield for a season, his only other club being Cliftonville, with whom he took part in a few games in 1919 and 1920. He played for the Irish FA on their tour to Norway in May 1922, and for the Irish League against the Scottish League at Parkhead on October 18th of the same year, and went on to win nine full caps for his country. On leaving Forest he signed for Luton Town, who were reported to have paid the biggest transfer fee in their history to secure his services. Within a matter of three months, he requested a transfer. Suffering in health since moving to Luton he felt unable to do himself justice, and he did in fact appear in only four League matches for the Hatters before joining Grantham in 1930.

Appearances: FL: 200 apps 6 gls FAC: 19 apps 0 gls Total: 219 apps 6 gls

Honours: N. Ireland International, 9 caps 1922-29. F.A. of Ireland tour to Norway May 1922. Irish League representative, 1 appearance 1922. (Linfield) Irish Cup winners 1922. Irish League champions 1922 and 1923.

MORGAN-OWEN, Morgan Maddox

Half back
Born: Cardiff,
26th February 1877
Died: Willington Hall,
Derbyshire,
14th August 1950
Debut v Blackburn
Rovers (h) 8.4.01, lost
0-1
CAREER: Colet
School, Rhyl.
Shrewsbury School
1891 to 1896. Oxford
University (Oriel
College). Corinthians.
**FOREST 20th
March 1901**.
Corinthians. Casuals.

Glossop amateur April 1904. Also assisted London Welsh, Rhyl and Oswestry.

Morgan-Owen was considered to be one of the outstanding centre halves of the Edwardian period. He was a schoolmaster at Forest School, Walthamstow until 1909, and later a House Master at Repton School until retirement in 1937. During the First World War he served as a Captain in the Essex Regiment, and was awarded the D.S.O. A life vice president of the F.A., he also served a magistrate and councillor until his death at the age of 73. A younger brother, Hugh, was also a Corinthian and won five Wales caps between 1901 and 1907.

Appearances: FL: 1 app 0 gls Total: 1 app 0 gls
Honours: Wales International, 12 caps, 1897-1907

MORRIS, Arthur **Grenville**

Centre or Inside-forward
5' 9½" 11st 8lbs
Born: Builth, Wales,
13th April 1877
Died: West Bridgford,
27th November 1959
Debut v Bury (a) 3.12.98,
lost 0-2
CAREER: Builth Town
August 1892. Aberystwyth
Town July 1893. Swindon
Town 21st October 1897.
**FOREST 25th
November 1898,
retired May 1913, fee
£200.**

Grenville Morris was only 18 years old when first capped by Wales. Born at Builth on 13th April 1877,

he played for Aberystwyth and his first big game was for Mid-Wales against Denbighshire. Transferred to Swindon Town and then to Forest in 1898, he played for 15 years in the red jersey. He captained the first Welsh side to win the International Championship, and scored nine goals in 21 matches for his country. An article in the 'Lancashire Evening Post' in 1899 revealed that Morris could not withstand hard training. Beyond walking about town he did little in the way of preparation, but when the match kicked-off at the weekend he was as dashing and vigorous as anybody, and if necessary would fight until he dropped. Ranked along with Billy Meredith as by far the finest forwards of their day, Morris at all times won admiration for his wonderful ball control, and he was equally good in combined play or in individual work. He was ever the marked man of the Forest team, but was usually clever enough to lose his opponents. Certainly his range of passing and first time shooting carried the Forest attack forward throughout his lengthy stay. In 1912-13 Forest endured a very lean season in Division Two, finishing with eight successive defeats. At this point Morris, their mainstay for so many years, announced his retirement from the game. Perhaps unsurprisingly, Forest finished at the foot of the Second Division table in the following season. Morris retired to concentrate on his other great love, lawn tennis, subsequently coaching at the Nottinghamshire Lawn Tennis Association.
Appearances: FL: 421 apps 199 gls FAC: 37 apps 18 gls Total: 458 apps 217 gls
Honours: Wales International, 21 caps 1896-19. (Forest) FL Division Two champions 1907.

MORRIS, Hugh

Utility forward 5' 7" 11st 6lbs
Born: Giffnock,
27th February 1894
Died: Whalley, Lancs, 23rd January 1962
Debut v Arsenal (h) 30.8.24, lost 0-2
CAREER: Rutherglen Glencairn. Clyde July 1915. Manchester City July 1922. **FOREST 4th July 1924**.
Notts County April 1925. Southend United September 1925. Newport County July 1929 to 1930.
Hugh Morris had the experience of 187 Scottish League matches with Clyde before first crossing the border to join Manchester City. In two seasons at Hyde Road he had the unenviable task of succeeding the great Welsh international, Billy Meredith, whose glittering career was reaching its conclusion. Morris appeared in 61 League and Cup matches for City before leaving to join Forest. Tried in every forward position except as attack

leader, he departed before the end of the season in which Forest were relegated from Division One. Without appearing in Notts County's first team, he moved on to Southend United, appearing in 137 League matches, scoring 15 goals. His lengthy career wound up with Newport County, where a mid-season leg injury restricted him to 22 League appearances and five goals.
Appearances: FL: 22 apps 1 gl FAC: 1 app 0 gls
Total: 23 apps 1 gl

MORTON, Robert 'Bobby'

Outside-left 5' 9" 11st 0lbs
Born: Widdrington, Northumberland, 3rd March 1906
Died: Widdrington, Northumberland, April 1990
Debut v Stoke City (h) 25.8.28, lost 1-5
CAREER: Widdrington F.C. Newbiggin F.C. Ashington amateur December 1922, professional July 1925. Bedlington United September 1926. Barnsley October 1927. **FOREST 31st May 1928**. Newark Town June 1930. Bradford Park Avenue May 1931. Port Vale May 1932. Throckley Welfare July 1935. Blyth Spartans May 1936. Jarrow November 1936. Blyth Spartans. North Shields May 1939.
Bobby Morton's debut in League football was not a memorable one, as the apprentice colliery surveyor made his bow in what was at that time Ashington's heaviest defeat at Portland Park under League auspices – a 2-6 defeat by Barrow. After just three League appearances and a season in the North-Eastern League with Bedlington United, he joined Barnsley. Despite a scoring debut – in a 1-1 draw against Forest at the City Ground – he was not afforded another opportunity. He must have impressed the Forest directorate, however, and he spent the next two seasons with the Reds. His first campaign was his best (27 League matches and three goals), but he played little in 1929-30 when Noah Burton dominated the left wing position. Two further spells in League football brought contrasting fortunes, after appearing in just six matches for Bradford Park Avenue, he enjoyed the best spell of his career with Port Vale, scoring 20 goals in 102 League and Cup matches.
Appearances: FL: 34 apps 3 gls FAC: 2 apps 0 gls
Total: 36 apps 3 gls

MUNRO, John Scott
Left full-back 5' 11" 11st 10lbs
Born: Burnside, 13th August 1914
Died: Perth, 3rd December 1992
Debut v Bradford Park Avenue (a) 31.10.36, lost 2-3
CAREER: Burnside Rangers. Scone Thistle. Dundee North End. Dundee Violet. Dundee. Birmingham (trial) September 1933. Heart of Midlothian December 1933. Hibernian (loan)

February 1936. **FOREST 2nd June 1936 to March 1940.**

Of ideal build, fair-haired John Munro improved season on season at the City Ground, and by 1938-39 was the first name on the team sheet, missing only one match. Three appearances in the aborted season 1939-40 brought up his century, but a few matches in the subsequent wartime East Midlands Section wound up his career. From earliest days a tremendous worker and strong tackler who proved a stumbling block to the best, he impressed everyone by the improvement in his positional play which ensured that he dominated the left full-back position for the best part of two seasons.
Appearances: FL: 93 apps 0 gls FAC: 4 apps 0 gls
Total: 97 apps 0 gls

MURRAY, Patrick 'Paddy'
Outside/Inside right
Born: Currie, 13th March 1874
Died: Cardenden, Fife, 25th December 1925
Debut v Wolverhampton Wanderers (a) 8.12.00, won 2-1
CAREER: Quarter Huttonbank. Royal Albert June 1895. Hibernian October 1895. Darwen 1897. East Stirlingshire 9th September 1897. Preston North End 22nd April 1898. East Stirlingshire June 1900. Wishaw Thistle January 1900. Royal Albert 13th October 1900. **FOREST December 1900.** Celtic November 1902. Portsmouth 1903. East Stirlingshire November 1904. Royal Albert March 1905.
Paddy Murray was a Scottish League representative after no more than a handful of games for Hibernian, and he quickly crossed the border to join Darwen. After just five appearances and one goal, he returned to Scotland, but a second spell in England brought better results – nine goals in 51 matches for Preston North End. Another wander around Scottish football preceded his transfer to Forest, who were said to be concerned with the lack of first class reserve players. That said, he was soon found employment in the first team and reports of his debut at the Wolves were generally favourable. Having commenced on the right wing, he had a lengthy run from mid season at inside-right. In the following term the 'Nottingham Evening Post' observed that Murray was: "Not doing Forest much good this season, the old Preston North End man seems to have completely lost his form." He was released in the close season, having failed to score in 14 League appearances. A return to Scotland and a spell with Celtic brought a scoring debut against Partick Thistle and three goals in 16 League and Cup appearances. A marathon trek then took him to Portsmouth of the Southern League whom he assisted to a fourth place finish in Division One. A third, and final, spell with East Stirlingshire lasted for less than a season, and his career concluded with a second spell with Royal Albert.
Appearances: FL: 27 apps 2 gls FAC: 3 apps 0 gls
Total: 30 apps 2 gls
Honours: Scottish League representative, 1 cap 1897

MURRAY, Robert
Full-back
Debut v Preston North End (h) 4.10.94, lost 0-2
CAREER: Gordon Highlanders. **FOREST 26th September 1894.**
Prospects for the Forest club, reported in the 'Evening Post' in August 1894, revealed that the team's full-backs would be the same as last season – Scott and Ritchie – with the assistance of Murray as reserve. In the event, Messrs. Scott and Ritchie did not miss a single Division One match throughout the season and Murray's two senior appearances were made in the unaccustomed positions of centre-forward and outside-left.
Appearances: FL: 2 apps 0 gls Total: 2 apps 0 gls

MURRAY, Robert
Centre-half back
Born: East Benhar, near Fauldhouse, Linlithgowshire
Debut v Liverpool (a) 21.4.1900, lost 0-1
CAREER: FOREST 21st April 1899.
Airdrieonians August 1901.
Exactly twelve months on from signing for Forest, Robert Murray made his solitary Football League appearance. He deputised at centre-half for fellow Scot John McPherson at Anfield and played a fine game in the narrow 1-0 defeat. Murray did not get another opportunity in the following season, despite the fact that McPherson's long and distinguished career ended after he had made just 11 League appearances. England international Frank Forman taking over at centre-half. In August 1901 Murray joined Airdrieonians for a season in the Scottish League Division Two. He was not retained at the end of the season and his subsequent whereabouts remain untraced. There were, however, two players of the same name who appeared in official lists of Scottish transfers in 1902 – one transferred to Victoria United on 7th August, to other to Bathgate on 16th October.
Appearances: FL: 1 app 0 gls Total: 1 app 0 gls

NEEDHAM, George James

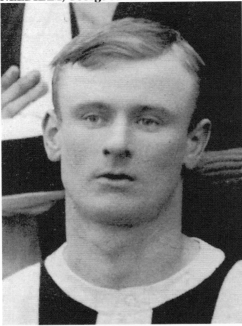

Centre half-back 5' 10" 11st 0lbs
Born: Shepshed, 26th November 1884
Died: Ruddington, Notts. 4th May 1971
Debut v Everton (a) 28.4.06, lost 1-4
CAREER: Shepshed Albion. **FOREST 8th May 1905 to May 1919.**
George Needham developed his game in Forest Reserves ranks before making his League debut in the final fixture of the 1905-06 season, showing promise despite appearing on the losing side. In the Division Two championship season that followed the wholehearted centre-half underlined his potential with a strong challenge for the first team jersey, appearing in 22 of the 38 League matches during the season. By season 1910-11 he was appearing regularly at left half-back, with George Wolfe and Joe Mercer contesting the role of pivot. From the commencement of the 1911-12 season, Needham did not miss a single League game for four seasons, a run of 152 consecutive appearances.
Appearances: FL: 275 apps 10 gls FAC: 16 apps 0 gls Total: 291 apps 10 gls
Honours: (**FOREST**) FL Division 2 champions 1907

NELIS, Patrick

Centre-forward
5' 9½" 12st 0lbs
Born: Londonderry, N. Ireland, 5th October 1898
Died: Londonderry, 22nd April 1970
Debut v Bradford Park Avenue (h) 18.3.22, won 4-1 (scored two)
CAREER:
Londonderry Distillery. Accrington Stanley December 1920. **FOREST 16th March 1922, fee £2,000**. Wigan Borough June 1925 to April 1926. Coleraine. Rossville Hall. Derry City player-coach to second eleven.
Pat Nelis was recommended to Accrington Stanley's directors by one of their players, his fellow countryman Pat Quigley. Described at the time as: "A pale-faced and rather sickly-looking Irishman" he nevertheless scored a hat trick against Durham City on his debut. He was dropped after his initial two matches and had three months to wait for another opportunity, when he seized his chance, scoring 11 goals in nine games, including two hat tricks. Not surprisingly, he was soon on his way from Peel Park, Forest paying what was then a record fee for a Third Division player. It proved to be money well spent as he immediately assisted Forest to win the Second Division championship. In April the Irish FA wished to include him in their side to play Wales, but out of loyalty to his new club, Nelis sacrificed his cap and helped lift Forest into the First Division. Happily, he was given another opportunity in Ireland's first international match of season 1922-23. Forest struggled in Division One and Nelis returned to Third Division football with Wigan Borough. He lasted for less than a season at Springfield Park before returning to Ireland, initially assisting Coleraine in the premier Irish League.
Appearances: FL: 59 apps 13 gls FAC: 1 app 0 gls Total: 60 apps 13 gls
Honours: N. Ireland International, one cap v England, 1922. (**FOREST**) FL Division 2 champions 1922

NEVE, Edwin 'Ned'

Outside-left
5' 8" 11st 6lbs
Born: Eccleston, Lancs.
3rd May 1885
Died: Prescot,
3rd August 1920
Debut v Birmingham (h)
2.9.14, drawn 1-1
CAREER: St. Helens
Recreation 29th December
1905. Hull City 7th May
1906. Derby County
July1912. **FOREST 14th July 1914.** Chesterfield April 1916.
*After just half of a season with St. Helens
Recreation, a Lancashire Combination Division
One team, Ted Neve was snapped up by Hull City
a matter of days beyond his 21st birthday. He
stayed long enough to share a benefit with two
other players in December 1911, and had
completed 102 League matches, scoring 12 goals,
when he was transferred to Derby County. He had
stiff competition for the outside-left berth at the
Baseball Ground, in the shape of England amateur
international and Olympics gold medal winner
Ivan Sharpe. Neve played in most matches in his
second season, however, but this coincided with
relegation from the top flight. He had appeared in
47 League matches, and scored just one goal, when
he was transferred to the Forest. He had been
offered terms by Derby but, according to the
'Nottingham Evening Post', he wanted a change.
Although it was five seasons earlier when Alf
Spouncer retired, Forest' left wing spot had never
been adequately filled. Neve gave every indication
that he was the man to succeed the Forest legend,
but World War One intervened, and he enlisted in
the Royal Garrison Artillery. He did not resume
his football career after the conflict, subsequently
working as a traveller for a brewery.*
Appearances: FL: 35 apps 3 gls FAC: 2 apps 1 gl
Total: 37 apps 4 gls

NEWBIGGING, Alexander 'Sandy'

Goalkeeper/Inside-right 5' 10" 12st 0lbs
Born: Larkhall, 27th December 1879
Debut v Stoke (a) 5.10.01, drawn 1-1
CAREER: Paisley Abercorn. Larkhall United.
Queen's Park Rangers 13th October 1900. **FOREST
7th June 1901.** Reading August 1905. Rangers May
1906, fee £200. Reading 7th May 1908. Coventry
City September 1909. Inverness Thistle 1910-11.
*Sandy Newbigging was a versatile performer, at
both ends of the pitch. He won Scottish junior
international recognition as a goalkeeper, but
joined Queen's Park Rangers as a forward. Forest
recruited him for the role of reserve goalkeeper,
but with Harry Linacre as competition, he found
few opportunities. Forest selectors kept him in
form by playing him as a forward in several Notts.*

*League matches, and on 15th February 1902 he
appeared at inside-right against Sunderland,
Forest winning 2-1. Of his early debut in goal one
match report confirmed that he had quite satisfied
his critics. "His clearances were clean and well
timed, and he evidently possesses coolness and
resource. It was unfortunate that the goal he
conceded was scored by a team mate, Iremonger's
mis-kick taking him totally unawares." He
certainly performed well in two seasons with
Rangers between 1906-08, being ever present in
Scottish League and Cup matches in his first
season and totalling 70 League and Cup matches.*
Appearances: FL: 7 apps 0 gls Total: 7 apps 0 gls
Honours: Scottish Junior International

NEWBIGGING, Harry

Inside-left 5' 8" 11st 2lbs
Born: Douglas, Lanarkshire, 22nd May 1893
Died: New York, USA, December 1966
Debut v Barnsley (a) 20.9.19, drawn 2-2 (scored
one)
CAREER: Douglas Water Thistle. Blantyre
Victoria. Cambuslang Rangers cs 1914. Hamilton
Academical December 1915. Raith Rovers 1915-16.
Larkhall Thistle. Royal Navy football. **FOREST
26th August 1919.** Stockport County July 1920 to
May 1921. Philadelphia Field Club 1923-24.
*Like his elder brother 'Sandy' (q.v.) Harry
Newbiggin won Scottish Junior international
honours. He was signed from Larkhall Thistle,
following his demobilisation from the Navy in
February 1919. He did not sign a Football League
form until August, after he had played in both pre-
season practice matches under the name of
"Newton." As football resumed under normal
conditions in 1919-20, Forest surprisingly
struggled in Division Two, considering the fact
that they had won the championship of the
Midland Section (Principle Tournament) in the
previous wartime campaign. Despite having
fielded 38 different players in League matches, a
winning blend remained elusive. Newbiggin
scored on his debut and held his place for just five
matches thereafter, making infrequent appearances
thereafter. Transferred to Stockport County, he
played his last game in late December, after
appearing quite regularly in early season. He was
released in the wake of relegation – to the new
Third Division North – having made 15 League
appearances and scored one goal.*
Appearances: FL: 9 apps 1 gl Total: 9 apps 1 gl
Honours: Scotland Junior International.

NIBLO, Thomas Bruce

Centre-forward/Outside-left
5' 8" 12st 7lbs
Born: Dunfermline, 24th September 1877
Died: Walker, Newcastle-on-Tyne, July 1933
Debut v Wolverhampton Wanderers (a) 3.9.04, lost 2-3
CAREER: Cadzow Oak F.C. 1893. Hamilton Academical 1894. Linthouse F.C. 23rd August 1896. Newcastle United 5th April 1898, fee £900. Middlesbrough (loan) 7th April 1900. Aston Villa 11th January 1902. **FOREST 29th April 1904**. Watford 3rd May 1906. Newcastle United 29th July 1907. **FOREST 14th May 1908**. Hebburn Argyle player-manager August 1908. Aberdeen December 1908. Raith Rovers August 1909. Cardiff City December 1910. Blyth Spartans February 1911. (Wartime guest player with Fulham and Crystal Palace.) Playing in Isle of Wight football in 1919.

A versatile forward of many clubs, Tom Niblo was a powerfully built stylish dribbler with a tendency to be too individualistic and volatile. He occupied four of the five forward positions in his season and a half at the City Ground, but rarely found the form that had earned him his cap against England, less than three weeks before his arrival in Nottingham. Four years after leaving to join Watford, he was back at the City Ground, but left without playing to take up a player-manager post with Hebburn Argyle. Ironically, his best performance at the City Ground was for Aston Villa when he netted a hat trick in Villa's 7-3 win on 19th December 1903.
Appearances: FL: 46 apps 9 gls FAC: 2 apps 0 gls
Total: 48 apps 9 gls
Honours: Scotland International, one cap v England 1904

NORRIS, Robert 'Bob'

Left half-back
Born: Preston, July quarter 1875
Died: Nottingham, 31st March 1940, age 64
Debut v Sheffield Wednesday (a) 10.9.98, lost 1-2
CAREER: South Shore F.C. 27th April 1895. Blackpool 30th May 1896. **FOREST 17th May 1898**. Doncaster Rovers 9th July 1904. **FOREST, trainer, 10th May 1905**.
Bob Norris commenced with Blackpool, and had the experience of 51 League appearances when he commenced his Forest career in 1898-99, the season after the Reds had won the FA Cup. He seized his early opportunity after Willie Wragg had been left out after the opening match of the season, and he was never lost his place again,
except through injury. His excellent form was rewarded with a place in an international trial match in early March 1900. At the end of the same month he played for the Football League against the Scottish League at the Crystal Palace, when he had the misfortune to score on own goal in the 2-2 draw. More serious misfortune occurred in the following season when he suffered a broken leg on 23rd February in the Second round FA Cup-tie against Aston Villa at Villa Park. He was sidelined for over a year, ironically returning on 1st April 1902, against Aston Villa, his form seemingly unimpaired after such a lengthy lay-off. After six years at the City Ground, Norris spent a season with Doncaster Rovers, scoring three goals in 21 matches, before being welcomed back to Forest as trainer. He later became one of the best-known figures in local bowls circles, being a member and sometimes captain of the Victoria Embankment Club and representing his County. In doubles competitions he was regularly partnered by another old Forest footballer, Archie Ritchie. A licensed victualler, Bob Norris was for some years mine host at the Sir Richard Arkwright, Nottingham.
Appearances: FL: 129 apps 7 gls FAC: 18 apps 0 gls
Total: 147 apps 7 gls
Honours: FL representative, one appearance,1900.
.

OAKES, John 'Jack'

Centre half-back
5' 11" 12st 4lbs
Born: Winsford, Cheshire, 13th September 1905
Died: Perth, Australia, 20th March 1992
Debut v Millwall (a) 21.9.29, drawn 2-2
CAREER: Chilton Colliery. Cargo Fleet & Cochrane F.C. (South Bank League) May 1928. **FOREST amateur 15th May, professional 23rd August 1928**. Newark Town August 1930. Clapton Orient (trial) September 1930. Crook Town October 1930. Southend United May 1931. Crook Town July 1932. Spennymoor United February 1933. Workington cs 1933. Middlesbrough Police F.C. 1933. Aldershot Town May 1934. Charlton Athletic March 1936, fee £1,144. (Wartime guest player with Brentford, Clapton Orient, Crystal Palace, Millwall and Tottenham Hotspur.) Plymouth Argyle July 1947. Snowdon Colliery Welfare player-manager July 1949 to February 1953. Gravesend & Northfleet trainer July 1953. Coaching appointment in Sweden until 1959.
It took quite some time for Jack Oakes to make his mark in senior football, as he had played only

twice each for Forest and Southend United before joining Aldershot where he scored 19 goals in 61 League matches. He next assisted Charlton Athletic, and starting at centre-forward he scored on his debut but was soon switched to centre-half and held the position without challenge until after the Second World War. He represented England against South Africa in 1939, but this was not ranked as a full international. He was a member of Charlton Athletic's Football League (South) Cup winning team in 1944, and in 1946 became one of the oldest players to appear in an FA Cup Final. His lengthy career wound up with Plymouth Argyle, for whom he made his final appearance at the age of 42. He was later employed in a Kent paper mill before emigrating to the USA and later Australia, where he died at the age of 86.

Appearances: FL: 2 apps 0 gls Total: 2 apps 0 gls
Honours: England Wartime International v Wales in 1940. (Charlton Athletic) FL (South) Cup winners 1944. FA Cup finalists 1946. Also represented England against South Africa in 1939, but this was not ranked as a 'full' international.

OAKTON, Albert Eric

Outside-left
5' 9½" 11st 4lbs
Born: Kiveton Park, 28th December 1906
Died: Sheffield, 5th August 1981
Debut v Sheffield United (a) 28.8.37, lost 1-2
CAREER: Kiveton Park Colliery. Grimsby Town November 1924. Rotherham United July 1926. Worksop Town May 1927. Sheffield United October 1928, fee £700. Scunthorpe & Lindsey United August 1930. Bristol Rovers May 1931, fee £200. Chelsea May 1932, fee £250. **FOREST 12th June 1937.** Boston United August 1938.

A very promising youngster, Eric Oakton had passed through two League clubs plus Worksop Town by the time he reached 20. He did not make the League side with Sheffield United, but a good season with Bristol Rovers (40 appearances and nine goals) earned him a move to Chelsea where he remained for five years, scoring 27 goals in 107 League matches. At Stamford Bridge, his first two seasons were his best, but he did not play regularly thereafter. He also failed to hold down a first team place in his season with Forest, who only avoided relegation by taking a point from the last match of the season at Barnsley, who accompanied Stockport County in to the Third Division North.

Appearances: FL: 7 apps 1 gl Total: 7 apps 1 gl

ORME, Joseph Henry

Goalkeeper
5' 9½" 11st 7lbs
Born: Staveley, Derbyshire, 8th November 1884
Died: Nottingham, June 1935
Debut v Tottenham Hotspur (h) 22.11.19, drawn 1-1
CAREER: New Tupton St. John's. Clay Cross Zingari May 1904. New Tupton Ivanhoe May 1906. Clay Cross Zingari May 1907. North Wingfield Red Rose May 1908. Chesterfield Town cs 1909. Pinxton Colliery cs 1910. Watford June 1911. Millwall May 1913, fee £100. (Wartime guest with Notts County and **FOREST**). Ilkeston United September 1919. **FOREST 22nd November 1919.** Heanor Town. Shirebrook May 1922. Butterley Works reinstated amateur December 1927.

Joe Orme began in local junior football as a centre-forward with New Tupton St. John's, but was suddenly called upon to play in goal, owing to an injury sustained by the team's regular custodian. He then spent two seasons each with Watford and Millwall, up to his enlistment into the Footballers' Battalion in 1914. Following his discharge from the army, he took up government appointment in Nottingham, and this prevented him from playing regularly. When his appointment ended he joined Ilkeston United, but very shortly afterwards he was signed by Forest, following an injury sustained by regular goalkeeper Josh Johnson. Orme remained for a second season and made six consecutive appearances spanning September and October, but then found himself as third choice with Johnson and the emerging Alf Bennett sharing the first team jersey. A talented cricketer, he spent the summer of 1912 as professional with Rickmansworth C.C.

Appearances: FL: 11 apps 0 gls Total: 11 apps 0 gls

PAGE, Walter

Centre half-back
Debut v Wolverhampton Wanderers (h) 31.12.04, drawn 2-2
CAREER: Darlington amateur. **FOREST 1st December 1903-05.**

One trial run out for Forest Reserves against Doncaster Rovers in a Midland League match was sufficient for Walter Page to be offered a professional contract. The former Darlington amateur then had a year to wait for his New Years' Eve debut against the Wolves. Without adding to his first team appearance he was released at the end of the season.

Appearances: FL: 1 app 0 gls Total: 1 app 0 gls

PALMER, William 'Bill'
Outside-left 5' 9" 12st 0lbs
Born: Hemsworth, 22nd November 1887
Died: Hemsworth, April quarter 1958
Debut v Notts County (h) 4.9.09, won 2-1
CAREER: Ardsley Nelson August 1906. Barnsley
May 1907. Mexborough Town March 1908.
FOREST 9th June 1909. Rotherham County May
1910. Bristol Rovers June 1912. Everton May 1913,
fee £800. (Wartime guest player with Barnsley,
Notts County, Hull City and Chesterfield Town.)
Bristol Rovers July 1919. Gillingham August 1922.
Doncaster Rovers June 1923 to cs 1924.
*Bill Palmer was on Barnsley's list as a League
player, but moved to Mexborough at the close of
the 1907-08 season. He scored 22 Midland League
goals for his new team and figured in the forward
line of the Rest of the League X1 who played the
champions Lincoln City. His clever exhibition in
the match earned him his move to Forest, who
fielded five different players on the left wing in
efforts to find an adequate replacement for Alf
Spouncer who was in his final season at the City
Ground. Able to continue his career after World
War One Palmer had good spells with Bristol
Rovers (43 matches and 10 goals) and Gillingham
(36 matches and five goals.) He played only twice
for his final League club Doncaster Rovers before
hanging up his boots in his 37th year.*
Appearances: FL: 12 apps 1 gl FAC: 4 apps 0 gls
Total: 16 apps 1 gl

PARKER, Fred

Centre half-back
5' 11" 11st 3lbs
Born: New Seaham,
23rd October 1893
Died: Manchester,
July quarter 1959
Debut v Rotherham
County (a) 30.8.19,
lost 0-2
CAREER: Seaham
Young Albion.
Seaham Harbour
1910. Manchester
City amateur
October, professional
November 1913. (Wartime guest player with Stoke
and Port Vale.) **FOREST July 1919.** Southport
August 1926.
*Fred Parker played for Seaham Harbour in the
North-Eastern League at the age of seventeen. Tall
and rangy and with exactly the right build for his
position, he could attack and defend and was
quickly snapped up by Manchester City. He spent
almost six years on the books at Hyde Road, but
played almost all of his football as a wartime guest
player with Stoke and Port Vale. Joining Forest in
July 1919, he was a regular at centre-half for four
seasons before being injured and subsequently*

*losing his place to Gerry Morgan. Fred's elder
brother, Charlie, was capped by the Football
League and selected for a 'Victory' international.
Also a centre-half, he assisted Stoke, Sunderland
and Carlisle United, totalling 297 League
appearances and 16 goals.*
Appearances: FL: 157 apps 6 gls FAC: 7 apps 0 gls
Total: 164 apps 6 gls
Honours: **(FOREST)** FL Division 2 champions
1922

PARKER, John 'Jack'
Centre-forward 5' 11" 12st 10lbs
Born: Longton, Stoke-on-Trent, 6th August 1897
Died: Stoke-on-Trent, April quarter 1958
Debut v Grimsby Town (h) 14.2.20, won 2-0
CAREER: Longton. Army football. Port Vale
November 1918. Shrewsbury Town 1919. **FOREST
11th February 1920, fee £100.** Tranmere Rovers
(trial) August 1920. Port Sunlight September 1920.
Shrewsbury Town October 1920. Bristol Rovers
May 1922. Winsford United August 1924 to April
1930 plus.
*A heavily built centre-forward of direct methods
who enjoyed a winning debut with Forest but then
failed to hold his place in a side battling to avoid
relegation. He had scored 20 goals in 15 matches
for Shrewsbury Town prior to arriving at the City
Ground, but returned to non-League football after
his sojourn with the Reds. He was, however,
afforded another opportunity at senior level with
Bristol Rovers. The bulk of his first team
appearances for them were made in his first
season – 1922-23 - when he scored six League
goals in 25 Division 3 South matches, and one goal
in three FA Cup-ties. A native of the Potteries, he
worked in the local industry as a china pottery
thrower.*
Appearances: FL: 5 apps 0 gls Total: 5 apps 0 gls

PARKER, Robert Norris 'Bobby'

Centre-
forward/Inside-left
5' 9" 12st 0lbs
Born: Possilpark,
27th March 1891
Died: Glasgow,
28th December 1950
Debut v Crystal
Palace (a) 27.8.21,
lost 1-4
CAREER: Glasgow
Boys' Brigade.
Glasgow Ashfield.
Third Lanark (loan)
September 1908.
Glasgow Ashfield.
Rangers June 1910. Everton November 1913, player
exchange. (Wartime guest player with Rangers,
Morton and Rotherham County.) **FOREST 15th
May 1921.** Fraserburgh player-coach and secretary

July 1925. Bohemians trainer-coach April 1926 to 1930 plus.

Bobby Parker had the enviable record of winning championships throughout his career, commencing in junior Scottish competitions and continuing with Rangers, Everton, and finally Forest. Before the First World War he starred with Everton, scoring 36 goals in 35 League matches in 1914-15 to help them to lift the League championship. In August 1919 he returned from army service in Egypt, and was located in a hospital in Frodsham, recovering from an attack of malaria. He was never as prolific again, but he inspired the Reds to a blistering start to their Division Two championship season – seven wins and two draws in the opening ten fixtures of the campaign. His career record, covering Scottish and English football, amounted to 166 League appearances and 103 goals.

Appearances: FL: 46 apps 11 gls FAC: 5 apps 1 gl
Total: 51 apps 12 gls
Honours: (Everton) FL Division 1 champions 1915. (Rangers) Scottish League Division 1 champions 1913. (**FOREST**) FL Division 2 champions 1922.

PARKINSON, Robert 'Bob'

Centre-forward
Born: Preston, 27th April 1873
Debut v Bury (a) 3.12.98, lost 0-2
CAREER: Preston Ramblers. Preston Athletic. Fleetwood Rangers. Rotherham Town December 1894. Luton Town May 1893. Blackpool 26th May 1896. Warmley 20th August 1897. **FOREST 3rd October 1898.** Newton Heath 1st November 1899. Watford 26th November 1900. Swindon Town cs 1901.

Bob Parkinson became the third ex-Blackpool player to join Forest, although he had spent a season as captain with Warmley prior to joining the Reds. Despite winning 19 of their 22 league fixtures and scoring 108 goals and conceding 15, Warmley were pipped by one point by Royal Artillery (Portsmouth) for the championship of the Second Division of the Southern League. After appearing only twice for Forest, he did somewhat better with Newton Heath, for whom he scored seven goals in a run of 15 consecutive Second Division matches. Within his record, he scored the Heathens' last goal in the nineteenth century and their first in the twentieth. He assisted four different Football League clubs with moderate overall success, totalling 39 League matches and scoring 12 goals.

Appearances: FL: 2 apps 0 gls Total: 2 apps 0 gls

PEACOCK, Thomas

Inside-forward
5' 10" 11st 0lbs
Born: Morton, Derbyshire, 14th September 1912
Died: Chorley, December 1988
Debut v Oldham Athletic (h) 8.9.33, lost 1-3 (scored)
CAREER:
Tupton Hall Grammar School. Nottingham University.
Chesterfield amateur July 1931. Bath City. Melton Mowbray. **FOREST amateur 30th June to 4th August 1932, then professional from 25th August 1933 to October 1945.** (Wartime guest player with Southend United, Northampton Town, Birmingham, Wellington Town (Shropshire Senior Cup winner 1945) and Mansfield Town.)

Tom Peacock first attracted Forest's attention whilst a student at Nottingham University, whose team he assisted regularly. He left Nottingham to take up a scholastic appointment at Bath, and whilst there, played for Bath City. Returning to Nottingham in June 1932 he signed an amateur form with the Forest, signing a professional form in the following year. He scored on his Forest League debut, and in his first FA Cup-tie scored a hat-trick against Queen's Park Rangers. He was leading goal scorer in 1934-35 (21 League goals) and again with 20 League goals in 1935-36, when twelve of his total came in three matches. He netted four goals in matches against Port Vale, Barnsley and Doncaster Rovers. Earlier, he scored four goals against Port Vale in 1933-34. He was widely considered as the most constructive inside-left that Forest had had since the days of Grenville Morris and Charlie Jones. Sadly, a knee injury sustained at Plymouth Argyle on September 26th 1936 required surgery and he was unable to play again that season, his absence nearly costing Forest their place in the Second Division. It was over twelve months before he was able to resume first team duties, but he was never as effective as previously, having lost two knee cartilages. He was one of eleven players placed on the transfer list in May 1939, but he appeared as a guest player for several clubs whilst serving in the RAF as a flight-sergeant. In post war years he returned to his teaching profession, becoming headmaster of St. Edmond's Primary School at Mansfield Woodhouse.

Appearances: FL: 109 apps 57 gls FAC: 11 apps 5 gls
Total: 120 apps 62 gls

PEERS, Edward Henry 'Ted'

Full-back 5' 9" 12st 3lbs
Born: Wednesfield, near
Wolverhampton, 26th April 1873
Died: Stafford, 26th July 1905
Debut v Preston North End (h)
2.9.99, won 3-1
CAREER: Wednesfield Rovers.
Hednesford Rovers. West
Bromwich Albion 9th May 1895.
Walsall 24th June 1896. **FOREST 16th May 1899**.
Burton United 18th June 1901 to cs 1902. Swindon
Town 1903. Coventry City 11th July to October 1904.
*Ted Peers began with his local village team,
Wednesfield Rovers, and joined West Bromwich
Albion from Hednesford Rovers, but moved on to
Walsall after a season of reserve team football. A
speedy full-back with a splendid physique, he
made 73 League appearances for the Saddlers
before joining Forest, where he formed a successful
full-back partnership with Jimmy Iremonger for
two seasons. In the latter of which he missed a few
games in late season after an accident described
as: "A fearful smack on the head when heading a
heavy ball at the City Ground." On moving to
Burton United he was quickly in the wars again,
suffering a broken arm in an FA Cup-tie against
Northampton Town, and he did not play again
before being released in the close season. During
his time with the Forest, he was once described as:
"A youth of a curiously nervous and excitable
temperament." Sadly, he later spent some time in a
Staffordshire Asylum and his early death was
caused by suffocation, possibly self-inflicted.*
Appearances: FL: 56 apps 0 gls FAC: 9 apps 0 gls
Total: 65 apps 0 gls

PIKE, Horace

Outside or Inside-
forward
Born: Keyworth,
17th December 1869
Died: Germanstown,
Philadelphia, U.S.A. 1936
Debut v Chatham, FAC 2
replay (h) 23.2.1889,
drawn 2-2
CAREER: Keyworth
F.C. 1885. Notts Swifts.
**FOREST February
1889, registered for
FL matches 30th May
1892.** Loughborough
Athletic 11th June 1897. Keyworth F.C. (Emigrated
1911). Philadelphia & Reading Athletic.
*Horace Pike was a key figure in Forest's early
success in winning the championship of the
Football Alliance in 1892. It was the goal scoring
wingman's third full season with the Reds, his
outstanding record in Alliance matches amounting
to 29 goals in 59 matches. He missed only five*

*matches in the three seasons and netted two hat
tricks in season 1890-91, against Newton Heath
and Small Heath. When Forest entered the
Football League in 1892-93, Pike was moved to
inside-left to enable new signing Tommy McInnes,
the Scottish international, to take up his usual
position in the attack. In subsequent seasons he
settled at outside-right, a position he retained until
January 1896, when he was superseded by Fred
Forman. Horace Pike was awarded a benefit in
January of the following year and joined
Loughborough, assisting them for two seasons
before emigrating to the USA where he became an
early pioneer of football in Philadelphia.*
Appearances: FL: 91 apps 22 gls FAC: 19 apps 4 gls
Total: 110 apps 26 gls
Honours: (**FOREST**) Football Alliance champions,
1892.

POOLE, Harold

Centre-forward
Born: Bulwell, 30th July 1894
Died: Don Valley, October quarter 1971
Debut v Barnsley (h) 13.4.12, lost 0-2
CAREER: Newstead Rangers. **FOREST amateur
12th April 1912.** Coventry City August 1912. Sutton
Town August 1913.
*In the final three fixtures of season 1911-12, Forest
rang the changes, trying three different players at
centre-forward – a problem position throughout
the season. Teenage coal miner Harold Poole had
enjoyed a successful season with Newstead Byron,
but the step up to Division Two of the Football
League proved to be unrewarding. One of the three
trialists for the centre-forward slot in April 1912
was full-back Tommy Gibson who blossomed in his
unaccustomed role in the following term, leading
the scoring charts with 18 League goals.*
Appearances: FL: 1 app 0 gls Total: 1 app 0 gls

PORTER, William Carr

Centre half-back 6' 1½" 13st 0lbs
Born: Sunderland, 24th January 1908
Died: Norwich, 11th February 1987
Debut v Stoke (a) 25.12.31, lost 1-2
CAREER: Hylton Villa F.C. Nottingham
University. **FOREST amateur 28th July,
professional 28th August 1931.** Skegness United
December 1935.
*The former Nottingham University student had the
ideal physique for the role of centre-half, and it
was considered that, with a little more speed, he
would have been a great acquisition. He found few
opportunities, however, with the likes of Tommy
Graham and Harry Smith his chief competition.
Billy Porter combined his football with scholastic
duties at Skegness, and when he left the City
Ground he signed for his local club, Skegness
United.*
Appearances: FL: 14 apps 0 gls Total: 14 apps 0 gls

POWELL, Alfred Frank
Inside-left
Born: Cardiff, October quarter 1883
Debut v Sunderland (h) 15.10.04, lost 2-3
CAREER: Newport County. **FOREST 2nd
September to 1905**
*With fellow Welshman Grenville Morris a fixture
at inside-left, Alfred Powell lacked opportunities in
his season with the Reds. He was released at the
close of the 1904-05 season but Forest retained his
registration by placing him on the open to transfer
list with a fee of £25 on his head. At a meeting of
the Football League Management Committee on 5th
November 1906 it was ruled that his transfer fee
should be reduced to £10. As far as is known,
however, there were no takers!*
Appearances: FL: 1 app 0 gls Total: 1 app 0 gls

POWELL, John
Goalkeeper 5' 11½" 12st 4lbs
Born: Burslem, 3rd June 1892
Died: Chesterton, 7th February 1961
Debut v Barnsley (h) 24.10.14, won 2-1
CAREER: Port Vale cs 1911. Walsall March 1914.
FOREST 23rd October 1914. Port Vale August
1916 to May 1918.
*Associated with Port Vale and Walsall whilst both
were operating outside the Football League, 23
year-old goalkeeper John Powell stepped up into
Division Two when he joined Forest in October
1914. He replaced Harry Iremonger on arrival and
held his place for much of the remainder of the
season, although further cover in the form of Bill
Fiske might have brought more serious
competition, had the ex-Blackpool custodian not
been called up at the start of the season. His five
appearances being made when he was on leave
from the army in France.*
Appearances: FL: 24 apps 0 gls FAC: 1 app 0 gls
Total: 25 apps 0 gls

PRICE, Ernest Clifford 'Cliff'

Inside-forward
5' 9" 10st 10lbs
Born: Market Bosworth,
13th June 1900
Died: Market Bosworth,
30th July 1959
Debut v Portsmouth (a)
25.12.26, drawn 0-0
CAREER: Ibstock Albion.
Coalville Swifts. Leicester
Fosse January 1917.
Coalville Swifts (loan)
November 1919. Leicester
City professional October 1920. Halifax Town June
1922. Southampton December 1923. **FOREST 1st
June 1926.** Loughborough Corinthians September
1928. Nuneaton Town cs 1929. Gresley Rovers
February 1932. Snibston United October 1933.

*While working as a coalminer during the World
War One period, Cliff Price netted 33 goals in 75
appearances for Leicester Fosse. He also scored
twice on his Football League debut against the
Spurs in September 1919, but he departed Filbert
Street after 28 League appearances and eight
goals. A scoring debut for Halifax Town kicked-off
a successful first season at The Shay, with 15 goals
in 35 League matches and five in five FA Cup-ties
including a hat trick in the fourth qualifying round
against Rotherham Town. There then followed a
two and a half year spell in Division Two with
Southampton that was curtailed by injury in his
final season after he had completed 65 League and
Cup appearances and scored 18 goals. He was
again unfortunate to be injured in his first
appearance in a Forest shirt in the pre-season
practice match and missed half of the season, his
delayed debut coming on Christmas Day 1926.
Nominally an inside-left, Price played very well as
an emergency centre-forward in the later matches
of his first season, controlling the ball well and
opening out the play. Cliff's uncle, Fred Price, was
an outside-left who played for Leicester City,
Southampton, Wolverhampton Wanderers and
Chesterfield.*
Appearances: FL: 20 apps 5 gls FAC: 2 apps 0 gls
Total: 22 apps 5 gls

PRITTY, George Joseph

Wing half-back
5' 10½" 12st 7lbs
Born: Netchells,
Birmingham, 4th
March 1915
Died: Birmingham,
July 3rd 1996
Debut v Sheffield
United (a) 24.12.38,
won 1-0
CAREER: HB
Metropolitan Works
Old Boys. Newport
County May 1933.
Aston Villa May 1933.
**FOREST 22nd
December 1938.**
(Wartime guest player
with Solihull Town
and Wrexham.) Cheltenham Town August 1948.
*Said to have cost Forest a substantial fee, despite
having played in only three League matches for
Aston Villa, George Pritty helped to lift a
struggling side from the threat of relegation from
Division Two. Improving with every game,
towards the end of the campaign he produced
exceptional form when Forest were extremely hard
pressed, escaping the dreaded drop only on goal
average. Resuming after the war, he appeared in
26 League and four FA Cup-ties in 1946-47,
including Forest's shock 2-0 defeat of Manchester*

United at Old Trafford in round four. In August 1948 he was released and joined Cheltenham Town. He was living in Birmingham at the time, and training at Villa Park.
Appearances: FL: 49 apps 1 gl FAC: 5 apps 0 gls
Total: 54 apps 1 gl

PUGH, Robert Archibald Lewis

Inside-left
6' 0" 11st 12lbs
Born: Symonds Yat,
16th September 1909
Died: Newport, 2nd January 1986
Debut v Stoke City (a) 17.1.31, lost 0-1
CAREER: Whitebrook. Symonds Yat. Chepstow. Hereford United (trial). Symonds Yat. Newport County amateur cs 1925, professional October 1926. Bury 17th August 1929. **FOREST 9th January 1931, fee £300. Retired due to injury in 1938.**
Bob Pugh began in senior football with Newport County. A robust centre-forward in earliest days, he scored 13 goals in 66 matches prior to his move to Gigg Lane where he did not play regularly until his second season in which he made 19 of his League appearances and scored seven goals. His move to Nottingham Forest proved highly successful. The 'Nottingham Football Post Annual' for 1933-34 gave a rather graphic illustration of his style of play: "There are no parlour tricks about Pugh. He believes in bundling in and booting the ball about." At various times he appeared at outside and inside-left, centre-forward and left-half, but the middle line suited him best and he clocked up 263 League and Cup appearances and scored 19 goals before injury terminated his career in 1938. He then worked in the Nottingham Employment Exchange and later at the Royal Ordnance factory in Nottingham, continuing his association with Forest as a scout.
Appearances: FL: 248 apps 19 gls FAC: 15 apps 0 gls Total: 263 apps 19 gls
Honours: Welsh FA Tour to Canada 1929

QUANTRILL, Alfred Edward

Outside-left
5' 9½" 11st 8lbs
Born: Rawalpindi, India, 22nd January 1897
Died: Trefriw, 19th April 1968
Debut v Wolverhampton Wanderers (h) 30.8.30, lost 3-4
CAREER: St. James' School. Wanderers F.C. Liberals F.C. Haycroft Rovers. Boston Swifts. Derby County August 1914. Preston North End June 1921, fee £4,000. Chorley July 1924. Bradford Park Avenue September 1924. **FOREST 12th May 1930 to May 1932.** Old Altrincham's November 1934.
Alf Quantrill commenced with Derby County, making three appearances in the 1914-15 Division Two championship season. He was then called up, serving with the 7th Derbyshire Yeomanry. He contracted malaria in Salonika, but recommenced his career in 1919 and within six months was selected to play for England. He joined Preston North End following the Rams relegation from Division One, and was unfortunate to miss the 1922 FA Cup Final due to a cartilage injury. After a season in the Lancashire Combination with Chorley, Quantrill returned to League action with Bradford Park Avenue and enjoyed the best spell of his career, appearing in 202 League and Cup matches and scoring 58 goals. Approaching the veteran stage when signed by Forest, and after appearing in the first seven fixtures of 1930-31, he was injured and replaced by Billy Simpson, playing only infrequently thereafter. A son-in-law of the celebrated Steve Bloomer of Derby County and England fame, on leaving football Alf Quantrill worked as a manager with the Scottish Union Insurance Company in Manchester.
Appearances: FL: 15 apps 2 gls Total: 15 apps 2 gls
Honours: England International, 4 caps 1920-21. (Bradford Park Avenue) FL Division 3 North champions 1928.

RACE, Henry 'Harry'

Inside-forward
5' 8" 11st 5lbs
Born: Evenwood, Durham, 7th January 1906
Died: El Alamein, 24th October 1942
Debut v Brentford (h) 26.8.33, drawn 1-1
CAREER: Staindrop F.C. Bishop Auckland August 1926. Evenwood Town amateur November 1927, professional January 1928. Raby United (County Durham). Liverpool October 1927. Manchester City July 1930, fee £3,000. **FOREST 27th June 1933.** Shrewsbury Town July 1937. Hartlepools United August 1938. Rhyl September 1938.

Harry Race had seen considerable service with Liverpool and Manchester City before he joined Forest. He scored 18 goals in 43 appearances for Liverpool before Manchester City paid a then substantial fee to take him to Maine Road, where he became an almost permanent reserve, playing in only 10 League matches in a three-year stay. By contrast, he was rarely absent from the Forest front line for his first three seasons before injuries blighted his final campaign. A hard working inside-forward, particularly effective on heavy grounds, he was a schemer who made openings for others, although it was suggested that he might have done more shooting himself. He was placed on the transfer list in April 1937 and moved into non-League football up to the Second World War, when he enlisted into the 6th Battalion, Queen's Own Cameron Highlanders.
Appearances: FL: 115 apps 26 gls FAC: 9 apps 4 gls
Total: 124 apps 30 gls
Honours: (Shrewsbury Town) Welsh Cup winners 1938.

RADFORD, Arthur Greasley

Outside-left
Born: Eastwood, October quarter 1877
Debut v Bury (a) 4.4.98, drawn 2-2
CAREER: FOREST 24th April 1898.
Gainsborough Trinity 13th May 1899. Arnold F.C. 5th September 1899. Gainsborough Trinity. Arnold F.C. 23rd August 1900. Ilkeston Town 21st August 1921. Arnold F.C. 14th September 1901. Ilkeston Town 1st September 1902. Somercotes United 9th April 1903 to 1904.
An Eastwood coalminer, Arthur Radford deputised at outside-left for Alf Spouncer on his Football League debut against Bury and showed sufficient promise to be retained for the following season. There was, however, stiff competition for the left wing berth, and despite the fact that Tom McInnes was injured in November and was out for the season, it was Alf Spouncer and Fred Forman who subsequently shared the role. Transferred, along with reserve centre-half John Thornley, to Gainsborough Trinity, both players found more opportunities in Division Two football, Radford making 64 League appearances, scoring 21 goals, defender Thornley appearing in 88 League matches.
Appearances: FL: 4 apps 0 gls Total: 4 apps 0 gls

RADNELL, Charles Henry

Goalkeeper 5' 9" 11st 0lbs
Born: Arnold, 5th June 1886
Died: Nottingham, December 1942, age 56
Debut v Lincoln City (h) 24.4.07, won 3-1
CAREER: Ripley Athletic 5th May 1905. **FOREST April 1907, professional 10th March 1908.**
As the 'Post Football Guide' pointed out in 1907: "Radnell is a smart 'keeper, but up to now, understudying Linacre has not been a very profitable engagement for an ambitious youngster." His one senior appearance was made in the final fixture of Forest's Division Two championship season which wound up with a 3-1 win against Lincoln City, who finished just one place above Burton United who failed to gain re-election and finally disbanded in 1910.
Appearances: FL: 1 app 0 gls Total: 1 app 0 gls

RANSFORD, Herbert

Inside-left
Born: Blackwell, Derbyshire, 25th September 1901
Died: Chesterfield, April quarter 1983
Debut v West Ham United (a) 22.12.23, lost 2-3
CAREER: South Normanton. **FOREST amateur 24th November, professional 27th December 1923.** Alfreton Town August 1924. Sutton Town cs 1925. Matlock Town August 1926. South Normanton August 1927. Matlock Town August 1928. Pleasley Colliery September 1929. Heanor Town June 1930. South Normanton Welfare August 1934. South Normanton Victoria August 1935.
Signed as a professional after first team outings against West Ham United, and a 2-0 win against Chelsea on Christmas Day, Herbert Ransford was afforded only two more opportunities. Appearing in back-to-back fixtures against Birmingham in January, he scored in the 2-1 win at St. Andrews and retained his place for the return, a 1-1- draw at the City Ground. Forest came close to relegation from the top flight, avoiding the drop only on goal average over Chelsea, who accompanied Middlesbrough into Division Two. A lengthy career in local non-League football followed, which he combined with his work as a coalminer.
Appearances: FL: 4 apps 1 gl Total: 4 apps 1 gl

REED, Ebor

Left half-back 5' 10" 11st 10lbs
Born: Quarlington Hill, 30th November 1899
Died: Durham, 14th November 1971
Debut v Fulham (a) 30.8.26, lost 1-2
CAREER: Spennymoor Mount Pleasant School.
Tradesmen's F.C. Spennymoor United. Newcastle
United (trial) November 1921. Barnsley (trial)
January 1922. Newcastle United February 1922.
Cardiff City May 1925, fee £250. FOREST 10th
May 1926. Rotherham United June 1927.
Wallsend (trial) August 1929. Derry City August
1929. Dundalk 1930. Portadown July 1932.
Spennymoor Committee member October 1953.
*It took some time for Ebor Reed to establish
himself beyond reserve team football, which had
largely been his lot with Newcastle United (0
appearances), Cardiff City (six appearances) and
five with Forest when he failed to make much
impression on the regular middle line selection of
Belton, Morgan and Wallace. His move to
Rotherham United afforded more opportunities
with 60 League appearances in two seasons. He
then moved to Ireland where he played for the
Irish League against the League of Ireland at
Dalymount Park, Dublin, on 1st March 1930 and
helped his team to a 6-1 victory.*
Appearances: FL: 5 apps 0 gls Total: 5 apps 0 gls
Honours: Irish League representative, 1 app.
(Dundalk) FA Ireland Cup finalist 1931.

REID, Robert Thomson

Inside-right
Born: Larkhall, Glasgow, 1890
Debut v Fulham (a) 21.12.12, drawn 0-0
CAREER: Larkhall. FOREST 16th December
1912 to May 1915.
*Before crossing the border, Robert Reid had
represented the Lanarkshire League against the
Irish League. He was given an early debut on
arrival at the City Ground and all of his
appearances came in his first season when his
distribution was usually accurate, but he lacked a
scoring finish to complement his constructive
abilities.*
Appearances: FL: 9 apps 1 gl FAC: 1 app 0 gls Total:
10 apps 1 gl

RICHARDS, Charles Henry

Inside-right
5' 6" 11st 11lbs
Born: Burton-on-
Trent, 9th August
1875
Debut v Bolton
Wanderers (h)
11.1.96, drawn 0-0
CAREER:
Blackwell F.C.
Gresley Rovers.
Newstead Byron.
Notts County July
1894. Blackwell F.C.
24th January 1895.
Gresley Rovers.
FOREST 2nd January 1896. Grimsby Town
January 1899. Leicester Fosse July 1901.
Manchester United August 1902. Doncaster Rovers
March 1903.
*In January 1896, the 'Sheffield Independent'
reported that Gresley Rovers had transferred their
centre-forward, Richards, who used to play for
Blackwell, to Nottingham Forest for a fee of £21,
plus the proceeds of a match. On 28th April of the
same year, the match took place, Forest only
managing to make a draw of one goal each
against their modest opponents. In his three years
at the City Ground, 1897-98 was the most
memorable for the powerful inside-forward who
held on to the ball extremely well, and knew when
to part with it. On March 5th he won his England
cap in the 3-2 win against Ireland, and one month
later he was an FA Cup winner as Forest beat
Derby County 3-1 at the Crystal Palace.
Subsequently, he was Grimsby Town's joint
leading scorer when they won the championship of
the Second Division, and later again he was the
scorer of Manchester United's first-ever goal in the
Football League. His strike, five minutes from time
against Gainsborough Trinity on 6th September
1902, ensuring him a permanent place in the club's
history.*
Appearances: FL: 74 apps 20 gls FAC: 10 apps 6 gls
Total: 84 apps 26 gls
Honours: England International, one cap v Ireland
March 1898. (FOREST) FA Cup winners 1898.
(Grimsby Town) FL Division 2 champions 1901

RICHARDS, Stanley

Full-back 5' 10½" 12st 4lbs
Born: Beeston, Notts. 15th April 1916
Died: Nottingham, 14th March 1978
Debut v Blackburn Rovers (a) 16.4.38, lost 1-5
CAREER: Beeston St. John's. FOREST amateur 28th October, signing professional 20th November 1937 to May 1943. (Wartime guest with Mansfield Town 1940-41.)
A local find from Beeston St. John's, Stan Richards played in several Midland League matches for Forest Reserves before being signed on a professional form. His performances in the Midland League distinguished him as a cool and resourceful back with a stout physique and a powerful kick. Sadly, he never progressed further than reserve team football, his one senior appearance, on Easter Saturday 1938, was made in the unaccustomed position of right half-back and he struggled in a heavy defeat at Blackburn Rovers, the Second Division champions-elect.
Appearances: FL: 1 app 0 gls Total: 1 app 0 gls

RICHARDSON, George

Right half-back
Debut v Sunderland (a) 23.4.98, lost 0-4
CAREER: All Saints Methodists. Churchill Swifts. West Bromwich Albion September 1892. FOREST 5th April 1898 to May 1899.
Forest fielded a fairly settled middle line throughout the 1897-98 season, but the directorate took the opportunity to experiment once the FA Cup had been safely won, and the League position safe. George Richardson, a reserve half from West Bromwich Albion, was the second of four different right half-backs fielded in the last four Division One fixtures of the season, and three of the matches resulted in heavy defeats with no goals scored and eleven conceded. Richardson remained on the books throughout the following season but was not afforded a second opportunity in the League side.
Appearances: FL: 1 app 0 gls Total: 1 app 0 gls

RIDLEY, James

Outside-left 5' 9" 12st 0lbs
Born: Newcastle-on-Tyne, 3rd November 1889
Died: Nottingham, October quarter 1956, age 66
Debut v Sunderland (h) 18.2.11, lost 1-3
CAREER: Byker East End. Willington Athletic 7th September 1906. Newcastle United 19th February 1907, fee £50. FOREST 16th February 1911, fee £150. Wallsend F.C. September 1911.
Reputed to be the fastest outside-left in the country, a few months before joining Forest, Ridley had issued a challenge to race any footballer for level stakes. He was the winner of several handicaps, including the Morpeth event. He received his early football training with Byker West End, but joined Newcastle United from Willington Athletic. He found few opportunities during four years spent with the Magpies (17 League appearances and two goals) but was expected to figure regularly for Forest in a position that had not been adequately filled throughout what transpired to be a relegation season. Forest had beaten Liverpool 2-0 at the City Ground on 21st January 1911, but they then took just one point from the remaining thirteen Division One fixtures. Ridley had a four-match run spanning February and March, scoring at Woolwich Arsenal in a 2-3 defeat on February 25th. He was not retained following relegation and failed to find another League club, despite his transfer fee being reduced from £50 to £25.
Appearances: FL: 4 apps 1 gl Total: 4 apps 1 gl

RITCHIE, Archibald 'Archie'

Full-back 5' 6"
Born: Kirkcaldy, Fife, 12th April 1872
Died: Nottingham, 18th January 1932
Debut v Stoke (h) 10.9.92, lost 3-4
CAREER: East Stirlingshire 1888. FOREST August 1891, registered for FL matches 28th May 1892, retired May 1899.
Archie Ritchie began with East Stirlingshire, and was capped by Scotland for their match against Wales, at Wrexham, in March 1891. Later in the same year he crossed the border to join Forest. He immediately struck up a fine full-back pairing with his fellow countryman, Adam Scott, who at 5' 5" tall was even shorter than Ritchie. The lack of physical advantage did not prevent the pair from forming a powerful and very effective last line of defence. An FA Cup medal was a fitting reward for Ritchie's loyalty, as it came towards the end of his career. When the following season opened, the cup-winning side was fielded, but it never did duty again, and Ritchie made few appearances, and did not play at all in the final five months of the season. When he was released in May 1899, the club gave him a present of £25, and promised to give him whatever fees were obtained for his transfer. This was never collected, however, as he decided to retire. Along with another ex-Forest player, Bob Norris, Archie Ritchie became a star in local bowling circles. He was licensee of the Sawyer's Arms, Greyfriargate, at the time of his death, at the age of 62.
Appearances: FL: 156 apps 0 gls FAC: 21 apps 0 gls
Total: 177 apps 0 gls
Honours: Scotland International, one cap v Wales 1891. (**FOREST**) Football Alliance champions 1892. FA Cup winners 1898.

RITCHIE, Samuel Joseph

Half-back
5' 9" 11st 7lbs
Born: Belfast, *circa* 1889
Debut v Leicester Fosse (h) 3.9.13, lost 1-3
CAREER: Glentoran 1910. **FOREST 7th May 1913**. Belfast Celtic August 1914. *Glentoran's captain in the latter half of season 1912-13, Sam Ritchie had appeared for the Irish League against its counterparts in England, Scotland and Wales. His signing was expected to stiffen Forest's intermediate line materially, but after a shaky start his position at centre-half was taken by Joe Mercer. It was certainly an unhappy season for the Irishman, whose seven first team outings resulted in six defeats and one draw. Returning to Ireland to join Belfast Celtic he made a final appearance for the Irish League versus the Southern League when he appeared as a substitute, replacing S. Burniston, the Distillery full-back, who had suffered a broken arm.*
Appearances: FL: 7 apps 0 gls Total: 7 apps 0 gls
Honours: Irish League representative, four apps, 1912-14

ROBERTS, Ernest **Thomas**

Inside-forward
Debut v Small Heath (a) 5.4.02, drawn 1-1
CAREER: FOREST 1st August 1901-03
A reserve forward who spent much of his first season as understudy to Arthur Capes for the inside-right berth before appearing in two late season 1-1 draws against Small Heath and Liverpool, following Capes' transfer to Stoke in April 1902. Despite the absence of his former rival, little changed for Tom Roberts in the following season, with John Calvey the main contender for the inside-right berth.
Appearances: FL: 6 apps 0 gls FAC: 1 app 0 gls
Total: 7 apps 0 gls

ROBERTS, Samuel **Grenville**

Inside-right 5' 9" 10st 4lbs
Born: Blackwell, Derbyshire, 16th August 1919
Died: K.I.A. Dunkirk, 3rd June 1940
Debut v Luton Town (h) 15.4.38, won 1-0
CAREER: Huthwaite Swifts. Huthwaite C.W.S. **FOREST amateur 17th September 1936, professional 25th September 1937 to May 1939.**

One of two players recruited from the works' team of Huthwaite C.W.S., Arthur Betts being the other, Grenville Roberts soon began to show real ability, and was well worth his first outing against Luton Town on Good Friday 1938. Still a youngster, the 'Post Guide' considered that: "He needs more timber and will then make his presence felt." Unfortunately, after five consecutive appearances in the early weeks of the following season, a leg injury put him out of action for much of the remainder of the campaign. In June 1940 the sad news reached Nottingham that Private Roberts had been killed in action at Dunkirk while serving with the 2/5th Battalion of the Yorkshire Regiment.
Appearances: FL: 6 apps 0 gls Total: 6 apps 0 gls

ROBERTSON, Peter

Centre half-back 5' 10" 12st 0lbs
Born: Dundee, 1881
Debut v Wolverhampton Wanderers (a) 3.9.04, lost 2-3
CAREER: Providence F.C. Dundee 16th May 1901. **FOREST (debut) 3rd September 1904 (No date of signing given in FL registrations).** Dundee.
Scottish international Peter Robinson had appeared in 51 Scottish League matches in three seasons with Dundee, but in the season prior to his move to Forest he had had a number of quite serious thigh and knee injuries. It seemed that his signing was something of a gamble and, in the event, he was dropped after appearing in the first five matches of the season. At a subsequent meeting of Forest directors, consideration was given to the value (or not) for money of various signings. Robertson was firmly on the debit side. Apart from his undisclosed transfer fee, he had cost £208 and turned out only seven times, costing over £29 per match – a goodly sum in 1905!
Appearances: FL: 7 apps 0 gls Total: 7 apps 0 gls
Honours: Scotland International, one cap 1903 v Ireland. Scottish League representative v Irish League, February 1902.

ROBERTSON, Thomas

Right half-back
Born: Torrance, near Glasgow, December 1864
Debut v Sunderland (a) 19.11.92, lost 0-1
CAREER: Renton United. Queen's Park amateur October 1888. **FOREST amateur 18th September 1892.** Queen's Park amateur January 1893 to 1894.
Although Tom Robertson achieved little in his brief association with Forest, he had earlier appeared in two Scottish Cup finals for Queen's Park. He was on the winning side in 1890, when Vale of Leven

were beaten in a replay. Two years later he finished on the losing side, again after a replay, Celtic winning by 5-1. Additionally, he collected Glasgow Cup medals in consecutive seasons for victories against Partick Thistle (8-0) and Celtic (3-2).

Appearances FL: 1 app 0 gls Total: 1 app 0 gls
Honours: (Queen's Park) Scottish Cup winners 1890, runners-up 1892. Glasgow Cup winners 1889 and 1890.

ROBINS, Robert **Walter** Vivian

Outside-right
Born: Stafford, 3rd June 1906
Died: Marylebone, London, 12th December 1968
Debut v Barnsley (h) 25.12.29, won 4-0
CAREER:
Highgate School. Cambridge University.
FOREST amateur 13th December 1929.

Much better known as a cricketer, Walter Robins was a Middlesex and England all-rounder who appeared in 19 Test Matches between 1929-37. He was awarded his Blue at Cambridge in both cricket and football, and as a Freshman Blue scored 308 runs, average 77, against Oxford University. He played in 258 matches for Middlesex as a forcing batsman, leg-break bowler and brilliant fielder. Between 1925 and 1951 he scored 1,000 runs in a season four times, and achieved the 'double' in 1929 when he took 162 wickets at an average of 21.53. He was also a Test Selector, and managed the 1959-60 side to the West Indies. He followed his Christmas Day debut for the Reds with a second appearance, one year later, in a Boxing Day 1-1 draw against Reading at the City Ground.

Appearances: FL: 2 apps 0 gls Total: 2 apps 0 gls

ROBINSON, George Henry

Half-back
Born: Basford, Notts. 3rd June 1875
Died: Bradford, March 1945
Debut v Bolton Wanderers (h) 8.4.99, lost 1-2
CAREER: Nottingham Jardine's Athletic.
FOREST 3rd January 1899. Bradford City June 1903 to May 1915,

subsequently appointed club trainer until June 1922.
The son of a local Councillor who was once described as: "A quiet and popular player, and geniality itself." Considered a wing-half of exceptional promise at the time of joining Forest, by season 1990-01 George Robinson was fully established as a first team regular. In the following campaign he was ever-present in the Cup run that took Forest to the semi-final at White Hart Lane, where they lost 1-3 to Southampton, the beaten finalists. Moving on to Bradford City, he enjoyed a twelve-year career at Valley Parade that included two benefits, a Second Division championship, and an FA Cup winners medal in 1911. His 343 Football League appearances set a club record that stood until 1972, a figure that was overtaken by midfielder Bruce Stowell, who went on to total 401. George Robinson was a muli-talented sportsman who also enjoyed a game of cricket, golf and baseball.

Appearances: FL: 85 apps 1 gl FAC: 7 apps 0 gls Total: 92 apps 1 gl
Honours: (Bradford City) FA Cup winners 1911. FL Division 2 champions 1908.

ROE, Thomas William "Tommy"

Centre-forward
5' 8" 11st 0lbs
Born: Evenwood, 8 December 1900
Died: Evenwood, December 1972
CAREER:
Evenwood Town. Cockfield. Esperley Rovers. Willington Athletic August 1922. Durham City amateur November 1922. Shildon Athletic July 1923. Cockfield F.C. November 1923. Northfleet United August 1924. Tottenham Hotspur July 1925.
FOREST 10th May 1927. Luton Town May 1928. Walsall May 1929. Coventry City May 1930. Heanor Town. Nottingham City Transport reinstated amateur December 1932.
Debut v Fulham (a) 15.9.27, lost 0-2
Tommy Roe's League career began with Durham City and the youthful attack leader showed early promise, his eight goals in 17 matches in his debut season made him the teams' leading scorer, the undoubted highlight being his hat trick in the 3-2 win against local rivals Hartlepools United. Once described as "A forward of the dainty type and, if lacking a little dash, he impresses in his approach work and ball control." He was signed by the Spurs who immediately sent him out to Northfleet

United in the Kent League for development. Subsequently he graduated to the Spurs Reserve team but was unable to establish himself in the League side despite scoring 5 goals in just eight League and Cup matches. Although he maintained a very respectable scoring record throughout his senior career (31 goals in 97 League matches) his only prolonged spell of first team football came with Walsall in season 1929-30. Missing only one match during the campaign he scored eight League and one FA Cup goal. A brother, Harry Roe, was on Luton Town's books in 1926.
Appearances: FL: 9 apps 4 gls Total: 9 apps 4 gls

RONALD, Peter Mann

Centre-forward 5' 11" 12st 2lbs.
Born: Wallsend-on-Tyne, 15th November 1889
Died: Watford, Herts, 21st April 1953
Debut v Hull City (a) 9.9.21, won 1-0
CAREER: Wallsend Park Villa. Backworth United. Hebburn Argyle. Watford June 1914.
FOREST 15th June 1921, fee £500. West Stanley May 1923. Watford 1924, assistant-trainer August 1925 to June 1946.
Peter Ronald joined Watford from Hebburn Argyle, and assisted them to the championship of the Southern League in his first season, scoring nine goals in 35 matches. In 1919-20 he scored 10 goals in 35 Southern League matches, and in 1920-21 he scored Watford's first-ever goal in the Football League against Crystal Palace, going on to score 10 goals in 29 matches. Arriving at the City Ground with a reputation for cleverness and goal-scoring ability, he nevertheless failed to impress appearing in only three matches in the 1921-22 Division Two championship side. He was given a trial at right-half in the final match of the season at Leeds United, but spent his second season on the sidelines until a final appearance in the last match of the campaign, a 1-3 defeat at Cardiff City.
Appearances: FL: 4 apps 0 gls Total: 4 apps 0 gls
Honours: (Watford) Southern League champions 1915

ROSE, Thomas
Centre-forward 5' 9" 11st 10lbs
Born: Ockbrook, Derbyshire, April quarter 1875
Debut v Newton Heath (h) 7.4.94, won 2-0
CAREER: Langley Mill Rangers. Heanor Town. **FOREST 18th January 1894.** Bulwell United 8th November 1895.
In his debut season Tommy Rose enjoyed a productive month of April, scoring four goals in five United Counties League matches, including a hat trick against Sheffield Wednesday. Earlier in the month, he had made his Football League debut against Newton Heath. When first signed by Forest from Heanor Town there must have been a loan agreement between the two clubs, as Rose played for Heanor Town against Forest in the first round of the FA Cup, nine days after signing professional forms at the City Ground. Although Forest progressed by beating Heanor 1-0, Tommy Rose was said to have played an exceptionally smart game at centre-forward, getting in a number of excellent shots on goal. He scored his first League goals in the opening fixture of 1894-95, netting both of Forest's goals in a 2-1 home win against Burnley. In the following season he repeated the feat, scoring twice in the opening fixture, a 5-0 home win against Bury, but by November he departed to Bulwell United, having lost his first team place to David Smellie, the new forward signing from Albion Rovers.
Appearances: FL: 30 apps 9 gls FAC: 2 apps 2 gls Total: 32 apps 11 gls

ROTHERY, Harry
Outside-left 5' 11" 11st 5lbs
Born: Royston, Barnsley, 25th February 1881
Died: Rawmarsh, April quarter 1965
Debut v Grimsby Town (a) 1.9.06, lost 1-3
CAREER: Wath Athletic 1900. Mexborough West End 1903. Mexborough Town. Sheffield United 31st December 1904. **FOREST 19th April 1906, fee £225.** Rawmarsh Albion 26th September 1908.
Considering the fact that Harry Rothery had played in only four League matches for Sheffield United, his transfer fee when joining Forest was quite a considerable sum at that time. Sheffield United, who had spotted him when playing in an FA Cup-tie between Mexborough and Gainsborough Trinity, had also paid a substantial fee for his services. Tall and strong, and said to be clever and speedy, he sadly lacked opportunities to justify his reputation, a broken leg effectively terminating his senior career.
Appearances: FL: 4 apps 0 gls Total: 4 apps 0 gls

ROWAN, Frederick Septimus

Outside-right 5' 7½"" 11st 4lbs
Born: Sunderland, 1st November 1883
Died: Sunderland, 9th June 1951, age 67
Debut v Manchester City (a) 13.4.09, lost 1-2
CAREER: Sunderland Royal Rovers 16th September 1906. **FOREST 6th June 1908 to May 1910.** Silksworth F.C.
In season 1907-08 Fred Rowan scored 22 goals for Sunderland Royal Rovers from the right wing, form that led to his recruitment by Forest in the close season. Although he remained for two seasons at the City Ground, the form of Bill Hooper restricted Rowan to just two first team opportunities, despite the 'Post Football Guide' reporting that he had "Accomplished excellent work with the Reserves."
Appearances: FL: 2 apps 0 gls Total: 2 apps 0 gls

ROWLANDS, Alfred Stanley

Centre-forward
5' 11" 11st 4lbs
Born: Coedway, near Welshpool, 12th November 1889
Died: Barnstaple, Devon, 7th October 1974
Debut v Sheffield Wednesday (h) 8.4.11, lost 0-1
CAREER: Snailbeach White Stars August 1905. Abbey Juniors. Welshpool.
Wellington Town cs 1909. Montgomery F.C. Birkenhead North End 1909. Wrexham (trial) September 1910. Liverpool (trial) December 1910. **FOREST 15th March to April 1911.** South Liverpool cs 1911. Wrexham May 1912. Tranmere Rovers July 1913. Reading May 1914. (Wartime guest with Crewe Alexandra and Tranmere Rovers). Wrexham June 1922 to August 1923. Oswestry Town August 1923. South Molton player-coach September 1924. Bideford August 1926. Ilfracombe Town August 1930.
In season 1910-11, Stan Rowlands scored 28 goals for Birkenhead North End, and had undergone trials with both Wrexham and Liverpool, before joining Forest. He appeared just once, but failed to agree terms to remain for the following season. After a season with South Liverpool he joined Wrexham – at that time operating in the Birmingham & District League – and scored 18 goals in 30 matches. He next joined Tranmere Rovers and scored 32 goals as they won the championship of the Lancashire Combination. In March of the same season he was capped by Wales. His move to Reading was cut short by the outbreak of World War One and he joined the

army and saw active service in France. He had appeared with Crewe Alexandra in wartime football, and was still with them when they gained entry to the Football League in 1921, scoring 10 goals in 23 appearances. Another spell with Wrexham, now playing in the Football League, brought just nine appearances, but a final highlight came with Oswestry Town, with whom he collected a Welsh National League championship medal.
Appearances: FL: 1 app 0 gls Total: 1 app 0 gls

RYALLS, Joseph

Outside-right
Born: Sheffield, 3rd January 1881
Died: Sheffield, January quarter 1952
Debut v Bolton Wanderers (h) 16.10.09, won 2-0
CAREER: Montrose Works.
Sheffield Wednesday 20th June 1901. Barnsley 9th May 1905, fee £30. Fulham 1906. Rotherham Town 25th June 1906. Brentford 1st September 1908. **FOREST May 1909, registered for FL matches 23rd October 1909.** Brentford 1910. Chesterfield Town September 1911.
Generally a reserve team player throughout his career, Forest omitted to register Joe Ryalls to play in League matches when he was initially signed in May 1909. They then fielded him in a Division One match against Bolton Wanderers on 16th October and were promptly fined one guinea by the Football League for his non-registration. With the paperwork then in order, Ryalls had a number of outings in the first team as deputy for Bill Hooper. Earlier in his career, Ryalls had partnered Tommy Marrison (q.v.) on the right wing at Rotherham Town.
Appearances: FL: 9 apps 0 gls Total: 9 apps 0 gls

SAUNDERS, Frank Victor

Centre-forward 5' 11½" 12st 7lbs
Born: Kate's Hill, Worcs, 24th May 1888
Died: Birmingham, October quarter 1946, age 58
Debut v Leeds City (h) 2.9.11, won 2-1
CAREER: Wednesbury Old Athletic. Coventry City August 1910. Wednesbury Old Athletic. **FOREST 25th May 1911.** Huddersfield Town June 1912 to January 1913.
A burly centre-forward who returned to Wednesbury Old Athletic from Coventry and helped the Staffordshire club to turn a bad corner. After his arrival seven consecutive matches were won, in which he scored 13 goals. In his season with the Forest he scored a total of 16 goals, seven of which came in League matches. Transferred to Huddersfield Town, his season was ended prematurely by injury before he had made a first team appearance.
Appearances: FL: 28 apps 7 gls Total: 28 apps 7 gls

SAXTON, Arthur William

Centre-forward
5' 7" 11st 7lbs
Born: Long Eaton,
28th August 1874
Died: Shardlow,
January quarter 1911
Debut v Sunderland (a)
19.10.01, lost 0-4
CAREER: Long Eaton
Athletic 1891. Long Eaton
Rangers 1891. Mansfield
Town 1892. Mansfield
Greenhalgh's 1893.
Loughborough May 1894.
Glossop North End May 1895. Stalybridge Rovers
June 1896. Sunderland June 1898. Bedminster May
1899. Luton Town August 1900. Northampton
Town May 1901. **FOREST 6th September 1901.**
Long Eaton St. Helen's August 1902. Perks Athletic
November 1902.
*Arthur Saxton's meandering path began locally
before spells with both Mansfield clubs, followed
by a season with Loughborough – where he was a
Midland League championship winner. Spells in
The Combination with Glossop North End, and the
Lancashire Combination with Stalybridge Rovers,
preceded his elevation, at the age of 24, to
Sunderland. He took the transition to major soccer
in his stride, sharing the outside-left berth with
Jim Chalmers, and later Colin McLatchie.
Thereafter, with Southern League clubs, his career
tapered off somewhat. A final spell in League
football with the Forest was not distinguished, his
one senior appearance, oddly enough against
Sunderland, resulting in a heavy defeat. In the
early 1890s he was employed in the local lace
manufacturing industry.*
Appearances: FL: 1 app 0 gls Total: 1 app 0 gls

SAXTON, Fred

Outside-right
Born: Mansfield, 6th March 1916
Died: Mansfield, December 2000, age 84
Debut v Blackpool (h) 8.9.34, drawn 0-0
CAREER: Mansfield Grammar School for Boys.
Nottingham University. Sutton-in-Ashfield F.C.
**FOREST amateur 20th November 1933.
Mansfield Town amateur May 1934.
FOREST professional 16th May 1934.** Ilkeston
Town.
*After assisting both the Forest and Mansfield
Town as an amateur in reserve team football, Fred
Saxton was taken on as a professional. The
eighteen-year old wingman was given an early
debut in Division Two when he deputised for
Arthur Masters in a goalless draw against
Blackpool. He did not get another opportunity
before leaving to join Ilkeston Town.*
Appearances: FL: 1 app 0 gls Total: 1 app 0 gls

SAXTON, John 'Jack'

Right half-back
5' 9" 11st 4lbs
Born: Kimberley,
Nottingham,
18th November 1902
Died: Bentley, Doncaster,
15th October 1964
Debut v Blackpool (h)
5.9.25, drawn 1-1
CAREER: Bentley Colliery
1924-25. **FOREST
amateur 6th February,
professional 3rd March 1925.** Southport June
1927. Scunthorpe & Lindsey United August 1928.
Bentley Colliery 1929 to *circa* 1936.
*Jack Saxton was working as a miner and playing
for the colliery team when he was first spotted by
Forest. In less than a month on amateur forms he
was signed as a professional, the 'Post Football
Guide' observing: "His methods suggest a
successful career. He kicks with power and
judgment, and clears well." As understudy to long
serving right-half Jack Belton, Saxton found few
opportunities, his best run of first team action
being seven consecutive appearances in his second
season. Moving on to Southport, he appeared in 35
matches before being released after one season.
His move to Midland League side Scunthorpe was
blighted by a broken leg injury after he had
appeared in just four matches. Subsequently he
started his own coal delivery business while
captaining his colliery team.*
Appearances: FL: 11 apps 0 gls FAC: 1 app 0 gls
Total: 12 apps 0 gls

SCOTT, Adam

Full-back
5'5"
Born:
Coatbridge,
1871
Debut v Everton
(a) 3.9.92,
drawn 2-2
CAREER:
Coatbridge
Albion.
**FOREST
August 1890,
registered for
FL matches
3rd June 1892,
retired May
1900.**
*A small full-
back with a large moustache, Adam Scott
compensated for his lack of inches by his grit and
tenacity. Together with Archie Ritchie, whose
height was recorded as 5' 6", they were
undoubtedly the smallest, and among the best full-*

back partnerships in the game. A match report for Forest's win at Burnley in November 1894 ran as follows: "Chief credit for the victory undoubtedly rests with Adam Scott. Time after time he literally took the ball clean off the toe of the opposing forwards, and was constantly being cheered by the spectators." Considered by many to be 'Man of the Match' in Forest's 1898 FA Cup Final victory, his medal was a fitting reward for his long and distinguished service to the club.

Appearances: FL: 179 apps 4 gls FAC: 31 apps 0 gls
Total: 210 apps 4 gls
Honours: (**FOREST**) FA Cup winners 1898.
Football Alliance champions 1892.

SCOTT, James

Left full-back 5' 10" 12st 0lbs
Born: West Greenock, 1907
Debut v Swansea Town (h) 27.2.26, lost 0-2
CAREER: St. Anthony's. **FOREST 27th October 1925.** Accrington Stanley (trial) September 1926. Charlton Athletic November 1926. Merthyr Town June 1928. Armadale August 1932.

Jim Scott had appeared in little senior football before arriving Pendarren Park, the home of the Merthyr Town club. His single appearance for Forest, when he was tried at centre-forward although he was a left full-back by training, was followed by one League appearance for Charlton Athletic. In two seasons with the 'Red & Greens' he was regular performer at left full-back, appearing in 66 League and three FA Cup matches. After finishing in 20th position in the Third Division South, they struggled again and finished at the foot of the table in 1929-30 and failed to gain re-election to the Football League. Their place taken by the equally ill-fated Thames F.C., who lasted for just two seasons as a Football League club.

Appearances: FL: 1 app 0 gls Total: 1 app 0 gls

SCOTT, John 'Jack'

Outside-right
5' 6" 10st 7lbs
Born: Sunderland, 5th February 1908
Died: Sunderland, November 1992
Debut v Bradford Park Avenue (h) 3.10.29, drawn 1-1
CAREER: Darden Tempest. Arcade Mission. Seaham Harbour. Sunderland amateur October, professional November 1926. Ryhope Colliery October 1927.

Crystal Palace August 1928. Kettering Town August 1929. **FOREST 3rd October 1929.** Northampton Town August 1931. Exeter City May 1932. Hartlepools United June 1936. Blyth Spartans August 1938.

At the age of 21, diminutive wingman Jack Scott had already had a variety of experience when he joined Forest who, on the same day, signed Johnny Dent from Huddersfield Town. Scott had been a regular on Kettering Town's right wing in 1928-29 and he quickly established himself at the City Ground. He must have been particularly pleased to score against his former club, Sunderland, in round five of the FA Cup, he also appeared in 29 League matches in his first season. He was less successful in 1930-31, sharing the right-wing berth with Noah Burton throughout the season. After a season with Northampton Town in which he appeared in 22 League matches, he joined Exeter City. Remaining at St. James' Park for four seasons he accumulated 139 League and Cup appearances and scored 21 goals. His senior career ended with Hartlepools United for whom he scored 20 goals in 70 League matches. Jack's brother, Thomas, also played for Hartlepools United in season 1936-37.

Appearances: FL: 47 apps 3 gls FAC: 7 apps 2 gls
Total: 54 apps 5 gls
Honours: (Exeter City) FL Division Three South Cup winners 1934

SEVERN, William

Goalkeeper
Born: Ilkeston, 29th January 1876
Died: Don Valley, January quarter 1965
Debut v Preston North End (h) 4.10.94, lost 0-2
CAREER: Hucknall Portland. **FOREST 6th May 1894.** Hucknall Portland 4th May 1895. Red Hill United 14th September 1896. Little Hallam Rangers 20th September 1897. Alfreton Town 10th August 1897.

Forest's reserve goalkeeper for one season as Dennis Allsop continued to dominate the position. Severn's two Football League outings were made consecutively, and following his debut day defeat against Preston North End, he had the satisfaction of finishing on the winning side two days later. Visitors Aston Villa were beaten 2-1, with Rose and MacPherson scoring Forest's goals. Aston Villa went on to lift the FA Cup later in the season, beating local rivals West Bromwich Albion by 1-0 at the Crystal Palace.

Appearances: FL: 2 apps 0 gls Total: 2 apps 0 gls

SHAW, Arthur Frederick

Inside-forward
Born: Clifton, Nottingham, 1st August 1869
Died: Woodborough, Notts. 11th March 1946
FL Debut v Preston North End (a) 17.10.92, lost 0-1
CAREER: Notts Rangers 1886. Notts County 1886. Mellors Ltd. Notts Rangers 1887. **FOREST October 1887**. Notts Rangers. **FOREST 1888**. Notts County. **FOREST 1889, registered for FL matches 20th July 1892**. . Loughborough May 1897. Newark F.C. 1899 to February 1901.

A son of the Nottinghamshire and England cricketer Alfred Shaw who captained his county to four consecutive Championship titles from 1883 to 1886, and was for many years a partner in the sports goods firm of Shaw and Shrewsbury. Son Arthur shone in a different sport, being a star in Nottinghamshire football, assisting Forest to the Alliance championship in 1892 and followed with a lengthy service in Forest's early days in the Football League. A clever inside-forward who fed his other forwards splendidly from a deep lying role, he was not often on the scoresheet, but his play in combination was of the highest order. In a final spell of League football with Loughborough, he scored three goals in 11 matches. He then captained Newark for the best part of two seasons, retiring in February 1901 owing to business considerations. At the time of his death he was mine host of the Nags Head Inn at Woodborough.
Appearances: FL: 79 apps 14 gls FAC: 19 apps 4 gls
Total: 98 apps 18 gls
Honours: (**FOREST**) Football Alliance champions 1892

SHEARMAN, Ben W

Outside-left
5' 7½" 11st 2lbs
Born: Knight's Place, Lincoln, 2nd December 1884
Died: Sheffield, January quarter 1969
Debut v Rotherham County (a) 30.8.19, lost 0-2
CAREER: Sheffield Schoolboys. Rotherham County May 1905. Worksop Town. Rotherham Town 9th April 1906. Bristol City April 1909. West Bromwich Albion May 1911, fee £100. (Wartime guest with Sheffield United, Lincoln City, Rotherham County and Bradford Park Avenue.) **FOREST June 1919, fee £250**. Gainsborough Trinity June 1920. Norton Woodseats trainer-coach 1922-38.

Although well into the veteran stage by the time he reached the City Ground, Ben Shearman was still a sprightly wingman, able to beat his man and deliver accurate crosses from the left flank. Earlier in his career, he appeared in 60 League matches for Bristol City, and 126 for West Bromwich Albion. He appeared twice, within the space of a week in October 1911, for the Football League in wins against the Southern League and Irish League. Later in the same season he appeared in the FA Cup Final, won by Second Division Barnsley by 1-0 after the first meeting at Crystal Palace had ended goalless.
Appearances: FL: 31 apps 1 gl FAC: 1 app 0 gls
Total: 32 apps 1 gl
Honours: FL representative, 2 apps 1911. (West Bromwich Albion) FA Cup finalists 1912.

SHEARMAN, William James

Inside-forward
5' 10½" 12st 0lbs
Born: Keswick, 22nd May 1879
Died: Victoria, British Columbia, March 1933
Debut v Sheffield Wednesday (a) 3.10.03, lost 1-2 (scored)
CAREER: Braithwaite F.C. (Keswick). Shepherd's Bush. **FOREST 25th September 1903, retired May 1909**.

Born at Keswick in 1879, Bill Shearman played for his local team before going to Shepherd's Bush. On joining Forest in 1903 he celebrated his debut by scoring at Sheffield Wednesday, and in the following year he twice represented the Football League in wins against the Scottish and Irish Leagues. Shearman was a bustling inside or centre-forward who delighted in a shoulder to shoulder charge, and was often seen to literally charge his way through the most hefty defenders and finish up with a goal or pass that supplied one to such colleagues as 'Gren' Morris. Capable of pulling a match out of the fire by himself, the meteoric Shearman certainly shone more in individual dashes than in combination, and his combative style brought more than a fair share of injuries. Later in his Forest career he appeared on the right-wing, but the injuries that he sustained saw him gradually fade, and he went into retirement at the end of the 1908-09 season. After leaving Forest and Nottingham, he went to British Columbia, and on the outbreak of the First World War joined up with the 67th Canadian Battalion and was overseas for three years.
Appearances: FL: 110 apps 39 gls FAC: 7 apps 6 gls
Total: 117 apps 45 gls
Honours: (**FOREST**) FL Division 2 champions 1907. Football League representative, 2 appearances, 1904.

SHREWSBURY, Thomas Peace
Right half-back
Born: Heanor, 22nd April 1872
Died: Greenwich, January quarter 1949, age 76
Debut v Everton (h) 22.9.94, lost 2-3
CAREER: Heanor Town. **FOREST 17th April 1894**. Derby County 25th February 1895, in exchange for Frank Forman. Darwen 15th June 1895. Woolwich Arsenal 20th August 1896 to May 1900.
Tom Shrewsbury began with his hometown club, Heanor Town, and remained with them until the close of the 1893-94 season. In what proved to be his last season with them, he performed so well at right half-back against Forest in the first round FA Cup-tie on 27th January – which Forest won 1-0 – that he was signed by the Reds later in the same season. After less than a year he was released to join Derby County, Forest receiving Frank Forman in exchange. It has to be said that Forest came out best in the deal, as Forman subsequently won nine England caps and served Forest for eleven seasons. Without appearing in a League match for Derby County, Shrewsbury was transferred to Darwen, and after just three first team appearances he was on the move again. Another three first team appearances for the Gunners bringing his modest career to a close.
Appearances: FL: 4 apps 0 gls Total: 4 apps 0 gls

SIMMS, Willard
Centre-forward   5' 7½"   11st 0lbs
Born: Sutton-in-Ashfield, October quarter 1891
Died: Nottingham, 16th August 1935
Debut v Glossop (a) 13.12.13, lost 0-3
CAREER: Sutton Town. South Normanton Colliery. **FOREST 11th December 1913 to May 1915.**
After commencing with Sutton Town, Willard Simms played for the works' team of South Normanton Colliery, members of the Derbyshire League, where he worked as a miner. He was given an early debut in Division Two but was then unable to establish himself in what proved to be a dire season for the Reds. Winning only seven of 38 League matches, they scored only 37 goals and finished at the bottom of the table and were obliged to seek re-election.
Appearances: FL: 3 apps 0 gls Total: 3 apps 0 gls

SIMPSON, William 'Billy'

Outside-left
5' 8"   11st 7lbs
Born: Jarrow, 26th January 1907
Died: Registered at Durham North East, October quarter 1970
Debut v Cardiff City (a) 12.4.30, drawn 1-1
CAREER: Howden British Legion. Jarrow F.C. Sheffield Wednesday January 1928. Jarrow F.C. August 1928. Barrow June 1929. Washington Colliery Welfare November 1929. **FOREST 9th April 1930**. Jarrow F.C. August 1937. North Shields June 1938.
Flame-haired Billy Simpson was released by Sheffield Wednesday without appearing at first team level, but he made a bright start with Barrow, scoring on his debut against New Brighton, but he was then released into non-League football after just eight League appearances and two goals. His form with Washington Colliery led to his joining Forest, and his pluck and pace, combined with deadly centring, made him a very dangerous customer on the wing. He formed a particularly effective wing partnership with Tom Peacock, whose prompting led to many an opening for his wing partner to cut in and take a shot at goal. After seven years at the City Ground he was released and moved back to the North-East. Billy's father, George Simpson, assisted Sheffield Wednesday and West Bromwich Albion before the Great War, appearing in 160 League matches and scoring 36 goals.
Appearances: FL: 229 apps 36 gls FAC: 14 apps 3 gls Total: 243 apps 39 gls

SLATER, Herbert

Centre-forward
5' 9"   11st 11lbs
Born: Aston, Birmingham, 2nd May 1888
Died: Stapleford, 20th May 1967
Debut v Preston North End (a) 1.9.10, won 2-0
CAREER: Acock's Green St. Mary's 1906. Erdington F.C. 1907. Atherstone Town 1908. Stourbridge F.C. Aston Villa September 1909. **FOREST 16th July 1910 to April 1911.**

Herbert Slater commenced in 1906-07 with Acock's Green St. Mary's, the runners-up in the Birmingham Suburban League. During the following season he played for Erdington, and in 1908-09 he joined Atherstone Town, remaining for half a season, scoring 35 goals in League matches. He then joined Stourbridge, and in the second half of the season netted 14 goals. In 1909-10 he played regularly at centre-forward for Aston Villa Reserves in the Birmingham & District League. In that competition he scored 32 goals. He also played in the junior international v Scottish Juniors in April 1909. Despite his previously admirable record he played only twice for Forest, at Preston North End and Notts County, and failing to impress was released at the close of the relegation season.

Appearances: FL: 2 apps 0 gls Total: 2 apps 0 gls
Honours: England Junior International v Scotland, April 1909.

SMELLIE, Richard **David**
Centre-forward
Born: In Scotland
Debut v Small Heath (a) 9.11.95, lost 0-1
CAREER: Pollockshields Athletic. Albion Rovers. **FOREST 4ᵗʰ October 1895.** Newcastle United July 1896. Motherwell. Albion Rovers 4ᵗʰ December 1897. Eastville Rovers 9ᵗʰ March 1898.
A hard working centre-forward, but one who did not discover his 'shooting boots' until he joined Newcastle United. On Tyneside he enjoyed a memorable season, scoring a hat trick against Small Heath on his home debut, and followed with a four-goal blast against Darwen on his fifth appearance. He ended the campaign as leading scorer with 15 goals in 26 League matches, but surprisingly he returned to Scotland in the summer. His final move took him to Bristol to join Eastville Rovers, members of the Birmingham & District League. In the following year the club's title was changed to Bristol Rovers and they became members of the Southern League.

Appearances: FL: 16 apps 3 gls FAC: 1 app 0 gls
Total: 17 apps 3 gls

SMITH, Albert W

Wing half-back
Born: Nottingham, 23ʳᵈ July 1869
Died: Nottingham, 18ᵗʰ April 1921
FA Cup Debut in Round One v Linfield Athletic, 2.2.89, drawn 2-2
FL Debut v Everton (a) 3.9.92, drawn 2-2
CAREER: Notts Rangers. Long Eaton Rangers. Derby

County 1884. **FOREST October 1888**. Notts County February 1890. **FOREST 1890**. Blackburn Rovers November 1891. **FOREST 13ᵗʰ July 1892, retired April 1894.**
In terms of League football, Albert Smith had a fleeting association with Notts County, but he had three separate spells with Forest, assisting them to win the championship of the Football Alliance in 1891-92. An amateur player throughout his career, the Nottingham boot factor was described in 1893 as: "One of the most forcible half-backs. Always working, and is a heavy but fair tackler." Albert was capped three times by England while on Forest's books, appearing against Scotland, Wales and Ireland. On 17ᵗʰ February 1894 the 'Nottingham Evening Post' reported that: "Albert Smith, the late captain of Nottingham Forest, was on Thursday married to Miss Page of Nottingham. Mr. Smith, who has retired from active football, secured the highest international honours. The Forest club intend to present their old captain with a beautiful epergne."
Appearances: FL: 23 apps 1 gl FAC: 17 apps 0 gls
Total: 40 apps 1 gl
Honours: England International, 3 caps, 1891-93. (FOREST) Football Alliance champions 1892.

SMITH, Ernest

Inside-left
5' 10" 11st 0lbs
Born: Shirebrook, 13ᵗʰ January 1912
Died: Chesterfield, November 1996
Debut v Bury (a) 15.9.34, lost 0-1
CAREER: Sutton Junction F.C. Burnley November 1931. **FOREST 13ᵗʰ June 1934.** Rotherham United July 1935. Yeovil & Petters United. Rotherham Town October 1936. Plymouth Argyle November 1938.
Ernie Smith joined Burnley as a nineteen year-old inside-forward but in a stay approaching three seasons he made only seven first team appearances, scoring one goal. With Forest, he scored one goal in only two appearances, but as understudy to Tom Peacock, who scored 21 League goals in 36 matches, his opportunities were naturally at a premium. Moving on, he enjoyed his best spell with Rotherham United (44 goals in 107 League matches) and his League career wound up in the final season of peacetime football with Plymouth Argyle, in which he scored five goals in 12 Division Two matches. Although he remained on the club's books throughout the war and made a number of appearances in 1945-46, he did not re-appear when normal League football resumed in 1946-47.
Appearances: FL: 2 apps 1 gl Total: 2 apps 1 gl

SMITH, Henry Stanley 'Harry'

Utility defender
5' 9½"   11st 6lbs
Born: Throckley,
11th October 1908
Died: Throckley,
13th June 1993
Debut v Chelsea (a)
28.12.29, drawn 0-0
CAREER:
Throckley Welfare.
**FOREST 20th
December 1928.**
Darlington 13th July
1937. Bristol Rovers
August 1939,
player-coach
November 1948,
then groundsman to 1982.

Signed from Throckley Welfare, a Tyneside League club, Harry Smith was able to fill the role of either half-back or full-back. It was generally considered that his best position was at centre-half, a position dominated by Tommy Graham, but Smith's performances as his deputy in 1934-35 vastly improved the Forest middle line. He left Forest after appearing in eight seasons, being released to join Darlington in July 1937. After 65 League appearances, he joined Bristol Rovers on the eve of the Second World War.

Appearances: FL: 157 apps 1 gl FAC: 13 apps 0 gls
Total: 170 apps 1 gl

SMITH, Horace

Left half-back   5' 11"   12st 0lbs
Born: Stourbridge, 5th July 1908
Died: Wollaston, Stourbridge, 28th October 1975
Debut v Coventry City (h) 19.9.36, drawn 1-1
CAREER: Holly Hall F.C. Brierley Hill Alliance cs 1925. Stourbridge F.C. Coventry City May 1930. Merthyr Town October 1931. Stoke City January 1935. **FOREST 7th July 1936.** Shrewsbury Town July 1937. Revo Electric August 1939.

Despite a lengthy career at various levels, Horace Smith failed to establish himself in League football, being restricted to five matches for Coventry City, and one against them, when he made his Forest debut. He was signed by Forest on the same day that Meynell Burgin was signed from Bournemouth. The inside-forward scored a hat trick at Southampton in the final fixture of the season which doubtless helped when the retained list was published. Horace Smith was less fortunate, but on release was quickly fixed up with Shrewsbury Town.

Appearances: FL: 1 app 0 gls Total: 1 app 0 gls

SMITH, John

Inside-right
Debut v West Bromwich Albion (a) 3.4.93, drawn 2-2
CAREER: FOREST 5th September 1892.
Understudy to his much better known namesake, William 'Tich' Smith, John was not afforded a chance in the League side until the final fixture of the season, when a side showing several changes made a creditable draw against West Bromwich Albion.

Appearances: FL: 1 app 0 gls Total: 1 app 0 gls

SMITH, John 'Jack'

Centre-forward
5' 7"   11st 0lbs
Born: Wardley, 15th
September 1886
Died: K.I.A. in
France, September
1916
Debut v Bolton
Wanderers (h)
16.10.11, won 2-0
CAREER: Hebburn
Argyle. Hull City
26th June 1905.
Sheffield United
November 1910.
**FOREST 16th
March 1911, fee**
£450. Nelson August 1911. York City August 1912. Hebburn Argyle January 1913. Heckmondwike F.C.

In his second season with Hull City, Jack Smith scored 32 goals to head the scoring list in Division Two, his form was recognised in the same season when he was selected to play for the Football League X1 versus the Scottish League at Villa Park on 29th February 1908. In 1909-10 his figures were 32 in 35 matches, and his overall record with the Tigers was an impressive 102 goals in 168 League and Cup matches. A brief spell with Sheffield United followed in which he scored six goals in 13 League and Cup matches. A similarly brief spell with Forest did not have the desired outcome, as Smith's introduction did nothing to lift a side destined for relegation from the top flight. A round of non-League football followed before he enlisted in the York & Leicester Regiment in 1915. In the following year he lost his life in early September, sadly leaving five children without a father.

Appearances: FL: 3 apps 1 gl Total: 3 apps 1 gl
Honours: FL representative one appearance, 1908.

SMITH, John William
Goalkeeper 5' 11" 12st 0lbs
Born: Beeston, Notts. *Circa* 1885
Debut v Woolwich Arsenal (a) 9.10.09, won 1-0
CAREER: Long Eaton St. Helen's. Derby County
November 1903. Newark Town March 1908.
FOREST May 1909, registered for FL matches 4th September 1909. Ilkeston United July 1911.
A reserve goalkeeper to Harry Makrey for almost five seasons, Smith was restricted to ten League and Cup appearances for Derby County. After a season in the Midland League with Newark Town, he was given another opportunity of League football when he joined Forest. He made an impressive start, remaining unbeaten in victories in his first three matches against Arsenal, Bolton Wanderers and Chelsea. In his second season, which ended in relegation from Division One, he was one of three goalkeepers fielded during the campaign, and all were released at the season's close
Appearances: FL: 27 apps 0 gls FAC: 1 app 0 gls
Total: 28 apps 0 gls

SMITH, William 'Tich'

Inside/Outside-right
5' 6" 12st 4lbs
Born: Sawley, Derbyshire, 10th November 1868
Died: Nottingham, 27th September 1907
Debut v Clapton F.C. FA Cup Round One (h) 17.1.91, won 14-0 (scored two)
CAREER: Long Eaton Rangers. (Derby County amateur) Long Eaton Rangers. Notts Rangers. Notts County cs 1889. Long Eaton Rangers. **FOREST June 1890, registered for FL matches 23rd July 1892 to August 1894.** Long Eaton Rangers. Notts County May 1896. Loughborough August 1897. Lincoln City July 1898. Burton Swifts 1899.
'Tich' Smith was Long Eaton Rangers' centre-forward when they won the Birmingham Cup in 1887, beating West Bromwich Albion 1-0 at Perry Bar. They were also runners-up for the Derbyshire Cup in the same year. The son of Mr. William Smith senior, A Long Eaton lace manufacturer, he represented England (and scored four goals in a 6-1 victory) against Canada in an unofficial international played at The Oval, Kennington, on 19th December 1891. In the same season he assisted Forest to win the championship of the Football Alliance, and was at inside-right in the first Forest team to contest a Football League match, at

Everton on 3rd September 1892. At about the same time he was a reserve for a place in the England team to meet Scotland, but he did not win a full cap. In Forest's first Football League season he completed 26 appearances and scored three goals, but in the following campaign he struggled with injuries and was released in the close season. In a second spell with Notts County, he scored four goals in eight matches in the Division Two championship season 1896-97. Latterly operating mainly at right half-back he enjoyed useful spells with Loughborough (28 appearances) and Lincoln City (33 appearances) before becoming a licensee in Long Eaton and Nottingham.
Appearances: FL: 36 apps 6 gls FAC: 15 apps 5 gls
Total: 51 apps 11 gls
Honours: **(FOREST)** Football Alliance champions 1892. Football Alliance representative, 1 app. v Football League, 20th April 1891

SPAVEN, John Richard 'Jack')

Inside-right
5' 9" 12st 0lbs
Born: Scarborough, 22nd November 1891
Died: Nottingham, 29th August 1971
Debut v Birmingham (h) 28.2.20, lost 1-2 (scored)
CAREER: St. James' F.C. 1902. Northend F.C. Goole Town. Scarborough Town. Scunthorpe & Lindsey United September 1919.
FOREST 28th February 1920. Grantham August 1926, and then trainer by 1930.
Signed from Scunthorpe & Lindsey United at a fee believed to be a record for a Midland League player, Jack Spaven had scored 22 Midland League goals in the season that he joined the Reds. Formerly with Goole Town and Scarborough Town, he served in the RFA during the war and was demobilised in July 1919. Forest's leading scorer with 18 goals in the 1921-22 championship season, he was the undisputed favourite of the City Ground spectators. Powerfully built and possessing any amount of courage he could force his way past most defenders, and shoot with exceptional pace and accuracy. His one weakness was in headwork, the 'Topical Times' reporting in March 1922: "If only Jack Spaven was as deadly with his head as he is with his feet, what a wonder he would be. There is no harder shot than the Forest inside man when he gets his boot on the ball, but his headwork lets him down." After a half century of goals in the red jersey, he was released

and moved into non-League football with Grantham F.C. He was later a licensee in the town.
Appearances: FL: 157 apps 46 gls FAC: 13 apps 4 gls
Total: 170 apps 50 gls
Honours: (FOREST) FL Division Two champions 1922

SPENCER, Fred

Outside/Inside-right 5' 5" 10st 8lbs
Born: Basford, January quarter 1871
Died: Woodthorpe, 12th August 1959
Debut v Small Heath (a) 9.11.95, lost 0-1
CAREER: FOREST 13th July 1893. Notts County September 1900. St. Andrew's (Nottingham) September 1903.

An early Football League debut for Fred Spencer followed his outstanding performance for the Reserves. In a Notts League fixture on 19th October 1895 he was the scorer of a double hat trick in the emphatic 9-0 win against Ruddington. Without ever winning a permanent place in the League side he was an extremely useful utility forward, typically scoring five goals in just eight Division One matches in 1896-97. His long association with the Forest ended when he moved across the Trent to join Notts County. He was again cast into the role of a deputy forward for the outside-right berth, in three seasons making 16 League and Cup appearances, scoring one goal. As the 'Football Post' commented in September 1903: "Fred Spencer will play in Notts Alliance Football with St. Andrew's this season. He has never quite realised expectations in League football."
Appearances: FL: 43 apps 19 gls FAC: 1 app 0 gls
Total: 44 apps 19 gls

SPOUNCER, William Alfred 'Alf'

Outside-left
5' 8" 10st 8lbs
Born: Gainsborough, 1st July 1877
Died: Indonesia, 31st August 1962
Debut v Notts County (h) 4.9.97, drawn 1-1
CAREER: Gainsborough Trinity August 1893. Sheffield United July 1894. Gainsborough Trinity 13th May 1896. FOREST 4th May 1897 to retirement June 1910, fee £125.

At the time of his signing, Alf Spouncer was the third Gainsborough native to move up into First Division football. The first was Booth, who joined the Wolves, and then Fred Spiksley joined Sheffield Wednesday. Spouncer's transfer was the subject of lengthy negotiations and in addition to the £125 paid in cash; Forest agreed to meet Gainsborough Trinity in a benefit match in Nottingham with a guarantee of £75. They also opened the 1897-98 season with a benefit match at Gainsborough, for which they charged bare expenses. The overall total was estimated to be £250, a huge amount at that time, but one that was well spent as he appeared in 13 seasons of League football, forming one of the best left wing partnerships in the game with Wales international Grenville Morris. He assisted Forest to win the FA Cup in 1898, was capped by England against Wales in 1900, and scored seven goals in 20 matches in 1907-08 when the Second Division championship was won. Retiring after exactly 300 League appearances, he later coached in Europe and served during the First World War with the Black Watch. He was the last surviving member of Forest's 1898 FA Cup winning side.
Appearances: FL: 300 apps 47 gls FAC: 36 apps 5 gls Total: 336 apps 52 gls
Honours: England International, one cap v Wales 1900. (FOREST) FA Cup winners 1898. FL Division 2 champions 1907.

STANLEY, Fred

Right half-back
5' 7" 11st 8lbs
Born: Tutbury, 4th November 1884
Died: Tutbury, 8th February 1947
Debut v Aston Villa (a) 25.12.07, lost 0-4
CAREER: Horninglow Rangers. Horninglow F.C. Burton United January 1906. FOREST 2nd July 1907. Burton United 13th July 1908. Crewe Alexandra March 1910 to April 1915.

Fred Stanley appeared in every Football League match for Burton United in 1906-07 when, despite his best efforts, the Brewers finished at the foot of Division Two and failed to gain re-election. His transfer to the Forest proved to be a disappointing move, as he was restricted to just one Football League outing, a 0-4 defeat at Aston Villa on Christmas Day 1907. He was welcomed back to Burton United, by this time operating in the Birmingham League. Financial difficulties led to his transfer to Crewe Alexandra in March 1910, and he remained with them until football was suspended by the outbreak of World War One. Fred Stanley was for many years the licensee of the Vine Inn, Ludgate Street, Tutbury, until his retirement in the Second World War period. In the

very severe winter of 1946-47 he was found collapsed in the snow at the side of the road in Tutbury and expired at the age of 62.
Appearances: FL: 1 app 0 gls Total: 1 app 0 gls

STANWAY, Reginald Ewart
Right half-back
Born: Langley Mill, 25th April 1892
Died: Mapperley, 12th September 1972
Debut v Fulham (h) 27.4.12, drawn 1-1
CAREER: FOREST 19th September 1911.
Introduced for the final fixture of season 1911-12, at home against Fulham on 27th April 1912, reserve half-back and colliery worker Reg Stanway was joined in defence with Prestwood Machin, also making his solitary bow in the League side. Coming in on the back of seven consecutive defeats, the pair had the satisfaction of assisting their team to earn a share of the points in a 1-1 draw.
Appearances: FL: 1 app 0 gls Total: 1 app 0 gls

STAPLETON, Laurence
Outside-left 5' 9½" 11st 0lbs.
Born: Nottingham, 19th May 1893
Died: Nottingham, 2nd July 1969
Debut v Stoke (a) 24.1.20, won 2-0
CAREER: Wallsend F.C. Army football. Basford United. **FOREST amateur 7th October 1919, professional 26th January 1920**. Heanor Town July 1921. Shirebrook June 1922.
Initially associated with Wallsend F.C. of the North-Eastern League, during military service Laurence Stapleton appeared regularly for the R.M.A. regimental team. He joined Forest from Basford United and combined football with his work as a coal miner at Eastwood Colliery. Signed as a professional within days of his first team debut at Stoke, he held his place in the side for a run of eight matches. Forest narrowly avoided relegation from the Second Division in both of Stapleton's seasons at the City Ground, in the second of which he appeared exclusively in the reserves.
Appearances: FL: 10 apps 0 gls Total: 10 apps 0 gls

STEVENSON, James
Inside-right 5' 8" 11st 4lbs
Born: Govan Church, 2nd February 1881
Died: Greenock, 9th July 1946
Debut v Everton (a) 25.10.02, drawn 2-2
CAREER: Abington F.C. Leith Athletic. Morton 1900. **FOREST 23rd May 1902**. New Brompton February 1903. Morton 1904. Belfast Celtic. Port Glasgow Athletic 1906. Arthurlie. Morton 1912. Kilmarnock (loan) 1918. Clyde (loan) 1918. Morton 1919. Arthurlie 1921.
Aside from his sojourn with Forest, and a similarly brief association with New Brompton – for whom he scored six goals in 28 Southern League matches – James Stevenson spent the remainder of his

lengthy professional career in his native Scotland. Five separate spells with Morton, at either side and during World War One accounted for much of his overall figures, his record being 110 matches and 18 goals. He was still turning out for Arthurlie, a Scottish Division Two side, in his 40th year.
Appearances: FL: 6 apps 1 gl Total: 6 apps 1 gl

STEWART, Alexander
Wing half-back 5' 8½" 11st 12lbs
Born: West Greenock, Renfrewshire, 1868
Debut v Wolverhampton Wanderers (h) 2.9.93, won 7-1
CAREER: Morton. Burnley December 1889. Everton December 1892. **FOREST June 1893**. Notts County 10th March 1897. Bedminster 14th May 1898. Northampton Town 13th October 1899. Burnley September 1901. Leicester Fosse trainer 11th December 1902 to 1905.
A report of Forest's AGM in July 1893 revealed that, of last season's players, the only one not retained was Scottish international half-back Tom Hamilton. In his place, Alex Stewart, late Burnley and Everton had been signed. The powerfully built Scot enjoyed a stunning debut in the 7-1 thrashing of the Wolves and missed only one League match during his first season, when Forest finished in 7th place in Division One. He was similarly consistent throughout his stay at the City Ground, passing a century of League and Cup appearances before crossing the Trent to join Notts County, whom he assisted to win promotion to the top flight in season 1896-97. In a career that totalled 211 League matches and 14 goals, his final appearance, and goal, was scored for Leicester Fosse when, as club trainer, he turned out in an emergency at Glossop on 10th April 1903 and helped his team to a 2-1 victory.
Appearances: FL: 97 apps 1 gl FAC: 8 apps 1 gl
Total: 105 apps 2 gls
Honours: (Everton) FA Cup finalists 1893

STOCKS, Cyril William

Outside/Inside-right
5' 8" 10st 7lbs
Born: Pinxton, Derbyshire, 3rd May 1905
Died: Sutton-in-Ashfield, 31st May 1989
Debut v Newcastle United (h) 4.10.24, drawn 1-1
CAREER: South Normanton Amateurs 1921. South Normanton Colliery 1922. **FOREST amateur 29th September 1922, professional**

30th May 1923. Grantham F.C. July 1934. Bentinck Welfare coach/assistant manager.
A lengthy association with the Forest began as a 17 year-old amateur. Cyril Stocks first entered competitive football with South Normanton Amateurs in season 1921-22, subsequently joining South Normanton Colliery where he worked as a timekeeper. He appeared in ten seasons of football at the City Ground, eight as a regular first team member. He made his debut, and completed just three League matches, in the 1924-25 season that ended in relegation from Division One. Thereafter he operated in Division Two, although his style was often considered more suitable to First Division football. Of light build, he lacked any physical advantage, his style being entirely scientific, lacking the generally more robust methods of Division Two. Clever on the ball and with a useful shot, he scored 15 League and Cup goals in successive seasons between 1926-28, and 13 in 1931-32. Certainly a valuable find by the Forest, an immensely popular player with over a decade of sterling service.
Appearances: FL: 241 apps 76 gls FAC: 15 apps 4 gls
Total: 256 apps 80 gls

STOKER, Lewis

Right half-back
Born: Wingate, 31st March 1910
Died: Edgbaston, Birmingham, 6th May 1979
Debut v Sheffield United (h) 27.8.38, lost 0-2
CAREER: Bear Park School. Brandon Juniors. Esh Winning Juniors. Bearpark F.C.
West Stanley August 1929. Birmingham, (trial) August, professional September 1930. **FOREST 28th May 1938 to May 1939.**
Lewis Stoker joined Birmingham at the age of 20 and developed into a fine wing half, tackling and passing in fine style. He completed 230 League appearances for the Blues and was capped against Wales in 1933, against Scotland in 1934, and Hungary in the same year. He was also an England reserve on numerous occasions. Moving to Forest, he failed to find his best form in a struggling side that only narrowly avoided relegation. He was transfer listed in May 1939 and in the same year became a Police Special Constable. Later again he worked as a chargehand at Wimbush Bakery in Birmingham. In earliest
days he attended Bear Park School, which also numbered Sammy Crooks, the Derby County and England outside-right, as one of its former pupils.
Appearances: FL: 11 apps 0 gls Total: 11 apps 0 gls
Honours: England International, 3 caps 1933-34.
FL representative, 1 app

.

STUBBS, Philip **Eric** Gordon

Winger
5' 11"   12st 0lbs
Born: Chester, 10th September 1912
Died: Chester, 25th January 2013, age 100
Debut v Bury (h) 35.8.35, drawn 2-2
CAREER: Chester February 1932. Nantwich F.C. August 1933. Bolton Wanderers January 1934. Wrexham September 1934. **FOREST 6th June 1935.** Leicester City 14th November 1936. (Wartime guest player with Wrexham, Chester and Barnsley). Chester December 1945 to May 1946.
Eric Stubbs was without League experience when he joined Wrexham from Bolton Wanderers in September 1934. He made his debut in a 3-0 win against New Brighton, and the powerfully built wingman generally gave Third Division defences a lot of trouble, netting 10 goals in 28 League matches. He was signed by Forest as part of a double swoop into the transfer market in June 1935, Dan Edgar from Sunderland joining the Forest ranks two days later. Stubbs' six goals in 20 Division Two matches in his first season included a hat trick in a 4-1 away win at Bradford Park Avenue on 1st February 1936. Early in the following season he was transferred to Leicester City and became a key element in the Foxes' Second Division championship season. Before World War Two caused League football to be abandoned, Stubbs completed 78 League and Cup appearances and scored 15 goals. He subsequently worked as a fruit farmer in Cheshire.
Appearances: FL: 22 apps 6 gls FAC: 1 app 0 gls
Total: 23 apps 6 gls
Honours: (Leicester City) FL Division Two champions 1937

STURTON, Thomas William
Left half-back
Born: Nuncargate, Notts. 25th September 1908
Died: Carlton, Notts. 8th September 1966, age 57
Debut v Leeds United (h) 21.1.28, drawn 2-2
CAREER: FOREST amateur 31st March, professional 15th October 1927. Colwick Loco. (Notts.) September 1932. Lawrence Athletic (Netherfield) August 1933.
In the season that local teenager Tom Sturton made his solitary Division Two appearance,

Forest's form went rapidly downhill from mid term. Having commenced with wins by 7-0 (against Fulham) and 7-2 (against South Shields) in the first two home matches, excellent home form suggested that a promotion push was a real possibility. At the turn of the year, a 4-3 win at South Shields was followed by a slump in form, culminating in a final nine-match winless run that left the side in a respectable, but disappointing, tenth position in the table. Tom Sturton was employed as a timber porter in a cabinet works.
Appearances: FL: 1 app 0 gls Total: 1 app 0 gls

SUDDICK, James
Outside-right 5' 9" 12st 0lbs
Born: Middlesbrough, 1st February 1878
Died: Middlesbrough, 14th January 1967
Debut v Everton (h) 1.10.98, drawn 0-0
CAREER: South Bank Juniors. Middlesbrough. Aston Villa 31st May 1897. **FOREST 26th September 1898**. Thornaby F.C. 14th January 1901. Middlesbrough April 1904. Thornaby F.C.
A young reserve winger signed from Aston Villa who was expected to make a useful forward, given the likelihood of more opportunities with the Forest. However, a report of his Forest debut against Everton stated: "Most interest surrounded the first appearance of Suddick, who did not come up to expectations. With a splendid physique, a good turn of speed, and youth on his side, he ought to make a useful forward. Although he displayed clever footwork occasionally, his work as a whole lacked the finish and resource of the school in which he has been trained." Subsequently tried at inside-right and on the right wing, he featured little in the second half of the campaign and was transfer listed at the end of the season. A very brief stay with Middlesbrough featured just one appearance, in which he scored in a 1-3 defeat at Sunderland in January 1904.
Appearances: 14 apps 4 gls Total: 14 apps 4 gls

SUGDEN, Sydney Herbert
Centre-forward
Born: Battersea, London, 30th October 1880
Died: Brompton Hospital, Chelsea, 17th December 1930
Debut v Derby County (a) 17.1.03, won 1-0
CAREER: Ilford F.C. West Ham United October 1902. **FOREST 10th January 1903**. Queen's Park Rangers August 1905. Brentford July 1908. Southend United 1910.
Forest' leading scorer in his first full season at the City Ground, Syd Sugden led the attack in 27 Division One matches and scored 13 goals. In the following season he was moved onto the right wing to accommodate newly signed Tom Niblo, the Aston Villa and England centre-forward. The move was hardly a success, as Sugden made only

13 appearances during the season and failed to score, while Niblo disappointed as a marksman, netting just six goals in 29 matches. Sugden returned to Southern League football, his best spell coming with Queen's Park Rangers, for whom he scored 21 goals in 65 League appearances.
Appearances: FL: 47 apps 15 gls FAC: 1 app 0 gls
Total: 48 apps 15 gls

SURTEES, John 'Jack'

Inside-forward
5' 11" 11st 7lbs
Born: Willington-on-Tyne, 1st July 1911
Died: Percy Main, 16th July 1992
Debut v Newcastle United (h) 24.10.36, lost 0-2
CAREER: Willington Juniors. Percy Main Amateurs F.C.
Middlesbrough March 1930. Portsmouth June 1932. Bournemouth & Boscombe Athletic July 1933. Northampton Town July 1934. Sheffield Wednesday November 1934. **FOREST 24th October 1936 to September 1939, fee £2,500.** (Wartime guest player with York City, Darlington, Newcastle United, Gateshead and Crystal Palace.) Darlington manager 1943. Sheffield Wednesday scout November 1948.
Jack Surtees was rejected in turn by four Football League clubs and had decided to abandon the idea of a career in football, and try his luck in America. He had actually obtained his passport when his brother, Albert, who used to play for Aston Villa when Billy Walker was a player there, wrote to the Sheffield Wednesday manager asking him to give his brother one last chance. After playing a few games on trial for the Reserves, he was handed his League debut against Birmingham on Christmas Day 1934. He never lost his place afterwards and ended the season with a Cup winner's medal. He was not too comfortable at the City Ground after leaving Sheffield Wednesday. The crowd, or at a least a misguided section, barracked him at the early period of his first season. Surtees had the last laugh, however, and at the close there was no more popular player on the field. The critics had become admirers. Notable for his strength and untiring work in both attack and defence he was once described as "the biggest-hearted player in the team."
Appearances: FL: 93 apps 23 gls FAC: 3 apps 0 gls
Total: 96 apps 23 gls
Honours: (Sheffield Wednesday) FA Cup winners 1935

TAYLOR, Joseph

Centre-forward
5' 11½" 11st 7lbs
Born: Nottingham,
13th April 1905
Debut v Wolverhampton
Wanderers (a) 8.2.26, lost
0-4
CAREER: Lenton United.
**FOREST 13th October
1925.** Ilkeston United July
1927. Blackpool May 1928. Oldham Athletic May
1929. Notts County (trial) January 1932. Hurst F.C.
March 1932. Ramsgate Press Wanderers February
1934. Yeovil & Petters United June 1934. Nuneaton
Town July 1935. Nottingham L.M.S. reinstated
amateur September 1936.
*Joe Taylor had only two first team outings for
Forest despite scoring 30 goals for the Reserves in
season 1926-27. When released he spent a season
with Ilkeston United, for whom he scored 43 goals.
In a season with Blackpool he scored once in four
matches, but with Oldham Athletic he attained
some measure of success in late season 1929-30.
His six goals in ten Division Two outings included
a hat trick in a 6-1 win against Bradford City in
March 1930. In the same season he played before
the all-time record appearance at Boundary Park,
when 46,471 spectators witnessed the fourth round
FA Cup-tie won 4-3 by Sheffield Wednesday.*
Appearances: 2 apps 0 gls Total: 2 apps 0 gls

TEBBETT, Thomas
Goalkeeper
Born: Linton Heath, Derbyshire, 21st January 1873
Died: Mansfield, 9th September 1945
Debut v Derby County (h) 3.10.95, lost 2-5
CAREER: Langley Mill Rangers. **FOREST 17th
June 1895.** Heanor Town 18th August 1896.
Langley Mill Rangers 4th September 1897. Bolsover
Colliery 1st July 1898.
*Although goalkeeper Tom Tebbett's height and
weight were not recorded, it seemed likely that he
was a hefty young man. The' Notts. Guardian'
reporting in August 1895: "He is looked upon as a
prototype of Foulke of Sheffield United." (At 6'2½"
'Fatty' Foulke was exceptionally tall by the
standards of the day and his weight ballooned to
over 19st during the course of his colourful career.)
Tebbett was just one of eight local players
recruited for reserve ranks in the summer of 1895.
In September, Forest played a friendly match at
Langley Mill Rangers in connection with the
transfer of their goalkeeper. Unfortunately for the
home side the match was entirely spoilt by a very
heavy rainstorm.*
Appearances: FL: 1 app 0 gls Total: 1 app 0 gls

THOMPSON, Frederick
Wing half-back
Born: Sheffield, 1870
Debut v Stoke (h) 10.9.92, lost 3-4
CAREER: Sheffield Hastings. Sheffield
Wednesday July 1890. Lincoln City October 1890.
Sheffield Wednesday July 1890. **FOREST August
1891, registered for FL matches 31st July
1892 to May 1893.**
*Fred Thompson played a full part in Forest's
Football Alliance championship, appearing in 16 of
the 22 League matches contested. He had made all
but one of his appearances at left half-back, but
when Forest commenced operations as a Football
League club in the following term, it was Peter
McCracken, a new signing from Sunderland
Albion, who dominated the position restricting
Thompson to a single outing.*
Appearances: FL: 1 app 0 gls Total: 1 app 0 gls
Honours: **(FOREST)** Football Alliance champions
1892.

THOMPSON, Norman

Inside-left
5' 8½" 11st 6lbs
Born: Forest Hall,
Newcastle-on-Tyne, 5th
September 1900
Died: Tavistock, Devon,
December 1989
Debut v Stoke City (h)
28.4.28, lost 0-2
CAREER: Denton Burn.
Newcastle United
November 1920. Seaton Delaval. Backworth
United. South Shields March 1923. Middlesbrough
June 1925, fee £1,500 Barnsley June 1926, fee
£500. West Stanley September 1927. **FOREST 5th
April 1928.** West Stanley September 1930.
Newcastle East End October 1932. Carlisle United
October 1932. West Stanley March 1933. Pretoria
Municipal (South Africa) March 1935.
*In two seasons with South Shields, Norman
Thompson scored seven goals in 43 League
matches. Middlesbrough paid a hefty fee for him
but gave him few opportunities (three goals in
eight matches). A season with Barnsley was
similarly disappointing (four appearances) but his
form with West Stanley, of the North-Eastern
League, brought him to Forest's attention after he
had scored 40 goals from inside-left and centre-
forward. He was unfortunate to sustain a knee
injury in 1928-29 that sidelined him from the end
of September until April, and although he was
reported to be fully recovered after surgery, he
played in only three first team matches in 1929-30,
his final season.*
Appearances: FL: 12 apps 3 gls Total: 12 apps 3 gls

THOMPSON, William Potter 'Bill'

Full-back 5' 9" 11st 8lbs
Born: Derby, 17th
September 1899
Died: Duffield, Derbyshire,
4th October 1959
Debut v Sunderland (h)
26.8.22, won 1-0
CAREER: Rolls Royce F.C.
**FOREST amateur 20th
August, professional
24th September 1920
(Re-signed 1st October
1931).** Burton Town August 1935.

A native of Derby, Bill Thompson was capped by England schoolboys against Wales and Scotland in 1914. He played for the Rolls Royce club, where he worked as a draughtsman during the First World War, and joined Forest in 1920. A finely built defender of considerable promise, he developed into splendid full-back, always cool, calm and resourceful, but with a biting tackle and, according to one correspondent, with a kick like a mule! He became a first team regular in 1923-24 and was appointed club captain in 1930. Alarm was caused when he refused to re-sign for the 1931-32 season owing to a dispute over a benefit. He went so far as to sign a form with Burton Town of the Birmingham League. They were ready to play him against Oswestry Town but were contacted by the Football League, who refused permission on the grounds that he was still on Forest's retained list. A matter of a few days later Forest announced that satisfactory terms had been arranged and Thompson had signed on again. He returned to the fold and continued to give some of the finest exhibitions in the rear line that he had ever produced in his many years of association with the club.
Appearances: FL: 364 apps 4 gls FAC: 26 apps 1 gl
Total: 390 apps 5 gls
Honours: England Schoolboy International, two caps 1914. FA Tour to South Africa 1929.

THORNHILL, J
Goalkeeper
Debut v Preston North End (a) 17.9.92, lost 0-1
CAREER: FOREST 25th August 1892.
One of three goalkeepers on the club's books in Forest's first season as a Football League club. Thornhill faced a difficult debut, as deputy for William Brown, but came through with great credit in the single goal defeat at Preston North End who, for the second season in a row, finished the season as runners-up to Sunderland for the championship. A 2-2 draw against Burnley on 10th December proved to be Thornhill's final outing at League level. A fortnight later, the introduction of
Dennis Allsop brought about a remarkable upturn, seven consecutive League victories ensuing.
Appearances: FL: 3 apps 0 gls Total: 3 apps 0 gls

THORNLEY, John Fearn
Centre half-back
Born: Coalville, July quarter 1875
Died: Basford, Notts. December 1956
Debut v Sheffield Wednesday (h) 22.1.98, won 1-0
CAREER: Hucknall St. John's 3rd June 1896.
FOREST 19th March 1897. Gainsborough Trinity
13th May 1899 to May 1902.
Coalville born miner John Thornley spent an unrewarding two years with the Forest as understudy to club captain and Scottish international, John McPherson. Along with inside-forward Arthur Radford, Thornley was transferred to Gainsborough Trinity in May 1899. Both found more opportunities in Second Division football, Thornley appearing in 88 League matches and Radford in 64.
Appearances: FL: 6 apps 0 gls Total: 6 apps 0 gls

TILFORD, Arthur
Left half-back 5' 10½" 11st 0lbs
Born: Ilkeston, 14th May 1903
Died: Ilkeston, 10th April 1993
Debut v Sunderland (h) 7.3.25, drawn 1-1
CAREER: Trowell Rectory. Trowell St. Helen's.
**FOREST amateur 29th February,
professional 9th May 1924.** Blackpool May 1926.
Coventry City May 1929. Fulham February 1932, fee
£750. Southampton (loan) February 1933. Walsall
June 1934. Ilkeston F.C. November 1935.
An injury sustained by Forest's captain, Bob Wallace, provided Arthur Tilford with his only real opportunity of first team football when he appeared at left half-back in six of the final seven matches of the 1925-26 season. Moving on to Blackpool, along with reserve outside-right Joe Ashworth, Tilford made the most of extended opportunities, after been switched to left full-back by manager Major Frank Buckley. He passed the landmark of 100 League appearances in Coventry's colours, and followed his manager James McIntyre to Fulham, for whom he made 14 appearances in their Third Division South championship season. A brief loan spell with Southampton was followed by a final season in League football with Walsall. His 30 appearances brought his career total to 195 League matches for seven clubs. Later the owner of a fish and chip shop, Arthur was within weeks of his 90th birthday when he died in his hometown of Ilkeston.
Appearances: FL: 8 apps 0 gls Total: 8 apps 0 gls
Honours: (Fulham) FL Division Three South champions 1932

TIMMINS, Samuel

Half-back 5' 8" 11st 0lbs
Born: Dudley, 4th May 1879
Died: Dudley, January quarter 1955
Debut v West Bromwich Albion (a) 13.3.01, lost 2-3
CAREER: Dudley Sports. Burnt Tree F.C. Dudley Town May 1899. Walsall 13th June 1899. **FOREST 5th March 1901.** West Bromwich Albion August 1906 to May 1911, fee £50.

Once described as the versatile man of the side, Sam Timmins spent five years with the Forest after his excellent form with Walsall saw him displace the celebrated Welsh international Caeser Jenkins in the Saddlers' half-back line. Some early reservations about his fitness levels were evident as the 'Nottingham Evening Post' reported: "He can play a good game up to half time, but seems unable to keep the pace up for the full 90 minutes." Obviously his stamina improved as he completed well in excess of a century of appearances for the Forest, before adding a further 111 matches in West Bromwich Albion's colours. His overall record of League appearances for his three clubs being 266 matches and eight goals.
Appearances: FL: 125 apps 5 gls FAC: 12 apps 0 gls
Total: 137 apps 5 gls

TINSLEY, Walter Edward

Inside-forward
5' 9½" 11st 7lbs
Born: Ironville, Derbyshire, 10th June 1891
Died: Ripley, Derbyshire, 7th March 1966
Debut v Crystal Palace (a) 27.8.21, lost 1-4 (scored)
CAREER: Ironville F.C. Alfreton Town. Sutton Town. Sunderland January 1912. Middlesbrough December 1913. (Wartime guest with Forest September 1915). **FOREST 25th May 1921.** Reading May 1924. Heanor Town October 1927.
Introduced to the senior game by Sunderland, but Walter Tinsley made his name with Middlesbrough, scoring 46 goals in 86 League outings. He was less prolific with Forest, but his head for strategy, and the ability to apply it, effectively kept Forest's attack on the move. He had earlier assisted Forest during the war, and made a great left wing with Harry Martin, a former playing colleague at Sunderland. He was approaching the veteran stage when he joined

Reading, but was a vital figure in their 1925-26 promotion season. His career aggregate figures where 212 League appearances and 75 goals.
Appearances: FL: 61 apps 13 gls FAC: 3 apps 0 gls
Total: 64 apps 13 gls
Honours: **(FOREST)** FL Division 2 champions 1922. (Reading) FL Division 3 South champions 1926.

TODD, Allan Calderwood McKinstrey

Goalkeeper
5' 11" 121st 3lbs
Born: Orwell Kinross, Fife, 5th October 1910
Died: Darlington, 8th December 1975
Debut v Swansea Town (h) 2.10.37, won 2-1
CAREER: Wellesley F.C. Leith Athletic September 1931. Cowdenbeath (trial). Port Vale October 1932. **FOREST 12th June 1937, in exchange for Arthur Masters.** Darlington January 1939.
An experienced Scottish goalkeeper who joined Port Vale from Leith Athletic and completed 78 League appearances before joining the Forest in a player exchange deal that took Arthur Masters to the Potteries. Todd's signing followed the retirement of goalkeeper Arthur Dexter after 14 seasons as a professional at the City Ground. Percy Ashton had provided stiff competition during the latter seasons of Dexter's tenure, and he held the first team jersey following Todd's arrival, although the newcomer created a favourable impression when called upon to deputise. World War Two effectively ended Todd's senior career after he had played for Darlington in the first three matches of the aborted season 1939-40.
Appearances: FL: 17 apps 0 gls FAC: 4 apps 0 gls
Total: 21 apps 0 gls

TOWNSEND, Alfred Harold

Outside-left
5' 9½" 10st 10lbs
Born: Newtown, Montgomeryshire, 25th August 1902
Died: Welshpool, 29th November 1980
Debut v Notts County (a) 18.9.26, won 2-1
CAREER: Montgomeryshire County amateur. Cardiff City. **FOREST 29th April 1926.** Stockport County June 1928, Connah's Quay & Shotton July 1929. Oswestry Town January 1930.
Alf Townsend made a name for himself as an amateur outside-left who represented his county in

all matches for three years. In consequence, he attracted a lot of attention from professional clubs, eventually joining Cardiff City. He had yet to make his Football League debut when he joined Forest and it was rather ironic that his best spell of first team football came in the late stages of his final season when he scored three goals in seven matches, his first senior goals coming within the space of three days. Two in a 5-3 home win against Reading being followed by one in the 2-2 draw against Chelsea. Moving on to Stockport County, Townsend lost his place in the side after appearing in the first seven League matches, in what proved to be a successful but ultimately frustrating season for his team who finished as runners-up by one point for the Third Division North title when only the champions (Bradford City) were promoted to Division Two.

Appearances: FL: 15 apps 4 gls Total: 15 apps 4 gls

TRIM, Reginald Frederick D.F.C.

Full-back
5' 9" 11st 2lbs
Born: Portsmouth,
1st October 1913
Died: Bournemouth,
1st June 1997
Debut v Sheffield United (a)
28.8.37, lost 1-2
CAREER: Winton &
Moordown School.
Bournemouth Schoolboys.
Bournemouth Postal Workers F.C. Winton & Moordown F.C. Bournemouth & Boscombe Athletic amateur July 1929, professional April 1931. Arsenal April 1933, fee £1,000. **FOREST 28th July 1937.** (Wartime guest player with Derby County, Notts County, Bournemouth & Boscombe Athletic.) Swindon Town 24th July to November 1946. Coaching appointments in Lisbon November 1946 and Sweden November 1947. Leyton Orient trainer March 1948-49.

Reggie Trim captained England Schoolboys versus Scotland in 1928, and worked as a Post Office messenger on leaving school. He then signed for his hometown club, and his brilliant displays earned him his move to Arsenal. He remained with the Gunners for four years, and only the brilliance of their backs Male and Hapgood kept him out of the first team. He cost Forest a hefty fee after prolonged negotiations, but initially the Nottingham air did not seem to suit him and he asked for a transfer on health reasons. Forest, however, were not prepared to part with him, and happily Trim consented to stay. Once settled, he was considered one of the best full-backs in the Second Division, and one of the speediest. When not playing, he was involved in flying as a member of the Air Defence Corps. As an RAF pilot he rose to the rank of squadron leader and was decorated with the DFC. In 1943, he was reported to be flying

fighter planes after many bombing sorties over the continent.

Appearances: FL: 70 apps 0 gls FAC: 2 apps 0 gls
Total: 72 apps 0 gls
Honours: England Schoolboy International v Scotland and Wales in 1928.

TURNER, Alfred Docwra

Outside-right
Born: Islington, London,
25th June 1879
Died: Probus, Cornwall,
2nd October 1926
Debut v Stoke (a) 14.2.03, lost 2-3
CAREER: Old Rossalians. West Herts April 1896. Crouch End Vampires. Watford amateur February 1899. Upton Park F.C. **FOREST amateur 2nd December 1902. Bristol City 25th January 1905.**

A.D. Turner was a talented amateur who represented London, Middlesex and Essex, and was only 16 years old when he played for Watford in three friendly matches. Just prior to leaving to South Africa with the Herts Company of the Imperial Yeomanry, he appeared in a further four Southern League matches, scoring one goal. Praised for his infectious energy and clever play on his Forest debut, he helped to solve a problem position on the right wing in the closing months of the 1902-03 campaign. His final Football League outing was a single appearance for Bristol City in a 1-2 defeat at Leicester Fosse on 11th February 1905.

Appearances: FL: 9 apps 0 gls Total: 9 apps 0 gls
Honours: Represented London, Middlesex and Essex as an amateur.

TURNER, Thomas

Left half-back
5' 10" 11st 7lbs
Born: Whittle-le-Woods, Lancs.
2nd April 1906
Died: Whittle-le-Woods, Lancs.
April quarter 1980
Debut v Blackpool (a) 2.2.29,
drawn 2-2
CAREER: Whittle-le-Woods.
Burscough Rangers 1925.
Chorley April 1926. **FOREST 31st March 1927.** Chorley June 1929. Lytham F.C. August 1930 Fleetwood August 1933.

One of two players signed in March 1927 from Chorley, leaders of the Lancashire Combination, who at that point had lost only three matches. Tom Turner accompanied Albert Harrison to the City Ground, but while Harrison was quickly established in the heart of Forest's defence, Turner failed to dislodge the full-back pairing of Thompson and Barratt and returned to Chorley and Lancashire Combination football.

Appearances: FL: 1 app 0 gls Total: 1 app 0 gls

VASEY, Robert Henry 'Bob'

Wing half-back
5' 8" 11st olbs
Born: Tanfield, County Durham,16th December 1907
Died: Dipton, County Durham, 4th December 1979
Debut v Tottenham Hotspur (h) 29.8.32, won 3-1
CAREER: Annfield Plain. Consett F.C. **FOREST amateur 1st January, professional 7th January 1932**. Notts County June 1936. Brighton & Hove Albion August 1938. (Wartime guest player with Chester March 1942).

Described as "quiet but effective" Bob Vasey remained at the City Ground for four seasons without mounting a serious challenge for a regular place in the League side. On crossing the Trent to join Notts County, his fitness levels were questioned, as the 'Football Post' commented in October 1936: "What a pity it is that Vasey is not stronger physically! He has put up some excellent first-half performances, but rarely is able to last out a game at top speed." That said, he had done enough in the Magpies' 1-0 win at Brighton & Hove Albion, and following his release, he moved to the Goldstone Ground. The outbreak of the Second World War effectively brought his senior career to an end, after he had made 15 League appearances in the 1938-39 season.
Appearances: FL: 23 apps 0 gls Total: 23 apps 0 gls

VAUGHAN, William

Outside-left 5' 7" 10st 8lbs
Born: *Circa* 1887 (Said to be aged 23 in 1910)
Debut v Woolwich Arsenal (h) 2.3.10, drawn 1-1
CAREER: Portmadog F.C. Whitchurch F.C. 16th May 1906. **FOREST 2nd March to May 1910.**
One of three players signed from Whitchurch F.C. – the others were Edward Thomason and Arthur Dean – William Vaughan was the only one of the trio to make a Football League appearance but his final three outings in April 1910 were best forgotten as Forest suffered successive defeats of 3-7 at Liverpool, 0-6 at home to Sheffield Wednesday and 0-4 at Bristol City.
Appearances: FL: 6 apps 0 gls Total: 6 apps 0 gls
Honours: (Portmadog) Welsh Amateur Cup finalists 1906

VENTERS, John Cook

Inside-right 5' 8" 11st olbs
Born: Cowdenbeath, 22nd August 1910
Died: Cowdenbeath, 28th April 1978
Debut v West Bromwich Albion (h) 12.10.29, lost 0-2
CAREER: Lochore Thistle. Dunnikier Juniors. Preston North End August 1927. **FOREST 20th June 1928**. Thames F.C. September 1930. Morton January 1931. Young Boys (Berne) October 1931.

Speedy inside forward John Venters had played in only three matches for Dunniker Juniors when he was signed by Preston North End, where he spent a season in the Central League side. Able to play at inside-right or left, he nevertheless made only one first team appearance in two seasons at the City Ground. He was just twenty years of age when he joined Thames, and again appeared only once before returning to Scotland to join Morton, for whom he appeared in six Scottish League matches without scoring. He was last traced when he moved abroad in attempts to give his football career a much- needed boost. His younger brother, Alexander, was also an inside-forward. He was capped three times by Scotland, played twice in Scottish wartime internationals, and made six appearances for the Scottish League. He won four Scottish League championships with the Rangers, and was a Scottish Cup winner with them in 1935 and 1936.
Appearances: FL: 1 app 0 gls Total: 1 app 0 gls

WADSWORTH, Harold

Winger 5' 6" 10st 8lbs
Born: Bootle, 1st October 1898
Died: Chesterfield, 2nd November 1975
Debut v Port Vale (a) 27.8.27, drawn 2-2 (scored one)
CAREER: Bootle St. Matthew's. Tranmere Rovers 1914. (Wartime guest player with Everton and Liverpool.) Liverpool August 1918. Leicester City June 1924. **FOREST 30th April 1927**. Millwall June 1928. Oswestry Town September 1932. Canterbury Waverley December 1932. Cray Wanderers November 1934.
Forest were much better in attack than defence in season 1927-28 when they opened the campaign by scoring 18 goals in the first three Division Two fixtures. Newly signed Harold Wadsworth scored on his debut and provided much of the ammunition for his inside partners. In fact, all five of Forest's

most regular forward players scored 10 or more goals during the season. A provider rather than a goal scorer on his own account, with a career total of 28 League goals in 252 matches, his goal ratio certainly peaked during his season at the City Ground. Wadsworth was ever-present on Leicester City's left wing throughout their 1925 Division Two championship win, and subsequently gave excellent service to Millwall in Division Two, following their Third Division South championship win in 1927-28. Harold had commenced, alongside his elder brother Walter, with Liverpool during the final season of football played under wartime conditions. Walter appeared in over two hundred League matches for the Reds, winning League championship medals in 1922 and 1923.
Appearances: FL: 30 apps 9 gls FAC: 5 apps 1 gl
Total: 35 apps 10 gls
Honours: (Leicester City) FL Division Two champions 1925

WAGSTAFF, John George
Goalkeeper
Born: Nottingham, 27th September 1899
Died: Nottingham, 1st December 1932
Debut v South Shields (a) 15.11.19, lost 2-5
CAREER: Arnold St. Mary's. **FOREST amateur 18th September 1919**. Arnold St. Mary's.
An injury to Joe Johnson at South Shields on 8th November, led to the introduction of Wagstaff, the young former Arnold St Mary's goalkeeper, who endured a torrid debut at Horsley Hill. The home side dominated throughout to record their best League victory at that point. Forest directors moved swiftly to provide extra cover by signing Joe Orme, the former Watford and Millwall goalkeeper, who had commenced the season with Ilkeston United. John Wagstaff was then allowed to return to assist Arnold St Mary's.
Appearances: FL: 1 app 0 gls Total: 1 app 0 gls

WALKER, Duncan Campbell 'Dunky'

Centre-forward
5' 9" 11st 7lbs
Born: Alloa, 12th September 1902
Died: Alloa, 9th September 1981
Debut v Everton (a) 25.8.24, lost 1-2
CAREER: Cowie Wanderers. Kilsyth Wanderers. Army football. Dumbarton F.C. March 1919. Bo'ness (loan) cs 1919. St. Mirren April 1921.
FOREST 28th May 1923, fee £2,500. Bo'ness F.C. July 1927. Larkhall Thistle. Thornbridge Waverley.
Scottish centre-forward Duncan Walker, showed while North of the Tweed that he could score goals and plenty of them. He joined St. Mirren from

Dumbarton at the close of 1920-21 season. He had done little in the scoring line for Dumbarton, but as soon as he arrived at the Paisley club he began to get goals, and continued doing so. In the course of 1921-22 he scored 45 goals in 38 League matches, and 11 in five Scottish Cup-ties, 56 in all, this being a record for a Scottish player at that time. In Scottish League games in 1922-23 he was less prolific but still scored 21 goals. Over medium height, Walker was powerfully built, and his pace in going through with the ball was always a threat. He was equally sure in picking up a pass either on the ground or in the air, and used his head with uncommon skill. He had a less profitable time in his first season in English football, but was still easily the top scorer for Forest, and with more suitable support it was felt that he would have largely increased his total of 17, among which were some very spectacular efforts. Sadly, he was seriously injured in the first minute of the opening day of season 1925-26 against Darlington at the Feethams, and did not reappear until Christmas Day but then completed only nine matches. He was transferred to Bo'ness in July 1927, and in later years became president of the club.
Appearances: FL: 82 apps 29 gls FAC: 6 apps 4 gls
Total: 88 apps 33 gls

WALKER, Thomas Tichbourne
Inside-left
Born: Radford, January quarter 1875
Died: Nottingham, January quarter 1929, age 54
Debut v Wolverhampton Wanderers (h) 13.4.95, lost 0-2
CAREER: FOREST 25th October 1894-96
Tom Walker's form in United Counties League matches (five goals in three matches, including a hat trick at Sheffield United) ensured that he was offered another contract for the new season, but he remained a reserve team player throughout, mustering just four League appearances in three seasons.
Appearances: FL: 4 apps 0 gls Total: 4 apps 0 gls

WALKER, Walter Wallis
Inside-left
Born: Nottingham, 1st July 1890
Died: Nottingham, October quarter 1943, age 53
Debut v Glossop (h) 30.3.12, lost 0-1
CAREER: FOREST amateur 30th March 1912.
As deputy for the injured Frank Saunders for the visit of Glossop to the City Ground, Walter Walker failed to shine in a disappointing display by the Reds. Although Glossop were struggling at the wrong end of Division Two, a goal from ex-Derby County forward Jim Moore gave Glossop the points and their first away victory of the season. Forest, meantime, were two games into a losing streak that saw them secure just one point from their final eight matches.
Appearances: FL: 1 app 0 gls Total: 1 app 0 gls

WALL, Tom Henry
Goalkeeper   6' 0"   12st 0lbs
Born: Nottingham, 29th May 1909
Died: Nottingham, 8th June 1989
Debut v Notts County (a) 29.9.34, won 5-3
CAREER: Ripley Town. Clifton Colliery. Notts County amateur May 1932. Tottenham Hotspur June 1933. **FOREST amateur trial 28th September to 25th October 1934**. Ripley Town September 1935.
Tom Wall was a reserve goalkeeper whose involvement in League football amounted to just four matches. Three appearances were made for Notts County, and one opposed to them on his Forest debut. He did not appear at senior level for Tottenham Hotspur, and his one outing for the Forest was made during a trial period when he conceded three goals but finished on the winning side in a 5-3 victory. His lack of success at senior level was revealed in the 'Football Post' who, in April 1933 stated: "Wall is good in anticipation and shot stopping, but his goal kicking and general clearing is a big weakness."
Appearances: FL: 1 app 0 gls Total: 1 app 0 gls

WALLACE, Robert Stewart 'Bob'

Left half-back
5' 8½"   11st 10lbs
Born: Greenock, 20th January 1893
Died: Nottingham, 16th October 1970
Debut v Everton (a) 25.8.23, lost 1-2
CAREER: Belleville F.C. Abercorn F.C. Regent Star F.C. Linfield January 1914. **FOREST 22nd June 1923**.
Burton Town August 1931. Raleigh Athletic December 1932 to 1937.
Although playing for an Irish club, Robert Wallace was a native of Greenock, Linfield being his only club of note after he left the army in March 1919. For two and a half years prior to joining Forest he captained Linfield and had played in every representative match for the past two seasons – five matches in all. He had also captained the Irish League against the Football League during the last two seasons. A polished and resourceful player, he was able to play on either flank in the middle line, but was seen more regularly on the left, from which position he captained the team. He had completed 113 consecutive appearances for Forest before he sustained an injury in the FA Cup-tie against Bradford City on 6th January 1926. Certainly one of Forest's most loyal servants, the 'Post Football Guide' for 1930-31 had this to say about him: "One of the evergreens is Robert, and his seeming youth is a perpetual as his smile."
Appearances: FL: 248 apps 2 gls FAC: 21 apps 0 gls Total: 269 apps 2 gls

Honours: Irish League representative, five apps. 1921-23. (Linfield) Irish Cup winners 1922 and 1923. City Cup winners 1922.

WALLBANKS, Frederick

Left full-back
5' 10"   11st 0lbs
Born: Platt Bridge, Wigan,
14th May 1908
Died: Consett, April 1938
Debut v Fulham (h) 11.9.35, drawn 1-1
CAREER: Crook Town. Consett F.C. Annfield Plain July 1928. Goole Town. Bury (trial) November, professional December 1928, fee £75.
Chesterfield August 1930. Scarborough July 1931. Bradford City May 1932. West Ham United December 1934. **FOREST 7th May 1935**. Northampton Town July 1936. Consett F.C. June 1937.
Hailing from a footballing family, Fred Wallbanks had brothers James and John who both appeared in much League football in the interwar period while Harry and Horace appeared in the early post war years. Fred was, in terms of League action, the least successful of the brothers, as he recorded very modest figures of 29 League matches and three goals in a career that spanned six Football League clubs. His hobbies included golf, tennis and swimming.
Appearances: FL: 8 apps 0 gls Total: 8 apps 0 gls

WAPLINGTON, Samuel
Right half-back
Born: Basford, Notts. 13th April 1896
Died: Basford, Notts. December 1976, age 80
Debut v Port Vale (a) 31.1.20, lost 1-4
CAREER: FOREST amateur 4th December 1919 to May 1921
One appearance at Port Vale as deputy for Fred 'Sticker' Banks, who was unfit, was the extent of Sam Waplington's first team involvement in a season and a half at the City Ground. It is thought that he was a player with North Street, in the Notts Alliance League, prior to joining Forest an amateur forms. His occupation, per Census returns, was that of a colliery hewer.
Appearances: FL: 1 app 0 gls Total: 1 app 0 gls

WARREN, Frederick
Centre half-back   5' 11½"   12st 6lbs
Born: Newhall, October quarter 1878
Died: Basford, Notts. July quarter 1964
Debut v Everton (a) 25.10.02, drawn 1-1 (scored)
CAREER: Derby Hills Ivanhoe. **FOREST 16th November 1901.** Alfreton Town 13th April 1904.
FOREST 27th September 1905.
Fred Warren spent three seasons with Derby Hills Ivanhoe, initially as a centre-forward, later switching to centre-half-back. In terms of physical presence alone he was a dominant figure, and two successful trials with Forest Reserves within the space of a week led to his immediate engagement. A cheque for an undisclosed amount was forwarded to Derby Hills Ivanhoe for the loss of their centre-half. The club received the donation with gratitude, as they ruefully admitted that they had generally had their players 'poached' without compensation. Despite a scoring debut at Everton, it was not until season 1903-04 that Warren became established, making 19 Division One appearances. Returning to the City Ground after a spell away with Alfreton Town, he did not add to his total of League appearances.
Appearances: FL: 25 apps 2 gls FAC: 2 apps 0 gls
Total: 27 apps 2 gls

WEST, Enoch James 'Knocker'

Inside/Centre-forward
5' 8"   12st 6lbs
Born: Hucknall Torkard, Notts. 31st March 1886
Died: Salford, Manchester, 14th September 1965
Debut v Bury (h) 16.9.05, won 3-2
CAREER: Linby. Sheffield United November 1903. Hucknall Constitutionals
1904. **FOREST 8th June 1905.** Manchester United June 1910, suspended sine-die April 1916.
Once described as 'The Hucknall Torkard nugget', former collier Enoch 'Knocker' West was a powerfully built centre-forward or outside-left of rare penetrative ability and a magnificent sharpshooter. He scored 14 League goals in 33 matches to assist Forest to the championship of Division Two in 1906-07, and had his best season in 1907-08 with 26 goals in 35 Division One matches. The next highest scorer managed just 10 goals, while West scored four against Sunderland and hat tricks against Chelsea and Blackburn Rovers. In April 1909 he was one of three Forest forwards who all scored hat tricks against Leicester Fosse in a 12-0 win which remains the
club's record win in League football. After scoring exactly 100 League and Cup goals for Forest, he was signed by Manchester United to replace Jimmy Turnbull as leader of United's attack. He scored on his debut and finished leading goal scorer with 19 League goals as United carried off their second championship title. His goalscoring touch deserted him in his final two seasons at Old Trafford and during 1914-15, when United battled to avoid relegation for the First Division, his career ended in disgrace. Two days prior to Christmas in 1915 the FA suspended him for his part in the 'fixing' of the 2nd April 1915 fixture against Liverpool (won 2-0 by United). Eight players were all suspended but 'Knocker' West's sentence was draconian in its extremity, as he was banned for life, and this was not lifted until December 1945, all of 30 years later.
Appearances: FL: 169 apps 93 gls FAC: 15 apps 7 gls
Total: 183 apps 100 gls
Honours: FL representative, two apps. (**FOREST**)
FL Division 2 champions 1907. (Manchester United) FL Division 1 champions 1911.

WHITCHURCH, Herbert

Centre/Inside-forward
5' 7½"   10st 6lbs
Born: Ilkeston, 23rd March 1886
Died: Derby, July quarter 1973
Debut v Blackburn Rovers (a) 2.12.05, drawn 1-1
CAREER: Notts County. **FOREST 28th January 1905.** Ilkeston Town May 1910.
The Forest club were fined two guineas following a meeting of the Midland Committee that had been called to consider a complaint from Notts County, who accused the Reds of inducing the player to leave his club. The player was Herbert Whitchurch who had played in a match for Notts County Reserves, and the Magpies had been keen to keep him, but the transfer was allowed to stand. The young local centre-forward was described as 'dashing' and despite his lack of experience was a prolific scorer in Midland League fixtures. Without ever establishing himself in the League side, he was regarded as one of the best Forest reserves over a lengthy period, always ready when wanted and giving excellent displays in almost any position in the forward line.
Appearances: FL: 24 apps 8 gls FAC: 4 apps 0 gls
Total: 32 apps 8 gls

WHITE, John William
Right full-back
Debut v Sheffield Wednesday (h) 9.11.01, drawn 1-1
CAREER: FOREST April 1901. New Brompton
May 1903.
*After forming a new full-back pairing with
McCurdy on his debut against Sheffield
Wednesday, John White was reintroduced in the
following month as partner to Jimmy Iremonger.
Three successive victories, and no goals conceded,
saw the partnership retained for the remainder of
the season. However, the signing of Charlie Craig
from West Ham United in the close season saw
White cast in the role of understudy, and after just
three League appearances in 1902-03 he moved
South to join New Brompton, where he teamed up
again with James Stevenson, the former Forest
inside-forward.*
Appearances: FL: 24 apps 0 gls FAC: 4 apps 0 gls
Total: 28 apps 0 gls

WILLIAMS, John Lewis James 'Jack'
Centre-forward
Born: Rhayader, 15th January 1890
Died: Mold, 22nd October 1969
Debut v Huddersfield Town (h) 16.3.12, won 3-0
(scored one)
**CAREER: Builth Wells FC. FOREST amateur
15th March 1912.** Tottenham Hotspur cs 1912.
Swansea Town September 1913. Army football.
Swansea Town December 1919. Mold Town June
1925.
*Amateur centre-forward Jack Williams scored on
his Forest debut against Huddersfield Town, but
made only four first team appearances in his brief
stay with the Forest. He moved on to Tottenham
Hotspur without adding to his total of League
appearances, but on joining Swansea Town his
career finally took off. Used either at left or right
half-back, he assisted the Swans at either side of
World War One, appearing in 29 Southern League
matches and 85 Football League fixtures, in which
he scored four goals.*
Appearances: FL: 4 apps 1 gl Total: 4 apps 1 gl

WOLFE, George

Centre half-back
5' 11" 12st 0lbs
Born: Northfleet, Kent, 18th
September 1881
Died: Northfleet, Kent, October
quarter 1958
Debut v Wolverhampton
Wanderers (h) 2.9.05, won 3-1
CAREER: Northfleet August
1897. Folkestone November
1898. Woolwich Arsenal March
1900. Swindon Town 18th May 1903. **FOREST 9th
May 1905.** Folkestone November 1911.
*In three seasons with Woolwich Arsenal, George
Wolfe captained their reserve team but made only*

*five first team appearances. He found more
opportunities on moving to Swindon Town,
appearing in 50 League and Cup matches. He
arrived at the City Ground with the reputation of
being a sure tackler, accurate in passing and
having few superiors in the Southern League. Said
to be quiet and unobtrusive, both on the field and
off, he was at his best on heavy grounds. He
arrived at the close of the relegation season 1905-
06, but his form in the second half of the following
season had much to do with Forest's recovery and
elevation back into the First Division. The top
flight stay ended with a whimper, only one point
being taken from the final 13 matches of season
1910-11 at which point 13 players, including
George Wolfe, were not re-engaged. Returning
south, he joined Folkestone and worked for the
London Passenger Board at Orpington.*
Appearances: FL: 128 apps 1 gl FAC: 10 apps 0 gls
Total: 138 apps 1 gl
Honours: **(FOREST)** FL Division 2 champions
1907

WOOD, Alexander 'Sandy'

Full-back
5' 9" 11st 7lbs
Born: Lochgelly, Fife,
12th June 1907
Died: Porter, Indiana,
U.S.A. 20th July 1987
Debut v Burnley (a)
29.8.36, lost 0-3
CAREER: Emerson
High School (Indiana).
Chicago Bricklayers
F.C. 1928. Holley
Carburetors F.C.
(Detroit) 1930.
Brooklyn Wanderers
November 1930. New York Wanderers 1931.
Leicester City amateur February 1933. **FOREST
14th May 1936, fee £750.** Colchester United July
1937. Chelmsford City cs 1938 to October 1939.
*Alex Wood was born at Lochgelly, and won a
Scottish cap against Wales as a schoolboy in May
1921 He than emigrated with his parents to
America, where he played football and was capped
on four occasions, including the three games that
took USA to the World Cup semi-final against
Uruguay in 1930. He returned to the UK in 1933,
and was signed as a professional by Leicester City.
However, the Board of Trade refused permission
for him play as a professional, but allowed him to
sign amateur forms. During his spell with the City
they reached the FA Cup semi-final for the first
time in their history. After appearing in 57 League
and Cup matches he was transferred to the Forest,
and appeared in half of the season's Division Two
matches, sharing first team duties with J.S.
Munro, the former Heart of Midlothian left full-
back. Off the field, Wood appeared at the*

Nottingham Bankruptcy Court in May 1937, when his address was given as 41, South Road, West Bridgford. He admitted a deficiency of £131.10s. 1d., arising out of a commission agent's claim of £57. 11s. 8d., to which the costs of a judgment against him had been added. His only assets were £1 in the bank. In May 1936 he had received £250 as his share of the fee paid by Forest for his transfer from Leicester City, but this had been used to pay off a loan from his father when he opened a small tobacco shop at 214a Hinckley Road, Leicester in February 1934, but the business closed in April 1935. The examination was closed with no agreement reached with the Official Receiver regarding the payment. In the following month he signed to play with Colchester United, and was quickly selected to represent the Southern League. He returned to the USA in October 1939 and worked for the USA Steel Corporation until retirement in 1970. He was inducted into the USA Hall of Fame in 1986.
Appearances: FL: 21 apps 0 gls FAC: 1 app 0 gls
Total: 22 apps 0 gls
Honours: U.S.A. International, 4 caps. Scotland Schoolboy International, 1921. Southern League representative v Cheshire League October 1937.

WOODLAND, Thomas Benjamin
Outside-left 5'10" 12st 0lbs
Born: Birchwood, 6th March 1881
Died: Belper, 1st January 1961
Debut v Burton United (h) 25.12.06, won 2-0
CAREER: Ridding St. James'. Doncaster Rovers April 1902. Chesterfield Town August 1903. Worksop Town 30th August 1904. Rotherham County 20th June 1905. **FOREST 10th November 1906**. Rotherham County 23rd May 1908. Alfreton Town cs 1910.
After 10 first team appearances and two goals, the Chesterfield Town club had allowed Tom Woodland to move into Midland League football. They had, however, kept him on their transfer list with a fee of £35 on his head. The 'Nottingham Evening Post' of 6th November 1906 reported that, at a meeting of the Football League Committee, the player was granted a free transfer. Within days he joined Forest, but appeared in only three League matches, scoring once, in his first season when Forest won promotion as champions of Division Two. In the following campaign he was restricted to just two late season outings, but scored in the

final match, a 1-2 home defeat by Bury. A lengthy association with the Alfreton club continued as a committee member after he retired as a player.
Appearances: FL: 5 apps 2 gls Total: 5 apps 2 gls

WRAGG, William A. 'Willie'

Left-half/Left-back
6' 0" 13st 4lbs
Born: Sneinton, Notts.
12th August 1875
Debut v Liverpool (h) 28.11.96, won 2-0
CAREER: Notts Olympic. Newstead Byron. Hucknall Portland March 1895. Stannington December 1895. **FOREST 16th April 1896.**
Leicester Fosse 24th March 1899. Small Heath 11th January 1901. Watford 23rd August 1901. Hinckley Town 30th August 1902. Chesterfield Town August 1903. Accrington Stanley 8th August 1904. Brighton & Hove Albion 14th September 1905 to May 1905.
Versatile Willie Wragg seized his opportunity when Forest transferred Alex Stewart to Notts County, leaving a vacancy at left half-back. The strapping local product enjoyed a memorable second season, scoring his first League goal against Sunderland in October 1897, and assisting in Forest's opening goal, scored by Arthur Capes, in the 3-1 FA Cup Final victory against Derby County at the Crystal Palace. Despite being twice in the wars, and finishing the match as a hobbling passenger on the left wing, he was recovered to see out the remainder of the season that concluded with Forest placed 8th in Division One. In the following season, new signing Bob Norris from Blackpool was handed the left-half spot and held the position, leaving Willie Wragg to deputise for Adam Scott in the left full-back position. The first of subsequent moves took him to Leicester Fosse, for whom he made 49 League appearances and scored four goals. He played only once for Small Heath and in 20 matches for Chesterfield Town. Between times he appeared in Southern and Midland League football without playing in much first team football. Back in Nottingham in 1910, he appeared at the Nottingham Empire music hall in a Fred Karno show that also included co-stars Stan Laurel and Charlie Chaplin!
Appearances: FL: 49 apps 1 gl FAC: 10 apps 0 gls
Total: 59 apps 1 gl
Honours: **(FOREST)** FA Cup winners 1898

WRIGHT, Ernest James

Outside-right
Born: Nottingham, *circa* 1881
Debut v Notts County (a) 25.12.03, lost 0-1
CAREER: FOREST 29th October 1903-04
*Injuries and a selection shake up, following a 3-7
home defeat by Aston Villa, led to the selection of
Ernest Wright at inside-right, and Harry Comery,
who made his sole League appearance on the left
wing. The mid season slump continued, however,
Forest being without a win in eight matches from
December 5th to January 9th. Wright was given
another opportunity on the right wing in place of
Tom Davies in a final run of four matches that
included the 3-1 defeat by Blackburn Rovers in the
2nd round FA Cup-tie at the City Ground.*
Appearances: FL: 4 apps 0 gls FAC: 1 app 0 gls
Total: 5 apps 0 gls

YATES, Levi

Centre-forward
5' 7½" 11st 0lbs
Born: Church Gresley,
17th June 1891
Died: Church Gresley,
1st March 1934
Debut v Blackpool (h) 18.10.13,
won 3-0
CAREER: Gresley Colliery.
Gresley Rovers. **FOREST 14th
October 1913, fee £100.**
*Coal miner Levi Yates earned his club, Gresley
Rovers, a then significant fee when he joined
Forest in October 1913. His form for the Rovers
had been outstanding; in the first match of the
season he scored four goals out of five against
Long Eaton St. Helen's. On the Saturday prior to
his move to the City Ground he scored two of three
goals against South Normanton. Given an early
debut in Division Two he held his place for five
matches but appeared infrequently thereafter, his
only goal coming in the 2-2 draw against local
rivals Notts County on Christmas Day 1913. Yates
was not re-engaged at the close of the season, and
his subsequent whereabouts remain unknown, but
he was known to have served in the Cheshire
Regiment during the First World War.* **Note:** *The
amount of his transfer fee was confirmed in an
article in the 'Sports Argus' of 20th June 1914.
Reporting on the AGM of the Gresley Rovers club,
it was stated that the balance in hand was
£72.12.5d. Total income was £699, including the
£100 received for L. Yates from Nottingham
Forest.*
Appearances: FL: 10 apps 1 gl Total: 10 apps 1 gl

THE NEARLY MEN

FOREST TOUR OF ARGENTINA AND URUGUAY 1905

Following Southern League Southampton's outing
to South America in 1904, Forest took 13 players
and two officials on a nine-game trip in the close
season of 1905, returning unbeaten and with a
profit of £200. John Barnsdale pulled out of the
tour at the last moment and the new signing
Thomas Clifford took his place. Clifford returned
from the trip with a leg injury; at first this was
thought to be minor, and that he would be fit for
the start of the new season. However, it proved to
be more serious and involved treatment in
Manchester. His injury was then aggravated during
light training in November. His debut for the
reserve team came in a Midland League game on
28th February 1906. He made regular appearances
for the reserves but never played in the first team.

CLIFFORD, Thomas

Centre half
5' 11" 12st 0lbs
Born: Kilbirnie, Ayrshire,
14th August 1874
Died: K.I.A. on the Somme,
19th January 1917, age 42,
when serving as a Private in
the 6th/7th Royal Scots
Fusiliers.
Debut v Blackpool (h)
3.9.1899, won 4-1
Career: Annbank. Newton
Heath 5th December 1896.
Ayr 13th April 1898. Glossop North End 31st May
1898. Luton Town 30th July 1900. Celtic 28th
August 1901. Beith September 1903. Motherwell
1904. Nottingham Forest 12th May 1905.
*One of any number of talented footballers whose
skills were honed in the tiny Ayrshire village of
Annbank. Stated to be an outside-left when signed
by Newton Heath, his height and weight suggested
that he might have been better suited to a
defensive role. He did not graduate to first team
football with the 'Heathens', but as Glossop North
End's centre half he marshalled his defence to
great effect in the initial promotion season.
Virtually ever-present from mid season, he missed
only two matches, following a sending-off and
fourteen days suspension from February 27th. In
the following relegation season, with the team
shipping goals at an alarming rate, Lupton, whose
first outing was an unqualified success, retained
the centre half position for the remainder of the
campaign. After 16 Scottish League appearances
for Motherwell he was signed by Forest for £208
in May 1905 and was immediately drafted in to
the club's tour of South America, where he played*

6 games before injuring a leg. The injury turned out to be serious, and after some reserve team appearances after February 1906 he was not retained and retired from the game. At the time of Tom Clifford's death on the Somme, his home address was given as Rankiston, Ayrshire. His younger brother Bob played 197 Football League games for Bolton Wanderers, Everton and Fulham between 1904 and 1912.

SEASON 1918-19

Football continued throughout the two World Wars of the 20th Century. The Football League organised regional competitions to simplify the clubs' travel arrangements. From seasons 1915-16 to 1918-19 Forest played in the Midland Section, finishing top in 1916 and 1919.

With the armistice signed in 1918, and men returning from service in the armed forces, the Football League organised a two-legged "championship" match with the champions of the Northern Section, Everton. Guest players were allowed during the war-time seasons, and although this was a contest between Second Division Forest and First Division Everton, Forest's guest players included English internationals Shea and Hardy. After a 0-0 draw at the City Ground the deciding game took place at Goodison Park on May 17th 1919, when a Burton goal gave Forest a 1-0 victory. League President McKenna presented Forest with the League champioship trophy after the game, and each player received two winners' medals, one for the Midland Section and one for the Championship win.

The Forest team in the second leg was Hardy; Billing, H Jones; Lowe, Wightman, Armstrong; Birch, Shea, Gibson, Burton, Martin. Tinsley played in the first match at the City Ground, not Gibson. Sam Hardy in goal was a guest player and later played for Forest. Two other guests who do not feature elsewhere in this book were Birch (Queen's Park Rangers) and Shea (Blackburn Rovers). Harry Wightman returned as club manager in 1936 but played no regular League games for the club.

BIRCH, Jimmy

Inside-forward
5' 7" 11st 2lbs
Born: Blackwell, Worcestershire 1888
Died: 1940
Career: Stourbridge 1907, Aston Villa 1911, Queen's Park Rangers (Southern League) 1912, (Football League) 1920. Brentford 1926.
Signed by Queen's Park Rangers after scoring prolifically for Aston Villa reserves, Birch went on to play 328 League games for the club and score 123 goals. Although slight and stocky in build, he had the skill of confusing opponent's defenders with a drop of the shoulder.

SHEA, Danny

Inside-forward
Born: Wapping
6th November 1887
Died: Wapping
25th December 1960
Career: Builders Arms 1904. Pearl United 1905, Manor Park Albion 1906. West Ham United (Southern League) 1907.
Blackburn Rovers 1912. West Ham United (Football League) 1920, Fulham 1920, Coventry City 1923. Clapton Orient 1925. Sheppey United 1926.
Shea made 306 Football League appearances for his 5 League clubs and scored 104 goals. His career record also includes 103 goals in 166 Southern League games for West Ham. Described as a "delicate dribbler" yet defenders came to realise he could turn and shoot with power and accuracy. He signed for the then-Champions Blackburn Rovers for a record fee at the time, £2,000. He won international caps for England,

WIGHTMAN, Harry

Centre-half
5' 11" 11st 10 lbs
Born: Sutton in Ashfield, Notts
19th June 1894
Died: Nottingham 5th April 1945
Career: Sutton Town 1911. Eastwood Rangers 1912. Chesterfield Town 1913. Nottingham Forest 1915. Derby County 1919. Chesterfield 1929.
Notts County 1930. Manager of Luton Town 1931, Mansfield Town 1935, Nottingham Forest 1936-1939.
After starting out as goal-scoring centre-forward with non-League Chesterfield Town, he moved to centre-half in Forest's first Midland Section season of 1915-16. He was a regular team member in Forest's four war-time seasons but moved to Derby County in May 1919. He made 180 League

appearances for Derby, scoring 9 goals, with 38 appearances and 2 goals on his return to Chesterfield in 1929. After management experience at Luton and Mansfield, he joined Forest for the 1936-37 season, but after his teams won only 32 of 114 League games he was replaced by Billy Walker in 1939.

SEASON 1939-40

Throughout the summer of 1939 everyone was aware that war with Hitler's Germany was quite likely. Preparations for the new football season went ahead as usual. Forest had made five new signings; Jackie Maund and Tom Perry (both Aston Villa), Andrew McCall (Huddersfield Town), Frank Shufflebottom (Ipswich Town), George Crisp (Colchester United).

When war was declared on Sunday 3rd September 1939 Forest had played three League games, with Maund, Perry and McCall playing in all of them. The League immediately abandoned the season, the three games were struck from the record, and the players' registrations were cancelled, leaving them unemployed. The debutants at the 92 clubs in 1939 became known as "the men who never were", with no official appearances for their new clubs. Perry was particularly unfortunate. He made no first team appearances at his previous League clubs, scored on his debut for Forest, lost this part of his career when the results were annulled, and died in action in 1942.

McCALL, Andrew Johnstone
Inside-forward 5' 8½" 11st 0lbs
Born Cumnock, 12th October 1908
Died: 1979
CAREER: Cumnock Juveniles. Cumnock Townhead Thistle. Ayr United July 1927, for a donation of £5. St Johnstone November 1935. Huddersfield Town January 1939, fee approx. £2,000. Nottingham Forest July 1939 (Wartime guest player with St. Johnstone May 1940, Ayr United May 1940, Elgin City November 1940. Third Lanark, Clyde Aug 1941, Aberdeen August 1941, Aldershot 1941-42, Hibernian and Dundee.) Huntley F.C. player-coach 1946. Dundee coach. Dundee United manager October 1958 to April 1959.
A stylish and polished inside-forward with the ability to link up the attack by shrewd passing, Andy McCall shone in Scottish football with Ayr United (228 appearances and 30 goals) and he did even better with St Johnstone, scoring lots of goals from free-kicks and penalties (117 appearances

nd 80 goals). He came very near to winning his Scottish cap, twice being selected as reserve against Wales in 1932 and against Austria in 1933. Sadly, he failed to settle at Leeds Road and did not continue his goal scoring exploits. The team's best form seemed reserved for FA Cup-ties, and a second, consecutive, Wembley appearance seemed a distinct possibility. The dream ended at Highbury when the eventual winners of the trophy, Portsmouth, beat Town by 2-1 in the semi-final before a 'gate' of over 60,000 spectators.
1939-40 appearance: FL: 3 apps 1 gl

MAUND, John Henry "Jackie"

Outside right/left
5' 5" 9st 7lbs
Born: Hednesford
5th January 1916
Died: Hednesford 1994
Debut v Barnsley 26th August 1939, lost 0-4
Career: Cannock Mining College 1933. Hednesford Oct 1933. Aston Villa Oct 1934. Nottingham Forest May 1939. Wartime guest appearances for Hednesford, Forest, Northampton, Walsall and Port Vale. Hednesford player-manager 1945. Walsall Oct 1946.
Small of stature but capable of bursts of speed down the wing, Maund's League debut for Villa came in January 1936. He was a regular choice the following season, but illness and injury restricted his opportunities in 1937-38, a promotion season for Villa. Back in Division One for 1938-39, the form of Frank Broome meant that Maund was restricted to 12th man duties and reserve team football. With new Forest manager Billy Walker looking to strengthen the Forest team, he naturally turned to his old club Villa, and negotiation a "pay by instalments" deal to take Maund and Perry to the City Ground. After the season was abandoned he became a Bevin Boy, working in the mine at Hednesford, which gave him opportunities for wartime football. He retuned to the Football League after the war with a few appearances for Walsall.
1939-40 appearance: FL: 3 apps 1 gl

PERRY, Colin

Outside right
5' 10" 11st 4lb
Born: Kiveton Park,
Sheffield 1916
Died: K.I.A. 28th November
1942
Career: Sheffield United
1933. Gainsborough Trinity
1934. Aston Villa 1936.
Nottingham Forest 1939
*17 year-old Perry made an
immediate impact in
Sheffield United's "A" and reserve teams, making
his debut against Wolves reserves in August 1933.
Unable to break into the first team, he joined
Midland League Gainsborough Trinity in 1934,
where his reported fast, direct runs and
goalscoring skills brought him to the attention of
Aston Villa, for whom he signed in November
1936. There was much greater competition for
places at his new club, where he started with the
Colts and the "A" team, before regular reserve
team appearances in 1938. When Walker came
calling in 1939, Perry was no doubt grateful for an
opportunity for first team football, and signed in
May 1939 along with Maund. He died in 1942
during war service as a driver for the Royal Army
Service Corps in the Middle East.*
1939-40 appearance: FL: 3 apps 2 gls

BOOKS BY GARTH DYKES

Oldham Athletic-A Complete Record, 1899-1988 (Breedon Books 1988)

New Brighton-A Complete Record, 1922-1951 (Breedon Books 1990)

Exeter City-A Complete Record, 1904-1990, with Alex Wilson and Maurice Golesworthy (Breedon Books 1990)

Accrington Stanley-A Complete Record, 1894-1962, with Mike Jackman (Breedon Books 1991)

The United Alphabet-A Complete Who's Who of Manchester United F.C. (ACL & Polar Publishing (UK) Ltd. 1994)

All the Lads-The Official Who's Who of Sunderland A.F.C., with Doug Lamming (Polar Publishing 1999)

Latics Lads-The Official Who's Who of Oldham Athletic A.F.C., 1907-2002 (Yore Publications)

Meadow Lane Men-The Complete Who's Who of Notts County F.C., 1888-2005 (Yore Publications)

The Legends of Oldham Athletic (Breedon Books 2006)

The Who's Who of Oldham Athletic (Breedon Books 2008)

The Who's Who of Barrow A.F.C.- Barrow's Football League Players 1921-72 (Soccerdata 2009)

Nelson F.C. in the Football League. A Complete Record and Who's Who 1921-31 (Soccerdata 2009)

Durham City in the Football League. A Complete Record and Who's Who 1921-28 (Soccerdata 2010)

A Spinner's Yarn. High Crompton St Mary's C.C. The Official History 1904-2010, with Allan Cadman (Soccerdata 2010)

Ashington A.F.C. in the Football League. A Complete Record and Who's Who 1921-1929 (Soccerdata 2011)

Wigan Borough in the Football League. A Complete Record and Who's Who 1921-31 (Soccerdata 2011)

A Spinner's Yarn Over and Out. High Crompton St Mary's C.C. The Official History 1904-2011, with Allan Cadman (Soccerdata 2012)

New Brighton in the Football League. A Complete Record and Who's Who 1923-51 (Soccerdata 2012)

Oldham Athletic A.F.C. 1895-1915 (Soccerdata 2012)

Oldham Athletic A.F.C. 1915-1939 (Soccerdata 2013)

Glossop F.C. in the Football League. A Complete Record and Who's Who 1898-1915 (Soccerdata 2013)

Huddersfield Town Who's Who 1909-1961 (Soccerdata 2015)

Bury Who's Who 18993-1954 (Soccerdata 2016)

PUBLISHER'S AFTERWORD

Our book starts with Forest's first appearance in the Football League in 1892. By this time, the club had played over 500 ordinary games since its first meetings with the Notts club in 1866, and some 400 players had worn the garibaldi red caps and shirts. Forest played in the three seasons of the Football Alliance, a league competition that ran from 1889 to 1892 (when its clubs joined the Football League to form a second division) and reached the semi-finals of the FA Cup in 1879 (the first season the club had entered), 1880, 1885 and 1892.

Consequently, we gave some thought to calling the book you have in your hands "Volume Two". After all, we will need another two volumes to cover the club's players from 1946 to the current season. However, the work involved in producing a possible "Volume One, 1866 to 1892" proved daunting. Not impossible, just lengthy and difficult. The 400 includes many well-known players, nine of whom played in international matches for England. Equally, the number contains many players about whom we know nothing at the moment, other than their surname.

Research into the early history of English football is much easier today that it was in previous times, thanks largely to the British Newspaper Archive, with its ever-expanding supply of newspapers of the time. Just a few years ago, the researcher's only options were to tour local libraries or visit the British Library's storage unit at Colindale, where you were limited to four newspapers an hour. Now you can examine four papers in a few minutes, sitting at home in front of your computer screen. Consequently, we are not ruling out a "Volume One", but please don't expect it anytime soon. We will of course be grateful to hear from any readers with material that can contribute to this work. Please write or email to the address on the title page.

The Forest v Aston Villa match of November 1892, as seen by "Out of Doors". Newspapers were dependent on etchings for their illustrations until the widespread use of rotogravure, a development of the photogravure process used for making prints.

AUTHOR'S ACKNOWLEDGEMENTS

I am, as ever, most grateful to Jim Creasy whose continuing and herculanean efforts in the field of football history and research has provided the bed-rock of this and numerous other works of a similar nature. Current research has owed much to Peter Holme, Collections Officer of the National Football Museum, for access to their records, and to friends Mike Jackman and Mike Davage. I am also most grateful for the assistance of Michael Braham, Dave Sullivan (Millwall F.C. Museum), Robert Reid (Partick Thistle historian), Dr. Steven Phillipps, Paul Plowman, Michael Joyce, Gordon Small, Rod Evans and last, but by no means least, my friend and publisher Tony Brown.

ABOUT THE AUTHOR

Garth Dykes was born at Mellor, near Blackburn, and was educated at Chadderton Grammar School. Following studies at Oldham Municipal Technical College a career in cotton yarn sales commenced in 1957 at the Wye Mills, Shaw. A career move took Garth to Leicestershire in November1960 and he retired in 1992 at the age of 58. A member of the Football Writers' Association, Garth's lifelong love of football has seen his involvement in twenty-five books to date. Cover caricatures for this book are the work of the author, whose artwork has appeared in football programmes, national magazines, and several sets of trade cards issued by David Rowland of Bury.

THE COVER

The front cover is a team group from 1905. From the left; Niblo, Henderson, Craggs, Wolfe, Dudley, Morris, Craig, Linacre, Timmins, Spouncer, West. On the back cover, left column; Ashton, Harrison, McCall. Centre column; Bedford, Dexter, Jack Scott, Nelis. Right column; Matthew Bell, Charlie Jones, Langford, Stocks. All caricatures are by the author.

THE ENGLISH NATIONAL FOOTBALL ARCHIVE
www.enfa.co.uk

All Nottingham Forest's results, line-ups and scorers are included in the database of the English National Football Archive. The database holds more than 430,000 line-ups, 625,000 scorers and 43,000 players and is fully indexed, so that a player's career can be followed game-by-game. Many pages are free-to-view, but some detail pages require a subscription, which starts at £2.